MINORIT

MINORITY REPORTER

Modern Scotland's bad attitude towards her own Irish

Phil Mac Giolla Bháin

Phil Mac Giolla Bháin is an author, blogger, journalist and writer based in County Donegal, Ireland. He is an active member of the National Union of Journalists, sitting on the Irish Executive Council and the New Media Industrial Council. He is also the editor of the *Irish Journalist*, the NUJ's in-house magazine for members in Ireland.

An established print journalist for many years, Phil has been a columnist with *An Phoblacht* and contributed to publications as diverse the *Guardian*, the *Irish Independent*, *Magill* magazine and the *Irish Post*; in recent years he has developed an online audience through his blog at www.philmacgiollabhain.ie.

His journalism in recent years has focused on highlighting the incidence of anti-Irish racism in Scotland.

This is his fourth book.

For my mother

This edition published 2013

by Frontline Noir, an imprint of Books Noir

Copyright © 2013 Phil Mac Giolla Bháin

All Rights Reserved

Print edition ISBN 978-1-904684-73-2

A CIP record for this book is available from the British Library

Typeset in Garamond by Park Productions

Cover design by James Hutcheson

Printed and bound in the EU

CONTENTS

FOREWORD

Donnacha DeLong

There's nothing new about anti-Irish racism. In fact, the language of racism in general can be found far back in Irish and British history. Gerald of Wales accompanied the Anglo-Norman invaders who first subjugated Ireland to rule under the king of England in the twelfth century. He wrote, in *The History and Topography of Ireland*, of the native Irish:

> They live on beasts only, and live like beasts. They have not
> progressed at all from the habits of pastoral living ... This
> is a filthy people, wallowing in vice. Of all peoples it is the
> least instructed in the rudiments of the faith.

The stereotyping of the native Irish and the defaming of local culture and practices was accompanied by forced anglicisation and regular military incursions. The Protestant reformation, in particular Henry XIII's rejection of the Catholic Church, gave religious sectarianism a new edge. Despite the missionaries from Ireland who had reintroduced Christianity to Britain after the collapse of the Roman Empire, the Irish were now cast as followers of a superstitious and brutal religion – and seen as too stupid to know better.

As the centuries passed, the racist rhetoric continued and expanded to justify the repression of native Irish resistance and, from the sixteenth century onwards, the plantations of Ireland – a programme of confiscation and colonisation of the land with settlers from England and the Scottish Lowlands. The combination of religious rhetoric and land confiscations reached fever pitch with Cromwell's conquest of Ireland in the seventeenth century. From this point onwards, British colonialism expanded globally.

The lessons learned in Ireland became a template for how to deal with other troublesome natives. As Noam Chomsky put it in one of the interviews in *The Prosperous Few and the Restless Many*:

There has always been racism. But it developed as a leading principle of thought and perception in the context of colonialism. That's understandable. When you have your boot on someone's neck, you have to justify it. The justification has to be their depravity.

It's very striking to see this in the case of people who aren't very different from one another. Take a look at the British conquest of Ireland, the earliest of the Western colonial conquests. It was described in the same terms as the conquest of Africa. The Irish were a different race. They weren't human. They weren't like us. We had to crush and destroy them.

The colonisation of Ireland was completed with the Act of Union in 1800, following the defeated 1798 Rebellion. Ireland became an unequal part of the United Kingdom and, as its small economy was suppressed to the advantage of the larger country to the east, a trickle of Irish people began moving to Britain seeking work. The Irish became farm labourers, dock workers, builders and, as the Industrial Revolution began to take hold, factory workers.

The trickle of Irish immigrants into Britain became a flood with the advent of An Gorta Mór (The Great Hunger) in the 1840s and 1850s. Often referred to as the Irish Famine, the death of approximately one million people and the emigration of at least the same number was not the result of natural causes, as the word famine implies. On the contrary, the island of Ireland was still exporting massive amounts of food during the same period. An Gorta Mór was a legacy of the colonial policies of the British state, which pushed much of the native population to the rocky land of Connacht, and the *laissez-faire* politics of the British government that prevented any realistic attempts to alleviate the suffering in Ireland.

Irish emigrants ended up across the world, from Australia and South Africa to Argentina and the United States. But many hundreds of thousands went no further than Britain – London, Birmingham, Manchester, Liverpool and Glasgow. The immigrants were a gift to the emergent capitalism of mid-nineteenth century Britain; destitute thousands powered the huge factories and populated the great industrial cities. However, the poverty and lack of education of many of the immigrants fed the historic prejudices.

The Irish lived in ghettos which were often little more than shanty towns. These areas – including Irish Town in Manchester, described by Friedrich Engels in *The Condition of the Working Class in England*, or Whitechapel in London, described by Rudolf Rocker in *The London Years* – were rightly regarded as barely fit for human inhabitation. However, for many in Britain, the Irish were seen as natural inhabitants of such squalor, unwilling and unable to improve themselves.

Similar oppressive social conditions in the United States drove many Irish west to the frontier, to become pioneers of the new territories and gradually to attain new status. There was no such option in Britain and, as a result, new issues emerged. Out of the ghettos emerged new kinds of activism. A new version of the Irish fight for independence from Britain emerged amongst the emigrants in a number of movements that would become known as Fenianism. The Irish Republican Brotherhood (IRB) had groups in Ireland and Britain, the Fenian Brotherhood and then Clan na Gael were their equivalent in the United States. At various times throughout their history, these Fenian groups engaged in bombings in Britain – the most notorious of which was the Clerkenwell bombing in 1867 when a botched prison break resulted in the death of twelve civilians.

Michael Barrett became the last man to be publicly hanged in Britain after he was convicted of participating in the bombing. Despite many doubts over his conviction and campaigns for clemency similar to those in Manchester on behalf of those who became the Manchester Martyrs, Barrett came to symbolise a new aspect of anti-Irish prejudice – the dangerous bomber. So much so that his execution is thought to be the origin of the use of the name Mick as an insulting generalisation for Irish people.

The 1880s saw a new flank in Irish activism that had a more positive effect on British society. The New Unionism wave that turned trade unions into mass organisations for the first time originated in the largely Irish community of East London. The Matchgirls' Strike of 1888 and the subsequent London Dockers' Strike that so nearly became a London general strike were solidly based amongst the Irish.

The Irish involvement in the trade union movement continued and produced such legendary figures as Jim Larkin from Liverpool and James Connolly from Edinburgh, both of whom ended up returning to Ireland, the land of their parents. The British trade union movement to this day contains an obvious preponderance of Irish names, including my own – I was born in Dublin, moved to London in 2012, and was, until recently, president of the National Union of Journalists.

The Fenian movement continued on its own path to Irish freedom, partially achieved in 1922, and Republican activities largely disappeared for decades, barring some sporadic actions in Ireland in relation to Northern Ireland. The trade union movement achieved improvements in the living standards of all, particularly after World War II. But, for the Irish, many aspects of the old prejudice remained. The treatment of Irish workers has been captured in song, in particular Dominic Behan's "McAlpine's Fusiliers", written in the 1960s about the treatment of builders working for Sir Robert McAlpine. "No blacks, no dogs, no Irish" signs were still to be seen in 1960s London.

In 1968, as the whole world seemed to be rising up and demanding equality and civil rights, the Catholic community of Northern Ireland did the same – and provoked a violent reaction, first from the Unionist and Loyalist majority, and then from the army, originally brought in to defend them. The remnants of the IRA split and the largely Northern Ireland-based Provisional IRA began its campaign against British rule. The Troubles began in 1969.

This had much the same effect on the Irish community in Britain as the IRB's actions a hundred years earlier. Every Irish man or woman was a suspect, and, as the cases of the Birmingham Six, the Guildford Four, the Maguire Seven and Judith Ward showed, any Irish person could be arrested and convicted regardless of whether or not they were involved in IRA activities. Border security in the 1970s and 1980s was notorious in its suspicion of all Irish people and the dehumanising and sometimes degrading actions of officials.

The end of the 1990s created a perfect storm that changed nearly everything. The economy of the Irish Republic was becoming the envy of the world, as the Celtic Tiger appeared to break every rule and grow beyond all expectations. Irish emigration, which had been a constant factor since the 1840s, quickly went into reverse when Ireland became a destination of choice for emigrants from other countries, first Nigeria, then China and then Eastern Europe.

At the same time, the Troubles were slowly coming to an end. Ceasefires and negotiations, first secret and then in the open, resulted in the Good Friday Agreement in 1998. Very quickly, the myths that underpinned the prejudice started to disappear – Irish people turned out to be well educated, cultured and, increasingly, financially well off. Dublin became a favourite stop for English stag and hen parties. Irish accents became commonplace on British television. Everyone loved Terry Wogan, Boyzone and *Riverdance*.

However, the old myths and prejudices persisted in one part of Britain, and this is what Phil Mac Giolla Bháin has been central to exposing and combating. The continued tolerance of racist bile like the Famine Song in Scottish football was unacceptable and Phil's success in creating an international issue out of it is to be commended. The fact that this made him the journalist of choice for people to reveal the state of Rangers' finances speaks to his professionalism and courage to tread where many others feared.

After the collapse of the Irish economy and the return of emigration as the only option for young Irish people, there is a danger of a resurgence of anti-Irish prejudice. There were hints of it in some of the reaction to the Pope's visit to the UK in 2010. Catholics were portrayed by some opponents of the visit as being superstitious and stupid, a strong echo of the descriptions of the thick Paddy of old. In 2012, an English Defence League splinter group calling themselves the North-West Infidels moved from attacking Muslims to targeting Irish community parades, accusing groups like the James Larkin Society in Liverpool of links to the IRA.

To be very clear, I'm not an Irish nationalist. I'm an anarchist who wants to see the eradication of all borders, not the creation of more. I'm not a Catholic – I have a letter from the Catholic Church to prove it. And I don't have a particular dislike of the Rangers football team or most of the fans – I don't like football at all. As far as I'm concerned, football represents my inability to get the bus home when I lived in Holloway and Arsenal were playing. I don't care whether a team succeeds or fails; it's a complete irrelevance to me.

What I do care about is racism and hatred. If you sing a song that expresses your hatred of me and people like me, I want you to stop. If you react to something written with threats of violence, then you deserve to be stopped. I oppose all forms of intolerance and prejudice, whether it be against Irish people, Muslims, LGBT people or any other group. It is the job of an ethical journalist to expose this kind of hatred and prejudice, and Phil Mac Giolla Bháin has done it well.

PREFACE

Kieron Brady

Those with a certain contempt in terms of identity endeavour, partly at least, to undermine the Irish identity by an assertion which states that Irishness cannot be acquired through "summer holidays to Donegal". For me it was never like that. As we crossed the Glenshane Pass from the west of Toomebridge through Dungiven and into Derry City, I always believed I was returning home.

This is not to infer that Coatbridge and Glasgow were not home; just that as we crossed the now vacated checkpoint straddling the boundaries of Derry and Donegal I always felt a sense of belonging and that the final ascent into the townlands of Meenlaragh and Derryconnor was a homecoming. Such emotions were frequently reinforced in the ensuing days when friends of the family, born and reared in Tír Chonaill, would ask me "when did you come home?" At no point did I ever feel that such a question was outlandish. This was home; not in the form of any particular dwelling but in the spiritual sense of culture, history and ancestry.

My upbringing, an urban metropolis in comparison, had Irish culture permeating its narrow streets. The love of Celtic Football Club co-existed with a cultural environment where music, dance, arts and native sport were being cultivated to ensure that the generations beyond us would always have that sense of Irishness. To that end it was no different to Boston or Birmingham; what was different was a consistent aura that, regardless of a present day where Irish culture is globally absorbed in such a favourable manner, there were objections, and deep-seated ones, to the Emerald Isle and the culture that has been, in part, born from its history, tragedy and infrequent triumph.

As the years passed and my football career blossomed I was confronted with a choice. Enviable in many ways, I had the options of representing Scotland, land of birth, or Ireland, land of family, ancestors and incontrovertible cultural identity. I had represented Scotland at schoolboy level. I was honoured to do so and scoring against Holland on a blisteringly cold night at Starks Park, Kirkcaldy, is still something I recall with great affection. There was, however, an element in my thinking that such representation was an extension of my schooling. I had made the progression from St Ambrose to Monklands to Lanarkshire and to the west of Scotland teams. The ultimate beyond this journey was playing for the national side and I felt privileged to be deemed good enough to do so.

Within several months of being at Sunderland AFC I made it known that, if I were considered to be of the necessary standard, my aspirations were to play for Ireland. I was subsequently informed that I would be selected at youth level. After some initial obstacles – the Scottish Football Association trying to stop this "transfer" – I was cleared by UEFA to don the green. And so I stood to sing "Amhrán na bhFiann", much to the bewilderment of many Irish-born teammates who could not, and within several months carried the national flag at the closing ceremony of a tournament in Israel. The latter came from my rapid response when the players were asked who would like to and my west of Scotland verbal lunge may just have had the necessary decibel level to compel the official to comply.

My Irishness is not something I measure, nor do I give succour to the notion that national and cultural identity is restricted to the immediate environs of where we first witness the light of day. I am perfectly content being an Irish citizen born in Coatbridge. Never has there been any internal angst that my harp-bearing passport does not state Donegal, Drogheda or Dundalk as place of birth. I am content in ancestral and cultural identity as much as I am in being reared in a part of the world that for size and population has given the globe so much.

To that end being a bairn o' Jock Tamson is a blessing. It does not seem to engender ire or ridicule elsewhere. Nor, however, does a pride being expressed at having Róisín Dubh as a "mother" – apart, sadly, from within the confines of Alba. To the outsider this may seem incomprehensible; an intra-Celtic intolerance that seeks to deny identity. To those of the Irish community in Scotland it is something they have absorbed to the point of acceptance. Or, in accepting it grudgingly, then seek to demonise parts of the culture in order to apportion blame for the social ills that pervade Scotland and have done so since before any major influx of Gaels.

One recurring theme regarding anti-Irish racism in Scotland is the inability to articulate it in any meaningful manner in public. With

widespread discrimination economically unviable through demographic changes and hate crime of a non-verbal and personal nature
at a minimum through the broad community being indistinguishable
from the host, it has left many bereft of the wherewithal to explain it.

Within the sphere of equality we can simplify issues by sub-catego-
rising racism into prejudice, discrimination and hate crime. That the
Irish in Scotland are a focal point for racism is incontrovertible. Their
visibility in the public arena is recognised for the most part within
the environs that Celtic Football Club operates. The culture of the
community is broadcast within this arena. The broad Scottish community encounter this involuntarily. Beyond that, to locate cultural
assembly would mean intent to venture into Coatbridge, the south
side or smaller enclaves where the immigrant Irish have cultivated
their heritage and families. To that end, the relatively depoliticised
components of that culture thrive, be that within Gaelic games, Irish
dancing or a music hall with emphasis on instruments associated with
the "old country".

The experience of the Irish in Scotland is in stark contrast to that in
many parts of the globe where a diaspora has settled. It is in looking at
the aforesaid town and cities that we can pinpoint just how the visibility
of an immigrant community differs from one land to another. From
London, the political belly of the beast in the context of Irish history,
to New York and beyond, the existence of the Irish of any generation is
one of acceptance, respect and success.

Yet, in crossing the Irish Sea the Irish met hostility, and although this
was replicated elsewhere it was temporary. However in Scotland, broadly
speaking, this form of racism achieved a sustainability that shows no
signs of expiration. In challenging such racism, the emergence of the
now infamous Famine Song was almost a blessing; it permitted the
phrase "anti-Irish racism" and provided an opportunity to open a discourse about Scotland, notably the west Central Belt, and its social ills.

Racism, whether through the presence of hostility or the absence
of equality, constantly seeks to undermine identity in some way. Yet,
within Irishness lies a quandary for the intolerant. In the lyrical content
of the Famine Song it is evident that its author(s) and choir seek to
illuminate their profound hatred towards those of Irish ancestry who
reside in Scotland, yet the internal conflict that afflicts them is manifest in persistent endeavours to assert that the same community has
no rights in labelling themselves as Irish. The latter, sourced from an
envy that sees Irishness as globally popular, represents a viewpoint that

contradicts the sentiments contained in the Famine Song and which so categorically made clear the entity of the Irish in Scotland.

This is not confined to the realms of professional football, which is so often and erroneously portrayed as the birthplace of all that afflicts Scotland regarding intra-Christian and intra-Celtic division. The contempt directed towards the Irish predates the arrival of the beautiful game and has been maintained through such attitudes permeating the fabric of life, from the press to the police and beyond. That still exists today.

In 2013 it is hard to gauge progress. Racist chanting in football – once widespread and weekly – has diminished, yet it is very difficult to establish if that is due to a metamorphosis within the footballing public. There is a general consensus within the Irish community that it is only a matter of time before stadia are again reverberating to sentiments that depict a ridicule, contempt or hatred for the sons and daughters of Erin.

The additional problem is the lack of will from the political elite to bring closure on many of the relevant equality matters. The broad community can operate in Scotland without any form of racism impacting on daily life, in terms of financial, physical or emotional wellbeing. This is the case until such time as an overt display of Irishness is brought to light in an appropriate environment. This is where we can dissect anti-Irish racism, certainly in part, with regards to where we are and the recent past. In essence, the broad message from the profoundly racist, but also the more casual, is: we know your family history, your ancestral background, but you can't show it. It is this perverted logic and cultural restriction that gives a reluctant tolerance to "The Fields of Athenry" but not to the songs that remember those whose sacrifice gave birth to the nation.

This form of racism is not evident anywhere else I know of; it stands as one of the many anomalies that pervade the issue. What exacerbates it is the constant preparedness to treat such songs and airs as being born of religious prejudice. Whether those who peddle this believe it or not becomes irrelevant; such distortions have entered the psyche so much so that it is manna from heaven for the bigots who in turn mimic the behavioural patterns of bigots everywhere and believe because they want to believe.

With the absence of more serious forms of racism it is actually understandable why some downplay the notion of anti-Irish racism. They constantly ask for examples which demonstrate their surroundings as a hotbed of hatred. The reality is that such examples may be few and far between. Attacks on property with an Irish association occur but lack of coverage means that such information is not readily accessible. This, however, is not a regular pattern of hate crime, and so the complainant may again be stifled in trying to support such claims.

Racism, religious prejudice and other forms of intolerance exist all over the planet. What does isolate Scotland is an endurance and profundity to this form of racism and prejudice that is hard to match anywhere else. It poisons publications, filters through football and pollutes the police.

Despite this, those within and on the periphery of the target group do little to address it. Each instance, serious or not, that is brought to public attention is met with verbal ire. That anger, however, subsides without any attempts to ensure the same, or alternatives, do not reappear. It remains to be seen just how much of an appetite there is to remove such prejudice.

In all of this there is a deep sadness; a divided working class that lies prostrate through a form of Divide and Rule and which sadly shows little sign of progress. Forever the optimist, I can but hope that a realisation will dawn that the wind that shakes the barley shakes the thistle and the rose.

ACKNOWLEDGEMENTS

Many people have helped me in getting this book to you. Once more, Bob Smith and his vibrant team at Frontline Noir were there for me when it mattered. This time round, we all knew each other a bit better and as veterans of the *Downfall* campaign the creation of this book was less of a step into the unknown.

Once more, a special mention must go to Angela Haggerty; as the first recipient of this script she has a huge say in what the finished product looks like. Angela is proof that Scotland can produce talented journalists who are brave and resourceful. The glass ceiling hasn't been constructed that will contain her. I know that she would only eat succulent lamb if she had cooked it herself so that won't be happening …

Alison Rae's judgement, as an editor, has also been vital in getting the script into book form.

Tá míle buíochas le Donnacha DeLong.

Donnacha only recently stepped down as President of the National Union of Journalists and I'm honoured that he provided the foreword for this book. We work closely in the NUJ on matters digital, so it is fitting that I asked him to present my online work in book form. It did not take us long to find out that we're related through rebellion and our kin were in the first Dáil Éireann together. His support to me in my journalism around anti-Irish racism in Scotland has been what I would expect from a relative of Harry Boland.

To Seamus Dooley and Paul Holleran of the NUJ – they have been steadfast in their support throughout this period and they have my gratitude and respect. My thanks must also go to Professor Tom Devine for his patience and encouragement in assisting me during the latter stages of this book. He sent me off in the direction of the appropriate academic references and this work is the better for that.

Gratitude is also due to the Reverend Douglas Gay of Glasgow University for guiding me through the details and nuances at work in the Kirk in the 1920s. I am also in the debt of Alison Gemmell at the Church of Scotland who was hugely helpful in assisting me to locate Kirk documents.

There are others to whom I owe thanks just for being themselves and one person has an entire section of this book devoted to him: Neil Lennon. Every decent person in Scotland owes him their thanks just for being himself, for being brave and by his example shining a light on a dark corner of an otherwise decent country. Had Lennon caved in to the klan and left Scotland in 2011 there would have been an indelible stain on the nation. Through his courage he won a great victory for Scotland.

There are many people in the Irish community who assisted and advised me with this work. A special mention must go to Danny Boyle of the Irish Heritage Foundation and Councillor Feargal Dalton of Glasgow City Council; *go raibh maith agaibh*. I was delighted when Kieron Brady agreed to provide a preface for this book. He has often shared with me his perspective as an Irishman from the West of Scotland who also represented his country at professional football. In his current work as an equality practitioner he has been an invaluable help to me in shaping much of the journalism that is reproduced in this book.

A huge *gracias* is due to Paco, an extraordinary man from Extremadura who fell in love with Athletic Bilbao in the Basque country just for the *craic*! He's been there and done it. An anti-Franco activist, a committed trade unionist and a brilliant journalist, he has my thanks for his friendship, encouragement and for reminding me that what we both do is part of something bigger. *Venceremos!*

My gratitude is also due to John Hedges for being another in a long line of *An Phoblacht* editors who have made my copy readable and for understanding that anti-Irish racism in Scotland is a Republican issue.

Writing is a lonely pursuit and there are times when the example of others sees you to the next summit. This book documents a five-year journey of campaigning journalism against anti-Irish racism in Scotland, and along the way many people told me to keep going and I'm grateful to all of them.

I have to mention Enda Fanning for his work against the Famine Song and for being a sound comrade. Also Carmen, who took the hand that life dealt her without complaint yet still worked out where all of the pieces of the jigsaw go. Her example continues to inspire me. Natalia, for teaching me that a smile can cross an ocean, and Vanda for giving me another reason to love Lisbon.

As ever my greatest debt is owed to those at the centre of my life. You read the output, but only they truly know the centrality of the role they all play in keeping me connected to what is truly valuable. To Cathal, Róisín and Aislinn *go raibh mile maith agaibh mo pháistí*. I am a very fortunate father. Their mother anchors us all down with a quiet wisdom through it all – she remains my indispensable in this life.

This book is dedicated to my own mother for her strength of character and for never forgetting who she was despite being in a society that tried to make her forget. She didn't. Some girl, Bridget!

And finally, Rusty, who reminds me constantly that I live among beautiful mountains and that they are covered in interesting smells. She knows stuff.

Phil Mac Giolla Bháin
Ireland
April 2013

INTRODUCTION

Anti-Irish racism has an old history in Scotland. There is, of course, little new about the hostility of a host community to a rapid influx of immigrants, especially if those newcomers seem utterly alien and bring with them the portent of trouble and social problems.

There was a time when Irish people arriving in Scotland in large numbers would have been celebrated by Scots. In the heroic age, Robert the Bruce's brother, Edward, was High King of Ireland, leading the clans against the common threat of English predatory expansionism. Some historians believe that the hero of Bannockburn spent the winter of 1306–07 in Ireland being sheltered by the Gaels of Ulster. As the Scottish ruling class started to move towards a *rapprochement* with their ancient enemy south of the border, the people in Scotland who were, ironically, the most distinctively Scottish started to be considered alien. Just as *Gaidhlig* started to become distinctively separate from the Irish language, people in positions of power in Edinburgh would sneer at the Highlanders and their "Irish tongue".

When Scotland was absorbed in the Hanoverian *Anschluss* of 1707, England had finally completed the long march to annex her neighbour to the north. It was, indeed, the end of an auld sang. In the afterglow, union-ambitious and upwardly mobile Scots became ardent and enthusiastic "North Britons".

When the starvelings of Mayo and Donegal arrived on the Clyde in 1848 they landed in a Scotland that was very different from the Alba of Bruce and Wallace. The Irish fleeing An Gorta Mór in the mid-nineteenth century were viewed as alien by Victorians of the industrialising Central Belt. This was the period of history when Friedrich Engels, Karl Marx's friend and colleague, wrote of the great slums of Manchester and how different, how "other" the Irish were in comparison to the English working class.

In Scotland the Famine Irish bore an uncomfortable resemblance to what the Scots used to be like before they were British, imperialist and "civilised". In the 1980s I was invited by the Irish unit at the Greater London Council to give one of the Terence MacSwiney memorial lectures. The theme that year was the Irish in Britain. My talk was on the

Irish in Scotland. The title was: *The Irish in Scotland: Despised Aliens or Guardians of the true Scotland?*

To borrow from Hugh MacDiarmid, Irish arriving in Victorian Glasgow could have been forgiven for observing that "this Scotland is not Scotland". It was as if a time machine from medieval Scotland had disgorged a glen full of Albannaigh on the Broomielaw. The Scotland that the Famine Irish arrived in was British and part of a global imperial project during its glory days. They were Catholic by faith but not all in the "mother church" were delighted with these new additions to the flock in Scotland. In the nineteenth century, Bishop Grey, a Scotsman, and Bishop Devine, an Irishman, disagreed about the nature of the Catholic Church. Was the church going to be immigrant in nature or was it to be truly Scottish? That dispute was settled when the Catholic Church in Scotland decided its duty was to strip the Irishness from her newly arrived flock.

The increasingly militarised stalemate over the Third Home Rule Bill and the run-up to the outbreak of the Great War infected the coal and steel towns of the west of Scotland. Catholic and Irish became virtually interchangeable terms. So much so that the ethnic was excised when dealing with Scotland's large, socially excluded Catholic minority population. However, it made no sense.

The Italian community was and is allowed to be publicly identifiable with their homeland and heritage. The Irish were certainly not afforded this space to self-define. From the time of An Gorta Mór, the Irish on Clydeside were seen as potential trouble, and political trouble at that. The War of Independence in Ireland had consigned the Irish to "otherness" within the British worldview. Association football was the main arena in which these differences were played out.

Once more, the dominant narrative was that this was a manifestation of sectarianism, not hostility to an Irish immigrant community. Given the evidence to sustain the view that this was racism rather than religion *simpliciter*, it remains remarkable that, as I write this, the sectarian framework is still in place.

When I spoke at the Changin Scotland conference in Ullapool in November 2011 I speculated that had my father been Italian and my mother's grandparents hailed from Italy in the late nineteenth century instead of County Carlow, my relationship with my native country would have been rather different. I would still have been reared in the Catholic tradition and the flag of my old country would have been a tricolour but it would not have been *that* tricolour. The respect and space afforded to Italian people in Scotland is not similarly given to the Irish.

It is a basic human right to be able to self-define, to say who you are. That is true of sexual orientation and of ethnic and national identity. Had I first saw the light of day in the 1950s in a culturally confident Scotland there would already be a Famine memorial in Glasgow and the city centre would be thronged with crowds on St Patrick's Day looking at the floats.

Professor Tom Devine has noted that census data proves that the Famine Irish achieved occupational parity in New York in 1901. The same ethnic group arriving in Glasgow at the same time did not reach that equality milestone until a century later. Now that the old economic barriers have been breached, what remains is what Professor Devine calls "attitudinal discrimination". As I will examine in this book, the cultural issues around the Irish and Irishness in Scotland are far from resolved.

The influence in Glasgow and the west of Scotland from beleaguered Ulster Loyalism cannot be discounted. The certainties of the old Stormont regime have gone, and nationalists in Northern Ireland demand equal treatment from the state and parity of esteem in matters like the Irish language. This is difficult for a subculture reared on *Herrenvolk* notions of supremacy. Instead, they now view themselves as victims of a *Kulturkampf* by Machiavellian Republicans. Meanwhile, the outside world just sees a society moving from institutional discrimination towards equality and mutual respect. Many of their leaders do not like this change. There is nothing unique about Eugène Terre'Blanche.

The experience of Irish people settling in England has been markedly different. In major cities south of the border there are huge Irish centres that are the hub of a myriad of community activities. Locals without Irish heritage join in if it takes their fancy. Subsequently, within a generation or two the Irish in England pretty much disappeared in the mass of white English people. Only the surname remained to hint at an Irish connection. That cannot be said of people in Scotland with a similar heritage.

The old chestnut of faith schools doesn't wash either. Many of the Irish in England send their children to faith schools and, strange to tell, there is no national navel gazing about Catholic schools in cities like Liverpool, London or Manchester. This is probably just a testament to the basic decency of English people. Aye, would some power the gift tae gie us, to see oursels as ithers see us, indeed!

However, this book is not about England or the English. No football crowd south of the border ever invented, let alone belted out, the Famine Song. Anti-Irish racism in Britain is a peculiarly Scottish phenomenon. Recently, the English Defence League tried to import this hatred into England after sampling the ambience of Glasgow. It fell flat. Only on the Clyde does it have roots in the soil.

This is a reality that many people in leadership positions in Scotland find uncomfortable. Raise this issue and the word "sectarianism" is used in reply. The utility function of the sectarian framework is multifold, with one of those functions being that it allows the conversation about the Irish in Scotland to be avoided.

This book deals with the Famine Song, however, this is not a work about Rangers Football Club or their supporters *in toto*, although it does focus on the subculture that has historically gathered around the Ibrox club and uses anti-Irish racism to self-define the values of their group.

Perhaps the Famine Irish in the nineteenth century were an unwelcome reminder of pre-British days as the Victorians larged it up on the imperial adventure. The Irish were like an embarrassing poor relative turning up uninvited just as the *nouveau riche* were attempting to impress some newly acquired friends. The Irish ethnicity at this specific historical juncture, as the British Empire was at its zenith, was particularly unwelcome.

Perhaps in the same way, the Lowland elite viewed the people of the Highlands as a block to closer union with England in the seventeenth century; the Irish arriving in the mid-nineteenth century in Glasgow in such numbers was a harbinger of trouble. Ireland had, within living memory, been shaken by a Republican uprising assisted by the revolutionary regicides in France. Glasgow had experienced its own radical shock in 1820 that had ended in public executions for Baird, Hardie and Wilson. The last thing the Scottish establishment needed was more anglophobia being dumped on its doorstep.

One Scotland, many cultures is a nice marketing slogan for Alex Salmond's "best small country in the world", but when the Irish in Scotland are mentioned it all gets a bit messy. Although the modern lexicon classifies the Famine Song as sectarian it is, quite clearly, racist and xenophobic towards the Irish and those of Irish heritage. Had the Famine Song been aimed at any other ethnic group in Scotland there would have been no squeamishness over using the R-word to so characterise the ditty. The utility function of much of the public discourse on the subject of sectarianism in Scotland in my lifetime has been to amputate the historical context and take the ethnic from the equation. The Famine song choir articulated a deep hatred of the Irish and of Irishness.

Yet, it is arguable that without outside interest, including questions in Dáil Éireann and, indeed, the European Parliament in late 2008, official Scotland may not have moved on this. By June 2009 it had been established – thanks to Lord Justice Carloway and his eminent colleagues – that the Famine Song was racist. The song encapsulated the paradoxical communication that Scottish psychiatrist RD Laing said was at the heart of the "double bind"; telling someone of Irish extraction to "go home" to Ireland while at the same time deriding that person when they sought to express or celebrate their Irishness. Why go home to Ireland if you're not, in some way, Irish? Racists are rarely rational and anyone singing the Famine Song is certainly singing a song that has been ruled racist in the highest court in Scotland.

It is the function of journalists to frame narrative and point the moral compass on such matters. They are not supposed to write permission slips for racists and explain away hate speech. However, that is what largely happened in Scotland during the time period that this book concerns itself with. How did the Irish come to lose their ethnicity in modern Scotland? This goes to the core of the issue and explains why, when asked to deal with the Famine Song in 2008 and 2009, only the forensic minds of the criminal justice system called this racism, for that is what it was.

Yet, the Fourth Estate in Scotland continued to cling to the sectarian framework. When I was introduced to the Famine Song in 2008 I immediately recognised the significance of it and that it had to be challenged. Rangers supporters had been told in June 2006 that they could no longer sing their favourite anthem, the Billy Boys, after a UEFA ruling when the club was fined £13,000 for singing the song at a Champions League match.

There was a need for a replacement that articulated what they were about. The Famine Song filled that void. Spokesmen for Rangers supporters' organisations felt confident enough to go on television to defend the song. It was breathtaking stuff. People outside Scotland, like politician and commentator George Galloway, stated again and again that if such a football song was aimed at Jewish people or black players then "it would be on CNN, it would be a scandal".

Yet, in Scotland the response was, at best, awkward and unsure. It was this incident that dragged me into reporting and writing about Scotland. The response in the years that followed showed me that I was better placed to comment and analyse than I had at first thought. A Glaswegian by birth and upbringing, I knew the city and the dynamics around Irishness.

I now know that my father wanted to settle in the USA with his kin there in the mid-1950s when he and my mother first married, but herself said no. She wanted to stay close to her mother, and in those days the USA was a journey that few could undertake with any regularity. It was my bad luck that I was born into a country where an Irish ethnicity was a form of social crime. I would go to school and grow into manhood in a city where occupational parity had not been achieved for people of my ethnic background.

The decisions taken for a child must be of the highest quality because a powerless little person will have to live with the consequences. My three children have grown up in Donegal. The youngest was born here and the other two never really knew anything else but Ireland. My first foray into writing about the Famine Song indicated that it made me glad that my three had little knowledge of Scotland and had not grown up there. This irked some racists and they had to concoct the "real reason" that I had taken my family to Ireland. As I was to learn, such people, indeed The People, have no moral boundaries, and when I wrote of these matters at the start of my reportage on the Famine Song those who would seek to defend that racist ditty needed to find a way to dismiss my criticism of their choice of song and what it said about them.

Personal attacks, threats and smears came to be part of my life. Rather than engage with what I was writing about, there seemed a desperate need to silence me. These chaps certainly seemed better at invective than investigation. Every day I would learn new, shocking details about my life that I had no idea of. I discovered that I had a sister and I did not live with my three children. Sadly, I remain an only child and this house, thankfully, has the happy soundtrack of my brood – minus the big guy, who has gone to the hallowed halls of Trinity College, Dublin, to be among his bright young peers.

The most bizarre revelation was that I had chosen to reside in Ireland because I was a fugitive from justice in Scotland. Of course, if I had been on the run from Scottish authorities I was rather ill advised in raising my profile in the Glasgow media village. Rather like ghost stories, what is of interest to me isn't the dearth of evidence to verify the existence of a spectre, but the deep emotional need that people had to believe that the fantasy was fact.

I styled these Rangers chaps part of an evidence-resistant subculture.

It seemed an appropriate sociological analysis of their behaviour as a human community. I don't think it makes them in any way unique but their level of group-think throughout the demise of their club was striking. In my writing about Scotland's racists I have been further reminded of the power of myth in human communities, even one as dysfunctional as the people who would sing and defend the Famine Song. In late 2008 the validity of their culture was being challenged. They did not take this well.

As I write this chapter, Belfast has seen the worst and most pro-longed rioting since the signing of the Good Friday Agreement in 1998, the cause being the decision taken in December 2012 by Belfast City Council to come into line with town halls across the UK and fly the union flag only on designated days. This sparked rioting that the police, at times, struggled to contain. It came from the same subculture that created the Famine Song and lauds the memory of the fascist Billy Fullerton. They have all the components in their belief system to be the Bosnian Serbs of the North Atlantic. Thankfully, they clearly lack the organisational smarts to do anything of note without an MI5 officer doing the arranging behind the scenes.

In Scotland this subculture has an acceptance and an inheritance from history that is not yet spent. The anti-Irish racism that this book examines has a stealth quality; it is not that it is whispered quietly, it is that it hides in plain sight. I cannot recall any mainstream journalist in Scotland in 2008 or 2009 who called out the Famine Song as a mani-festation of anti-Irish racism.

The Famine Song choir do not want people sent back to Vatican City; they want them put on the boat for Ireland. If that chant was aimed at the Italians it wouldn't be characterised sectarian, it would correctly be called out as racism. My grandfather once told me that a Scottish neighbour had remarked to him that she did not know that the Italians were Irish until she saw them going to the Catholic Church. The story is probably apocryphal, but it tells a greater truth about Irish ethnicity being equated with Catholicism to the point that, in the west of Scotland context, they were interchangeable terms.

This book could not have been written about people in North America. There, the term Irish American has a revered place in the lexi-con of the melting-pot nation. There is no equivalent term in Scotland, and that points to an inconvenient truth about the country I was born in. Sure, there is racism in the USA; sadly, lots of it. However, it is called out for what it is; there is no attempt to disguise it.

Conversely, the concept of an Irish Scot does not appear to have any generally accepted meaning. The term Glasgow Irish is in usage here in Ireland and people have their heads around that quite easily. To use that term in Glasgow to someone without that background or consciousness is to invite insult and challenge, so let's remove religious intolerance *simpliciter* from the analysis. What ails Scotland is an acceptance of a stealth racism that has been around all of my life and was one of the reasons that my wife and I did not want our brood being reared in the country we were both born in. An atheist since my teenage years, I saw anti-Irish racism as the issue impacting on people of my heritage within Scotland. The derogatory names for a Catholic within the Scottish lexicon tend to have Irish components; Fenian, Taig, etc.

In Scotland people will soon exercise their right to self-determination. The referendum of 2014 will be the demonstration that the people of Scotland, all of them, are sovereign. That in itself is historic. I suggested at the Changin Scotland conference in 2011 that the Scottish people needed to ask themselves what kind of country they wanted the new Scotland to be. I hope it is a more tolerant place than the one I grew up in and more at ease with itself. Confident cultures do not seek to exterminate an ethnicity or deny the existence of an identity. Hostile assimilation is not the same as integration, which would respect difference and promote active citizenship. The hostile response to the Irish and Irishness within modern Scotland is at the heart of this book. It explains the Famine Song, the victimisation of Glasgow Celtic manager Neil Lennon, the absence of a Famine memorial and much more besides.

But, there have been positive developments. The decision of Glasgow City Council in late 2012 to establish a working group to look into the nature and location of a memorial to the victims of An Gorta Mór was a huge step forward for my hometown. The prime mover in this project was Councillor Feargal Dalton of the SNP. A Dubliner and an ex-Royal Navy submariner, he was a PR nightmare for the klan to attempt to diss and so they didn't even try. Instead, the good ol' boys decided to try and put their own imprimatur on the proposed Famine memorial.

Professor Tom Devine indicated that he would come on board. One bizarre suggestion from the delusional world of Rangers message boards was that the memorial would have "mother Glasgow" simultaneously welcoming an Ulster Scot and an Irish Catholic. This attempt to sectarianise the history of An Gorta Mór is a first for me. I know of no other famine memorial where religiosity or politics have been built into the bronze, concrete or stone.

In the Famine, poor people starved. Their religion or politics – as if starving people had any energy to consider political debates – was irrelevant. In my journalistic work examining the absence of a Famine memorial in Glasgow my precedent was always the evocative statues on the Custom House Quay in Dublin.

As I was writing this book, the Scottish Government appointed an "anti-bigotry czar". Dr Duncan Morrow from the University of Ulster was brought in to guide the Scottish Government on matters sectarian. He was interviewed at length by the mainstream media on his appointment and the term anti-Irish racism never left his lips. This proved to me, sadly, that the political elite in Edinburgh are no further forward.

Anti-Catholic hatred in Scotland cannot be addressed without acknowledging the relationship it has to anti-Irish racism. When did Irishness and Catholicism become intertwined? By the time the Famine Irish arrived in Scotland any identifying mark of Catholicism was like a Star of David in the ghettoes of the Gorbals and the Calton.

In the mid-seventeenth century Oliver Cromwell decided that religion was the only basis upon which to divide the subjects of the Commonwealth and decide how they should be treated by the state. It was during the war crimes of the New Model Army that the Irish Catholic was socially constructed as the *Untermensch* of these islands – a view that is still extant on the Shankill Road and wherever Rangers supporters gather. There are, of course, followers of the Ibrox club who are appalled and embarrassed by the regular outpourings of the Rangers supporters who indulge in anti-Irish racism as part of their match-day experience.

What is atypical about anti-Irish racism in the modern Scottish context is that it is hidden from view by the sectarian framework. As English people regularly, and entirely unconsciously, interchange the words England and Britain, when Scots are engaged in conversation about anti-Irish racism the word sectarianism is usually used in response. Yet, stated hostility to Catholics within the west of Scotland often has a repatriation theme. The Famine Song was a recent example of the send-them-back impulse. Send who back to where?

There have been Catholics in Scotland since before Protestantism existed, so to suggest that people of the Catholic tradition are somehow alien in Scotland is nonsense. Where does one send the MacNeills of Barra back to? The destination for those that the Famine Song choir want repatriated to is, of course, Ireland. This is a xenophobic hatred that was incubated in Scotland from the demographic bulge created

by An Gorta Mór and the Irish Home Rule Crisis in the run-up to the
Great War. The Irish were "other", foreign, alien and just not properly
British. The Church and Nation Committee report of 1923 was not
some aberrant rant by an out of control bigot, but it spoke with the
authentic voice of the Scottish establishment. The title of the report
might give a clue to its contents: *The Menace of the Irish Race to our
Scottish Nationality*. The fear was not of Catholicism *per se*, but of large
numbers of Irish Catholics. Note that it mentions race and nationality
rather than religion.

The convenor of the Church and Nation Committee at that time
was John White. I believe he would have approved of the Famine Song.
He was racist and wanted the Irish to be sent back to Ireland. This is
xenophobia with a long history and it is within that context that the
Famine Song must be understood. What was heard from the Rangers
end was the stated belief that contemporary Scotland is much like the
one their great-grandfathers lived in. In some ways, sadly, they were not
mistaken.

When I started writing about the Famine Song in 2008 I started to
look at the place An Gorta Mór held in the officially sanctioned narrative of the country of my birth. As will be explored in the book, I do not
think it a coincidence that the country which gave the world the shameful Famine Song and which was a reception centre for Famine refugees
is also a country with no city centre memorial marking that fact in the
public space. It also, throughout my childhood, had no St Patrick's Day
parade in the city centre.

In the worldview of many of the Holyrood political elite, such a
move might be considered inflammatory or, whisper it, sectarian. Yet,
around the world on 17 March, cities with no Irish community to speak
of go the extra mile to put on a show for my country's patron saint. It is
a kitsch occasion with more anomalies than modern Christmas, but it
is the day for Irish exiles around the world. Glasgow doesn't have to do
much digging to unearth an Irish community.

I believe that the community activists in the city labour under conditions that no other part of the modern diaspora would recognise. The
Irishness of second-generation people is sneered at and wider society's
stance is to avoid mention of the presence of large numbers of people of
Irish ethnicity in the city and its hinterland.

This book also looks at the strange life of Neil Francis Lennon. You
may have heard of him. The young Armagh man was leading a successful, if rather uneventful life as a footballer with Leicester City. King

Lear, in ancient British legend, is the eponymous founder of Leicester. It is fitting because Lennon's life since leaving there for Scotland has been Shakespearean. When he joined Celtic Football Club in 2000 his life changed in many ways. It effectively signalled the end of his international football career with Northern Ireland. He was subjected to racist and sectarian abuse in almost every football ground he visited. When he became the manager of Celtic in 2010 and started to look like a success on the touchline, it was too much for the klan.

He was sent bullets in the mail and a package that the Crown's explosives expert said would have blown up had it been put together properly. He was later attacked at Tynecastle stadium while doing his job. Had Neil Francis Lennon been black his story would have been on CNN from the first few matches at Celtic when he was booed with every touch of the ball. Instead, it remained Scottish football's dirty little secret.

Then it was the turn of Celtic footballer Aiden McGeady. His crime was to be proudly Irish despite being born in Scotland. If this was being bracketed as an Old Firm thing by a venal and lazy sports media in Scotland it certainly did not explain the case of young James McCarthy. A starlet with Hamilton Academical, I sat among the visiting St Mirren fans at New Douglas Park in October 2008 as he was barracked every time he touched the ball. Chants about being a "plastic paddy" rose up if he was involved in the play for any length of time. Like McGeady, James's crime was to declare for the Republic of Ireland. It was dressed up as the misplaced patriotism of the so-called Tartan Army, but it was modern Scotland's oldest and most deeply entrenched hatred; anti-Irish racism. Football is the arena for much of the anti-Irish racism and this allows journalists operating in Scotland to dismiss it as sporting rivalry or the behaviour of a few yobs. Dr Morrow said that sectarianism in Scotland was not a "ned issue". Well, neither is anti-Irish racism.

I covered the self-destruction of Rangers in my previous book, *Downfall: How Rangers FC Self-Destructed*, and I will not revisit that particular tale in this book. However, any analysis of anti-Irish racism in Scotland that did not reference the importance of the Ibrox subculture would be absurd. Ironically, it was on St Patrick's Day 2011 that the club played PSV Eindhoven at Ibrox, a game which later resulted in the club being found guilty of "discriminatory chanting" for the fans' usual anti-Irish invective. I questioned UEFA persistently throughout that European campaign. After each match involving Rangers I submitted questions to the UEFA media office to see if the fans had been reported for their songs and chants. I suspected that the UEFA match delegates were not *au fait* with the nuances of the Ibrox song sheet and that discriminatory chanting was being missed. That night it was a chap from the Irish Football Association on point for the governing body, but apparently Mr Campbell heard nothing untoward. Fortunately, Fans Against Racism in Europe (FARE) had a representative in the stadium and their word was good enough for UEFA.

Only anti-Irish racism in Scottish football requires this level of effort to bring appropriate action. Moreover, it was up to UEFA, as the Scottish domestic authorities had been handed many opportunities to act on the racist chanting at Rangers matches and failed. As I was compiling this introduction I remarked to a colleague that the reception to my work in Ireland was strikingly different to the way it was characterised by the Fourth Estate in Scotland.

Writing in the *Scottish Review of Books* in 2012, journalist Kevin McKenna wrote the following: "If Mac Giolla Bháin had been employed as a staffer on any of Scotland's dozen or so national newspaper titles he would be a certainty to be crowned sportswriter of the year, news reporter of the year and journalist of the year for his work on the Rangers story. Yet not even the merest hint of his name will be breathed at the annual industry awards bash early next year. The reasons why not are not dissimilar to those that have prevented any review of *Downfall* yet having appeared in any Scottish newspaper at the time of writing."

I am a regular contributor on Irish radio and my work is published in Irish newspapers. In the land of my birth operating under the official fiction of the sectarian framework, there is no space for journalism of this sort. Subsequently, in 2008 I had the option of having my work on the Famine Song read in Ireland and among the Irish community in Britain through the pages of the *Irish Post* and leaving it at that or trying to influence the debate in Scotland through an online platform. My own website had existed since 2007 as an archive of my previously published work. From the summer of 2008 my site administrator had installed blogging software, so by the time the Famine Song controversy broke I was already writing for an online readership.

Last year, the site had over five million page views. Someone somewhere was paying attention. Since the site has been up and running as a blog there have been several not-too-subtle attempts to take it offline; spurious complaints to the web hosting company and two DOS attacks as well as the stream of invective, smears and threats from heroic chaps who never reveal their true identities. However, not all comments were hostile, and it appeared that I had stumbled upon people who had largely abandoned the mainstream media in Scotland and wanted to read news and comment that was not influenced by Rupert Murdoch or Sir David Murray.

As I look back across the period of time that is covered by this book I am more convinced than ever that modern Scotland has abnormalised itself *apropos* the Irish and Irishness. It seems to be self-evident to anyone outside the country when things like the Famine Song are brought to their attention. This book is a record of my work over several years of trying to highlight the extent of that abnormality to the people who are apparently blind to this racism in Scotland. The duty of a journalist is to bear witness, to hold the powerful to account and to try and make a difference. This is what I have tried to do.

PART I: THE FAMINE SONG

Introduction

You always remember how a person made you feel, even if you can't recall what it was they said to you. For me, that's how it was with the Famine Song. My memory is quite clear; I was incredulous. Here was a group of people who thought nothing of mocking An Gorta Mór.

When I started to analyse the lyrics of the Famine Song I knew immediately the importance of this new addition to the Rangers songbook. The song broke the sectarian framework and only the most historically illiterate journalist reporting on this could fail to see the ethnic component. The Famine Song was aimed at Celtic supporters; they were being asked why they didn't go home now that the Famine was over. Celtic Football Club was born from the Irish community that sprung up in Victorian Glasgow in the years following the Potato Famine of 1845–1849. The club is arguably the most visible evidence that Glasgow has of an Irish strand in its narrative. The Irishness of Celtic was built into the DNA of the club from the earliest days. For people in Glasgow unhappy that their city had suddenly become home to so many poor people from Ireland, Celtic, as a symbol of Irishness, was not something they welcomed.

That xenophobic hostility to the Irish in Glasgow has lasted generations and the Famine Song was only the most recent manifestation of that racism. The two words "famine" and "home" made it clear; this was about Ireland and the Irish. The send-them-back impulse is a common theme for racists when they perceive their country or city is being "swamped". What made the Famine Song more interesting was that Irish immigration to Scotland had dried up to a trickle from the 1970s onwards. This new addition to the Rangers song sheet was an echo from the 1923 Church and Nation Committee report which stated that the Irish race was a menace to the Scottish nationality. The document made it clear on page one that the Kirk did not consider the Roman Catholics from the Highlands to be such a menace, as they were of

the same race as other Scots. The report further called for the ending
of immigration of Irish Catholics to Scotland and the deportation of
any convicted of a criminal offence or living on state benefits. The convener of the Church and Nation Committee at the time of the report
was John White. White advocated a "racially pure" Scotland, declaring:
"Today there is a movement throughout the world towards the rejection of non-native constituents and the crystallisation of national life
from native elements." In the eyes of the men drafting the 1923 report,
this was about race, not religion. His role in the report did not adversely
impact his career, as two years later he was elected Moderator of the
General Assembly. In 1927, the Reverend John White congratulated
the General Assembly, saying: "They dealt with this very difficult, deli-
cate and important question entirely from the racial point of view. The
religious factor did not enter the question at all."

Of course, context, especially historical context, is vital to understanding such ideas and their currency. After the Second World War
ideas of "racial purity" and distinguishing people on the basis of race
was redolent of the Third Reich. Yet, even as late as 1952 the Church of
Scotland referred to the Irish in Scotland as an "alien race". Moreover,
this did not produce howls of outrage – it was not a resigning issue, it
was the common sense of the day. In Scotland the Irish were "other",
different and lesser. The very same year that the Church of Scotland
referred to the Irish in Scotland in such xenophobic terms, the Scottish
Football Association asked Celtic to take down the Irish tricolour from
the stand at Celtic Park. The referee committee of the SFA ruled that
"Celtic be asked to refrain from displaying in its park any flag or emblem
that had no association with the country or the sport" on match days.
The club chairman, Bob Kelly, faced the SFA down. The particular flag
in question had been presented to the club by Eamonn De Valera, the
Taoiseach of the Irish Republic. At the same time in the north of Ireland,
the unionist parliament at Stormont had passed the Flags and Emblems
Act. This made it, in effect, illegal to fly the Irish tricolour.

The close comparison was not lost on many of Celtic's supporters in
that part of Ireland. The Parkhead club no longer had to compete for
the support of those in Belfast with affection for a team in green-and-
white hoops. Belfast Celtic went out of business after suffering sustained violence from Loyalist mobs following Linfield FC. The club
believed that the Royal Ulster Constabulary was, at the very least, reticent about protecting their players. Belfast Celtic withdrew from the
league and would never again play a competitive match. Their final

friendly match on their home turf was against Glasgow Celtic in 1952. This was the Irish backdrop to the SFA's move in the same year to take the Irish tricolour down from the flagpole at Celtic Park. That episode summed up the central narrative of the Irish in Glasgow and not just Celtic's often fraught relationship with football officialdom. The Irish were barely tolerated, but not respected. These alien outsiders could remain in Scotland, in the lower reaches of society providing cheap labour, but their heritage and symbols would not be afforded space let alone respect.

I was reminded of this history when I sat with a senior member of Celtic media staff in the Jury's Inn on Custom House Quay in Dublin in the summer of 2011. The club was about to take part in the Dublin Super Cup, a pre-season tournament. Outside the hotel there is a memorial to the Famine comprising several life-sized figures. It was hard not to make the connections of Celtic, the Famine and Ireland. We discussed doing a small piece for Celtic TV at the memorial, but the schedule didn't allow it. The *Celtic View* had just published a piece I'd written on the need for a Famine memorial in Glasgow. As I stated the crushingly obvious about the club's strong Irish heritage he cut across me and reminded me of a basic fact: "Most of our season-ticket holders have Glasgow postcodes." The majority of those to whom the Famine Song choir were singing in 2008 were people born in Glasgow, living in Glasgow, and they were suggesting they "go home" to Ireland. It was part of the racist double bind that the second generation Irish in Scotland had endured all of my lifetime: "Go home to Ireland, but you're not Irish!" The Famine Song was telling Glaswegians to go home to Ireland; ipso facto, the people singing those words considered Ireland to be the home nation of the song's target group. However, if the subjects of the Famine Song wanted to, say, take part in St Patrick's Day celebrations, their connection to Ireland and Irishness would be denigrated and dismissed. Racism often has an internal logic that is difficult for the rest of us to grasp. The Famine Song choir thought they were making sense.

When the Rangers chaps first belted out the Famine Song at Celtic Park in August 2008, in the crowd was someone who had travelled that morning from Dublin with his young son. It was their first Glasgow derby match. The father, an architect, was appalled at what he heard and on his return to Dublin he contacted his local TD (MP). He also got in touch with me. He wasn't the only one to do so, and within a few weeks the Minister for Foreign Affairs, Micheál Martin, was being asked

about the Famine Song by a series of opposition TDs from various parties. Each TD's question specifically mentioned the anti-Irish racism of
the song, and Martin responded with written replies provided for him
by the Department of Foreign Affairs. These responses were drafted by
civil servants in Iveagh House and they consistently mentioned the work
being done to combat sectarianism in Scotland and the close ties that the
Irish Consulate in Edinburgh had with the Scottish Executive.

This founded the basis of a conversation I would have on several occasions with senior members of the Department of Foreign Affairs. I told
them that by replying with a quote on sectarianism when asked about
racism they were not being part of the solution in Scotland *apropos* anti-
Irish racism. Indeed, they were compounding the problem by using the
Scottish Government's preferred lexicon for dealing with matters Irish.

Another strand of the Famine Song story was the failure of publicly
funded bodies tasked with combating racism in sport. Show Racism
the Red Card (SRTRC) had an admirable track record of being quick
to denounce any incidents of skin-colour racism in the Scottish game.
Here, when faced with anti-Irish racism, they seemed, to this journalist, to be, at best, reticent. One ex-employee of SRTRC stated to me
that the non-governmental organisation "had no idea what to do about
anti-Irish racism in Scotland". The first obstacle I encountered when I
started working on the story was obtaining a statement from SRTRC
on the Famine Song. It proved to be an uphill battle.

I was aware that SRTRC was about to have a "week of action" in
Scotland in October 2008 so I decided to join in. An empty Tynecastle
stadium was the venue for a match between a SRTRC select, managed by SPL chief Lex Gold, and a motley crew of MSPs and policy
wonks from Holyrood. The SRTRC side had fitba luminaries like Chic
Charnely, Gary MacKay and SFA supremo Gordon Smith. The person
I was there to see was Billy Singh, the campaign director of SRTRC.
I introduced myself as he warmed up on the pitch readying himself
to take part in the match. I had a simple enough question for him:
why hadn't his organisation declared that the Famine Song was racist?
He told me I was wrong and it had always been called out as such. I
then asked why that wasn't on their website. The week after my visit
I noticed a new statement had appeared on the SRTRC website stating the organisation's opinion that the Famine Song was indeed racist.
When the Famine Song had first been "performed" several organisations from within Glasgow's Irish community approached SRTRC and
complained about it. My sources in the Irish community informed me

they were less than convinced about the ability of SRTRC to tackle the issue. By the time I was chasing the campaign director in Scotland, the organisation was well aware of the words and the import of the Famine Song, yet there was no statement on its website about it at that point, let alone any visible campaign.

The game was a walk-over for the ex-pros. I had an interesting chat during the match with Lex Gold about how he viewed the controversy. We spoke about Aiden McGeady, his visit to Croke Park in Dublin and his less than complimentary views of FIFA supremo Sepp Blatter. I recall getting the impression that he was hearing of the history of Croke Park for the first time and what the GAA generally meant to Irish people. When I told him of the events of Bloody Sunday 1920 I thought I heard a penny drop in an echo-filled Tynecastle as the SPL's top man in Scotland briefly viewed the world through Irish eyes. I left the home ground of Heart of Midlothian Football Club believing that I had been in the company of a fair-minded and decent man. A month later I saw a statement attributed to him in a Glasgow newspaper (the *Evening Times*) where he made the point that the Famine Song was racist, not sectarian: "Clubs know they need to be alert and make sure their fans are doing all they can to avoid sectarian or other offensive abuse. The verse of the song that has featured hugely is racist; it's not sectarian as such, it's racist. The rules were structured to help to try to tackle this. You don't start with points deduction. We have a range of sanctions which can be applied."

I told Lex Gold at Tynecastle that I feared if anti-Irish racism wasn't called out as such, the mob mentality that was being incubated – especially at matches involving Rangers – could authorise acts of violence in the deranged minds of some of the Famine Song choir. I said that I hoped that I was wrong, but I didn't see the racist targeting of Irish players ending well. What I could not know is that the spot I was standing on with the SPL's top guy was where John Wilson, a Hearts fan, would lunge at Neil Lennon on 11 May 2011. The world would see those images of a young football manager being attacked at his place of work. I do not believe that incident would have happened had it not become, in part, normal to demonise not just Neil Lennon, but Ireland and Irishness within Scottish football.

Down in the dugout after the SRTRC charity match, I asked Gordon Smith about the James McCarthy situation and he was admirably forthright. He said that the lad had made his choice and people should leave him alone. On the Famine Song, Smith said the SFA could not make a comment as it was the appellant body to the SPL, meaning if any SPL club was sanctioned by the league and disagreed with that punishment, the SFA was the court of appeal. Given the role of the Scottish Football Association in such matters it couldn't make any public comment about something it might later be called to adjudicate on.

I took an instant liking to Smith; I thought him to be a straight talker. We would bump into each other almost three years later in the media centre of the AVIVA stadium in Dublin and we enjoyed a wide-ranging chat about the brilliance of Spanish football and what had happened to the gene pool that once produced Jim Baxter, Billy Bremner, Jimmy Johnstone and Denis Law. A few weeks later he would be appointed Director of Football at Rangers by new owner Craig Whyte, a club that Smith played for and supported as a boy. I would break that story, much to the chagrin of the Glasgow sports desks, but by that time I didn't worry too much about their feelings. It was during the "Famine Song" story that I developed a rather low opinion of this section of the Fourth Estate in Scotland, and with good cause.

The day after the SRTRC match at Tynecastle I went to Hamilton to test Lex Gold's theory that anti-Irish racism, like the Famine Song and the abuse meted out to Celtic's Aiden McGeady for picking the Republic of Ireland as his national team, was merely an "Old Firm thing". Hamilton Academical were playing St Mirren. The clash of these two provincial West of Scotland teams could hardly be shoehorned into the Old Firm paradigm. The 'Accies had a young starlet, James McCarthy, on their books. Undeniably a talent, he had elected to play for the Republic of Ireland and was being subjected to the same "banter" as Aiden McGeady at Celtic. My experience sitting among the visiting chaps from Paisley confirmed to me that anti-Irish feeling was no preserve of the paying public at Ibrox on match day. Every time James McCarthy touched the ball he was booed. Sometimes this will happen in a match if a player has transgressed in the eyes of the opposition support. Usually the player has committed a bad foul on one of their players. He immediately becomes the panto baddy and it is all part of the fun. The red-haired, lanky eighteen-year-old midfielder was trying out his flicks and tricks on the wing. This was no hated enforcer dishing out the medicine. When McCarthy was on the ball for any length of time the "plastic paddy" chants would start from a determined clutch of St Mirren fans. The abuse aimed at young McCarthy did not make it into any of the match reports in the newspapers the next day and I wasn't surprised. However, if McCarthy had been black it would have been the Scottish football story of the weekend, of that I have no doubt. In fact, Hamilton ended the match with three black players on the field and there were some tasty tackles from two of them as the home team chased an equaliser. Yet the booing and chanting was only aimed at McCarthy. The following week Rangers visited New Douglas Park in the SPL. The Famine Song was altered for the day.

The visiting fans chanted throughout most of the match "James McCarthy, why don't you go home?" This did make it into the mainstream media, but there was always the minimisation and mitigation from the usual suspects on the sports desks. The Scottish mainstream media played a thoroughly dishonourable role in covering the Famine Song controversy. Their initial response to the news that the Irish Government had asked the Scottish Executive for clarification on this song was to undermine the very suggestion that the Famine Song was racist. James Traynor and Keith Jackson, both of the *Daily Record*, came particularly to the fore in defending this item of football "banter". Even when the Famine Song was criticised by one of the press pack it was kept within the sectarian framework, probably because they could not conceptualise anything else. They excised the ethnic from the analysis, therefore their reportage was nonsensical. What was unforgivable was the extent to which some tried to defend the song in print and on the airwaves.

While I was preparing this introduction I was also finishing off a piece of work for the European Council's Media Against Racism in Sports project (MARS). As part of my collaboration with a colleague in Spain we looked at anti-Irish racism in Scottish football and how ethnic and regional tensions were manifested in Spanish soccer. My partner on this project was a Canadian with a father from Aberdeenshire. He was a naturalised "Gallego" by marriage and parenthood. As we worked through the Famine Song and the Billy Boys it was hugely valuable to get his *súil eile* on the subject. The moment he heard of the Famine Song story he was intrigued. When he went away and studied YouTube footage of fans singing it and the reporting of the William Walls case he was clear that this song was as racist as anything he had seen or heard in Spain. The "banter" defence didn't work with him. This was the targeting of an ethnic minority by a racist subculture that was organised around a football club. He offered the observation that if Irish had been replaced with Jew and the country was Poland instead of Scotland no one would have been offering the explanation that this was some failed attempt at Holocaust humour. When we discussed that the Famine Song was introduced because of the banning of the Billy Boys from

2006, I had to explain the significance of that ditty within the Rangers subculture. That can't be achieved unless the life and world of Billy Fullerton is scrutinised.

The word fascist is a much over-used term in the modern lexicon of political discourse, but the man that Rangers fans laud in song – and the Billy Boys song made a comeback as recently as late 2012 at Hampden Park when New Rangers played Queen's Park – was indeed a fascist. To the tune of "Marching Through Georgia", the song lauding Glasgow gang-leader Fullerton was the preferred battle hymn of the Ibrox faithful since I had started watching football in the 1960s. The song emerged in the 1930s as the signature tune of Fullerton's eponymous street gang of razor-wielding thugs which, at its height during the inter-war period, had 800 members. During the General Strike in 1926 the Billy Boys were used to attack trade unionists and many of Fullerton's thugs received Certificates of Commendation from the Secretary of State for Scotland for services rendered during it. Billy Fullerton, who died in 1962, was a right-wing sociopath from central casting. As well as founding and leading the Billy Boys he joined Oswald Mosley's British Union of Fascists and started a Glasgow branch of the Ku Klux Klan. The man who led the Billy Boys in their street war against the Irish of Glasgow was the alpha male of the racist subculture that had been incubated at Ibrox in the days when the team on the field of play was "racially pure". A hatred of the immigrant Irish, conflated with a detestation of Catholicism and a suspicion of any left-wing view of the world defined much of the Rangers faithful. These supporters, who were often Empire Loyalists and protective of their employment privileges within craft unions, saw the Irish as a threat to their way of life. The song that was banned by UEFA in 2006, bringing censure down on Rangers, was an echo of an earlier Scotland that was still not completely extinguished. Although this is not a book about Rangers FC or the new club that now bears their name, one cannot write about anti-Irish racism in Scotland without reference to the collective consciousness of much of the Ibrox faithful.

Taking my colleague through the initial months of the Famine Song controversy and explaining what happened made me consider the amount of work that had gone into this story during those months. I hope that this section conveys a flavour of that effort and why I thought it was necessary. The role of a journalist in any democracy is to hold the powerful to account by questioning them and to bear witness to important events. Telling a truth that powerful people don't want you to tell is the only truth worth telling. As part of my work with the MARS project I worked for several days in November 2012 with a veteran Spanish TV journalist. We located the Latin American community in Bordeaux and examined the world from their perspective with regards to identity, integration and racism. At the end of the event my *compañero*, Paco, gave me a badge as a memento of our work together. It had a simple and incontestable statement for anyone who values this trade: *"Sin periodismo no hay democracia"*. Indeed, I cannot conceive of a functioning democracy without a free press. The role of journalism and journalists in any given situation where there is cultural or ethical confusion is to point the moral compass. In this the Scottish sports press signally failed. Perhaps because of where I lived and my vantage point I could do the country of my birth some service. It is incontrovertible that for a period in late 2008 and early 2009 I seemed to be the only journalist working on this story on an ongoing basis.

I knew how this story was playing in Ireland and it wasn't going well. Timing, as with most things in life, was crucial for the Famine Song story. In September 2008 RTÉ – Ireland's national broadcaster – was running a hugely successful series called *Where Was Your Family During The Famine?* Based on the BBC's genealogy series *Who Do You Think You Are?*, it too used well-known faces from the Irish media village and researched their families back to those dark times in our history. The three participants were TV presenter Eddie Hobbs, journalist John Waters and model Jasmine Guinness, a member of the aristocratic brewing dynasty.

When John Waters became the consulting editor of *Magill* in 2001 he commissioned me to write several articles in the early years of that decade. He also kindly agreed to write the foreword of my first book, *Preventable Death*, which is about male suicide in Ireland. The researchers on the show had found that John's great grand-uncle had died of starvation as a child in Sligo and that there had been no money available for a funeral. In a powerful piece to camera, Waters said that this "crime", multiplied by one million, was what the Famine was all about. He looked shattered as the information was revealed to him. I know that this wasn't a staged event. He was reacting in real time to what he was being told.

As I told this story to a police inspector at the City Chambers in Glasgow a couple of months later, I opined that the chaps in charge of the unofficial song book at Rangers had rather miscalculated – making jokes about An Gorta Mór wasn't such a good idea in the autumn of

2008. At first, the policeman, who was in charge of planning for the divisional area that included Hampden and Ibrox, thought that this whole Famine Song thing was just "hyperbole". It seemed an appropriate time to utilise the immortal words of Mr John Sacrimoni – it was indeed one of those moments: "Let me explain something to you again, but differently." I explained it was like trying to tell a Jewish person that jokes about Auschwitz were no big deal. He got it. The reason I was chatting to one of Strathclyde's finest in the citadel of municipal power in my native city in the first place was because of the Famine Song. The campaign against the song took a turn for the better when Eoin Ryan, the MEP for the Dublin constituency, raised the issue on the floor of the European Parliament. He had heard me being interviewed about the song by Matt Cooper on Today FM's *The Last Word*, a nationwide drive-time radio show. Ryan then read my piece in the *Irish Post* and decided that the Famine Song was appalling and had to be opposed. He was invited on a fact-finding mission to Scotland by Scottish MEP Alyn Smith. A member of the ruling Fianna Fáil party, Ryan jetted into Scotland and was given an "everything is okay here" tour. SNP MEP Smith said: "A lot of good work has been done in Scotland to combat sectarianism on all sides, and I am not going to stand by and watch a limited few mindless thugs damage our special relationship with the Irish."

It was interesting that not one single hack sought to seek clarification on why hatred aimed at a nation wasn't racism. Here was the core of the problem: anti-Irish racism in Scotland could not be called that. It magically became "sectarianism". No media was allowed into the meeting at the City Chambers, although Alyn Smith's young press officer, Grant Baskerville, did give me a lovely quote: "We're not sweeping anything under the carpet in there," he told me outside the meeting room. At this point I had only stated my name, shown my press card and told him that I was writing a piece for the *Irish Post*. I explained to him that the *Irish Post* was the weekly newspaper for the Irish community in Britain and that I would be filing to the Irish dailies later that day. Ryan's savvy press officer rarely left his guy's side, but he did do it long enough for me to brief him about what this disinformation day was all about. I explained to him, using terms that he would instinctively understand, that "this sectarianism/racism thing, it's a Derry/Londonderry issue; the Scots won't call it racism because that means recognising the Irish community here, something they don't seem too keen on. However, this is really important to the Irish community here. Remember that when you're preparing Eoin's statement." My work for *An Phoblacht* – the newspaper of the Republican Movement in Ireland, effectively Sinn Féin's official organ – over the years made briefing a politician's press officer second nature. He thanked me for the help and I duly saw some traces of our conversation in the statement that Ryan put out at the end of the day.

The quick chat with Ryan's press guy actually got to the crux of this whole controversy. People of Irish heritage were being told to go home to Ireland in a country that had, throughout most of the twentieth century, simultaneously denied their right to their ethnicity and a place in society based on equality. This was the Ibrox klan's Enoch Powell moment. The Clyde, unlike the Tiber, did not run red, but that was the colour of some faces within the Scottish political elite as questions were asked in Dáil Éireann and the European Parliament. Had the Famine Song been aimed at Italians in Scotland it would not have been characterised sectarian.

November 2008 was a good month for those of us who wanted to eradicate the Famine Song from Scottish soccer stadia, indeed from Scottish society. As well as the visit of Eoin Ryan MEP to Glasgow, Rangers supporter William Walls found himself in front of Sheriff McDonald at Kilmarnock Sheriff Court. He was convicted for chanting the lines of the Famine Song.

The charge read:

> *On 9 November 2008 at Rugby Park ... Kilmarnock you ... did conduct yourself in a disorderly manner, shout, swear, sing sectarian songs, shout remarks of a religious and racial nature and commit a breach of the peace; you ... did commit this offence while on bail, ... and it will be proved in terms of section 74 of the Criminal Justice (Scotland) Act 2003 that the aforesaid offence was aggravated by religious prejudice and it will be proved in terms of section 96 of the Crime and Disorder Act 1998 that the aforesaid offence was racially aggravated.*

He decided to appeal his conviction and this decision did the state some service. His case was heard at the High Court of Justiciary in June 2009. The appeal failed and the illegality of the Famine Song was no longer in question in Scots law. It was a good day for the good guys. The idea that the Famine Song could bring one of the choristers before the courts had been scoffed at on Rangers message boards. My view since I had first heard the ditty was that it had to be illegal – it was undoubtedly a hate crime, aimed at an ethnic minority. Lord Carloway ruled that "the court does not consider that the lyrics of this refrain bear any reasonable comparison to those of 'Flower Of Scotland' or indeed 'God Save The Queen'. Rather they are racist in calling upon people native to Scotland to leave the country because of their racial origins. This is a sentiment which ... many persons will find offensive." Lord Carloway added that the appeal judges accepted the sheriff's conclusion that singing the song's chorus "displays malice and ill-will towards people of Irish descent living in Scotland".

The Famine was a massive psychic wound on the collective consciousness of the Irish people – all of us. Those million corpses in mass graves held a million stories. I hadn't always known about mine, but I was sure that there was something there. It would have been almost actuarially impossible for my Mayo family not to have lost someone during An Gorta Mór. Taking my lead from John Waters I looked into my own family history. John and I are around the same age and both with family in the west of Ireland. John was born in Castlereagh, Roscommon, and my father was born in Westport, County Mayo. It did not surprise me to find that the genealogist considered the disappearance of my great-grandfather's brother from the household in those years likely to have been a Famine death. John and I were both three generations removed from this crime against our people. My grandmother never knew her father's brother as he died as a child. Philip Derrig was with his kin in the 1841 Census, but, although the family was at the same abode, a decade later he was absent. I was puzzled that the genealogist could not track down a death certificate until I read Tim Pat Coogan's masterful book (*The Famine Plot: England's Role in Ireland's Greatest Tragedy*, Palgrave Macmillan, 2012), and then I finally understood. The level of death sweeping over my father's county in those years meant that the basic governance of recording mortality effectively collapsed.

The scenes that Coogan depicted, using primary sources from the time, challenged my capacity to grasp the enormity of this holocaust on the Irish people, on my people. The British overlords seemed quite happy for this unnatural disaster to consume the "mere Irish". In some North American universities, An Gorta Mór is taught within courses of genocide studies. British Prime Minister Tony Blair apologised in 1997, on the 150th anniversary of the Famine, for the inadequate relief effort by the London government of the day. Some historians are of the view that the starvation was a weapon of war that was far more effective in dealing with the often rebellious Irish than bayonets or cannon fire. There is an old Irish saying, "It is easy to sleep on another man's wound", and I'm sure that the Famine Song choir slept like babies while sniggering over a million dead.

As Prime Minister Blair had apologised in 1997 for Britain's failings as ruler of all of Ireland in 1847 then so in May 2011 did a far more symbolic act of closure take place in Dublin. The British head of state, Queen Elizabeth II, bowed her head before a monument honouring Ireland's patriot dead in the Garden of Remembrance only a few hundred yards from the GPO where the insurgents had fought her grandfather's loyal troops. During that state visit, the first to the Republic by a British monarch, she came very close in a carefully crafted speech to saying sorry to the Irish people. In this age of reconciliation and atonement, the Famine Song was totally out of sync with the new Zeitgeist emerging within these islands.

The Famine Song and the response of the Fourth Estate in those months during 2008 told me a lot about the state of play in the place I was born and reared. It convinced me that my wife and I had made the correct decision to move our young family to Ireland in the mid-1990s. I brought my young family to Ireland in 1996 and we settled in Donegal. The county where I have reared my brood, like Mayo, has mass graves from the time of the Famine. Some academics believe that the folk memory of an atrocity is around ninety years, essentially three generations. The shame of the Famine caused it to be a largely taboo subject among people in rural Ireland. There is, of course, the guilt of survival. My grandmother's father survived, but his brother did not. Such psychological scars can be passed down the generations like ripples in a pool. If he did speak about this to his daughter, she never passed it down to her children and grandchildren. As the impact of these awful events recedes into the past they only exercise historians and academics until, of course, someone makes reference to them in the here and now. That is what the Famine Song did.

The controversy had a momentary impact in Ireland, which was remarkable given the timing. In the autumn of 2008 the global banking crisis was just starting to unravel. Celtic Tiger Ireland, with its huge financial services industry, was hugely engaged with what was happening on Wall Street. Another factor which made the coverage given to the story even more unlikely was the long-term effect in the Dublin media of many journalists having come into the trade during a prolonged period of state censorship against Republicans and Republicanism.

Section 31 of the 1960 Broadcasting Authority Act in the Republic of Ireland banned anyone from the airwaves if they represented Sinn Féin, even if they were elected politicians like county councillors. Anything that could be perceived to give succour and support to the Provisional IRA or its political wing had to be kept off the airwaves. This included avoiding any stories that might reinforce the beliefs of earlier generations that Ireland had been a victim of British imperialism and the only language that "Perfidious Albion" understood was physical force. The ban on members of Sinn Féin was lifted in 1993 by the Minister for Arts, Culture and the Gaeltacht, Michael D Higgins, as part of the Northern Ireland peace process. During the Section 31 years, many in Irish journalism learned to self-censor because it was good for their prospects. By the time of the Famine Song, most of the careers of senior people in the Dublin media had been established during that era.

There were very few people around in any positions of power that would be well disposed to a story about an Irish community in Britain suffering racism from British Loyalists. This was part of a wider movement called revisionism, which had started in the early 1970s and sought to look again at the accepted wisdom of Irish nationalism. Revisionists were, and remain, hugely influential in politics, media and the arts in the Republic of Ireland. This, coupled with the Section 31 mindset, made many in the Irish media uneasy about running with any story that might nourish the old Republican narrative that they were eager to see die. Despite all of this, and during the biggest global financial story since the Wall Street Crash, the national titles and national radio *did* run with the Famine Song story. It was a testament to the enduring cultural wound that is An Gorta Mór that the song could become a major news item in the midst of the Lehman Brothers collapse.

The idea of expelling Irish people from where they live actually pre-dates the modern diaspora. It happened here in Ireland first. The slow colonisation of the island from eastern bridgeheads in the east of the country by English, then British settlers has a long history. Today, even in post-Good Friday Agreement Belfast, the impulse to expel the "natives" remains strong. On the twelfth of July 2012, a Loyalist band wearing paramilitary uniforms stopped outside St Patrick's Church on Donegall Street in north Belfast during the parade. The band was recorded walking in circles outside the church by two different people. They played the tune of the Famine Song – borrowed from the Beach Boys' "Sloop John B" – and the following group took the cue and belted out the racist ditty. It was sadly instructive that the musical weapon of choice for Ulster Loyalists who wished to tell the Irish to get out of "their country" was the Famine Song.

A local community activist filmed this racist performance art on a mobile phone and, despite being threatened by a steward for his trouble, made good his escape. He duly got the footage onto YouTube and it was picked up by the mainstream. The Loyalist band apologised, but it did show that the impulse to expel Irish people "back home" even exists in parts of Ireland. There really isn't anything to be done with that. This weapons-grade stupidity is impossible to reason with. That is why police and courts exist. Any solution to this ancient and atavistic hatred will be multi-generational. In the city that spawned the Famine Song, people increasingly state that they will not put up with what their parents and grandparents endured. A clear element of the way forward is that the socially excluded group that has historically suffered this abuse realise, collectively, that they no longer have to go through what generations before them did. That is true for nationalists in the north of Ireland and it is also true of the Glasgow Irish. The Famine Song is not the sound of the mobilisation of a large xenophobic movement; rather it is the death rattle of an old culture where Paddy knew his place.

As I continued to write on the Famine Song, I realised that Glasgow was atypical, perhaps even unique. The city was a major reception centre for survivors of Black '47 and yet it did not have a city-centre Famine memorial. The more I considered this, the more I thought it unlikely to be a coincidence that the city that gave the world the Famine Song was without a memorial to An Gorta Mór. Subsequently, in the summer of 2011 I began to write about the lack of a memorial in Glasgow. In this section there are pieces from the *Celtic View*, the *Irish Post* and the *Mayo News* as well as from my own site, posing the question about the absence of a permanent memorial to An Gorta Mór. In November 2011 I was invited to speak to the Changin Scotland conference in Ullapool by political commentator and policy wonk Gerry Hassan. These twice-yearly gatherings have grown in significance over the years. I put a question to the crowd of locals and Central Belt politicos during my talk: What kind of country do you want this new Scotland to be? Unlike the famously unanswerable West Lothian Question, this one could be dealt with if there was sufficient will inside that room in the Highlands and, indeed, within the Scottish political village. I described how I had been born into a country, their country, in the 1950s, one that didn't want me. Moreover, any expression of Irishness was strictly *verboten*. Throughout my life, the city witnessed no St Patrick's Day parade, erected no Famine memorial. There was a complete lack of the respect for Irish ethnicity that is found in the great cities of North America. I left that question with them. What kind of country is it that wouldn't have a memorial to An Gorta Mór despite being home to the city most hugely affected by that event?

I was contacted in early 2012 by a couple of young members of the SNP in Glasgow and they told me that they had taken on board the issue of the Famine memorial for Glasgow. At that time, I was immersed in the Rangers meltdown story so I wished them well and left them to it. There was little more I could do at that point. I had written in various publications in Ireland and Scotland, both print and online, about the need and desirability for a Famine memorial in Glasgow. It was for others to make this happen. All I could do from my perch in the west of Ireland was point certain things out.

I then got an opportunity to do so in a great city where it isn't a cultural crime to be Irish. In August 2012 I was invited by leading members of the Irish community in the city of brotherly love, Philadelphia, to speak at the impressive Famine memorial there. I was already in Philly to attend a friendly match between Celtic and Real Madrid, and the Glasgow club were represented at the memorial ceremony by Dubliner Anthony Stokes. Local state representative Kevin Boyle spoke passionately at the monument about the lack of cultural respect shown to Irish people in Glasgow. The young politician was not the poorly informed Irish American from central casting. Earlier in the day I had been introduced to him at the pre-match press conference. He asked where I had travelled from and I said Donegal. He was flanked by his perceptive chief of staff. When I asked about Kevin's own Irish roots he told me Glencolmcille. I shared with him that I had worked there as a hillwalking guide for the *Oideas Gael* language school. I asked him if he knew the owner and director of the project, Liam Ó Cuinneagáin. Kevin beamed and said: "First cousin." His young chief of staff was agog.

The day after the friendly match Kevin and I got a chance to sit down at a table outside the Fadó Irish pub and discuss the twists and turns of life that saw him a young up-and-coming state representative and not a Glaswegian. His father had been in Glasgow, but decided it wasn't for him and made the journey to the land of the free. It was a smart move. I said that it was a journey that my own father wanted to make but my mother wouldn't travel so far away from her mother. In the 1950s, emigrating to America had the feel of a permanent goodbye to it, unlike today. I told Kevin that he got the better deal. If he'd grown up in

Glasgow as Kevin Boyle with a Donegal father, he would be starting out life in a city where his ethnic group did not achieve occupational parity until 2001, a hundred years after the Irish in New York. It would also be a city where the central tragedy that created modern Ireland was mocked in soccer stadia and where racism was regularly overlooked in the media.

I had no idea what private conversations took place within the SNP or across the political spectrum in Glasgow, but in September 2012 Councillor Feargal Dalton of the SNP introduced a motion to Glasgow City Council and it was passed unanimously. Dalton, a Dubliner and ex-Royal Navy submariner said: "A [Famine] memorial will bring us into line with other great cities such as New York, where they make sure to acknowledge and celebrate their diversity. We do too in Glasgow and any memorial will simply be a physical recognition of that fact. A memorial will highlight that in a world of continuing poverty and famine, Glasgow is very firmly on the side of justice and is a beacon of hope to those in the world who continue to suffer."

The people who had been singing the Famine Song suddenly had a decision to make. Some of them tried to put their mark on any permanent memorial to the dead and displaced of An Gorta Mór. One idea that was seriously discussed on a Rangers message board was that the proposed Famine memorial should have an Irish Catholic and an Ulster Scot being welcomed by "Mother Glasgow". This was an attempt to sectarianise the entire project. My own writing on the subject stressed from day one that any memorial to An Gorta Mór should be secular and non-political. With the apology on behalf of the British Government and, ipso facto, the British people, by Prime Minister Tony Blair in 1997, the politics of this had been put to bed. As part of the Good Friday Agreement these parts of Britain and Ireland's difficult, entangled history were being laid to rest. Blair, for Britain, apologised. I wanted Glasgow's Famine memorial, like the one at Custom House Quay in Dublin and those across the world, to make no political statement. These memorials to An Gorta Mór do not make any reference to the political views or the religious beliefs of those who died in the Famine or had to flee Ireland to survive. They were poor and starving. The Famine in Ireland killed the poor, by starvation and disease. Rich Catholics survived; poor Protestants died. It was not a religiously specific genocide. The Famine did not discriminate on the basis of religion, only income.

At time of writing, Professor Tom Devine's name has been floated as the historian to advise the working party created to organise the erection of a lasting Famine memorial in Glasgow. Professor Devine

OBE is considered by many to be Scotland's greatest living historian and he is currently Personal Senior Research Chair of History at the University of Edinburgh. He is the acknowledged expert in his field of Irish–Scottish Studies. In 2001 Devine was presented by Her Majesty the Queen with the Royal Gold Medal, Scotland's supreme academic accolade, and appointed OBE in the New Year honours list of 2005 for services to Scottish history. He is the only UK historian elected to all three national academies within the British Isles, and it was no secret that Devine was delighted to be mentioned as possibly having a formal role in advising the Famine memorial working party.

The Rangers Supporters Assembly welcomed the move for a Famine memorial in Glasgow and said they would donate to the cost. If anyone had said to me in 2008 that a group of Rangers supporters, who at that time were stoutly defending the Famine Song, would perform such a *volte-face* then I would have laughed out loud. Where we are now, with a Famine memorial in prospect and the Famine Song declared illegal in Scotland, can only be portrayed as a victory over racism. Glasgow will come of age as a mature intercultural city when it finally acknowledges, in a way that a foreign visitor can witness and understand, that Scotland's greatest metropolis has much to thank the Irish for. The old days of parochial racism towards the Irish in Glasgow are gone. A future society based on respect is something which inhabits the nightmares of the Ibrox choristers. One day I might, just might, visit the city of my birth and when I think of the Famine Song I will smile at a battle won and a job well done. I know I will have a good feeling when I finally look at Glasgow's monument to the dead and displaced of An Gorta Mór. We're not there yet, but the good guys won a major battle against anti-Irish racism back in 2009 and we shouldn't lose sight of that. I certainly will not forget. My Mayo blood won't let me.

The laughter of my children

17 September 2008

If you are reading this and you are a parent you will instantly get what I'm saying. If you are not a parent then you will either dismiss the statement I am about to make or take my word for it, because you certainly won't get it. This is a parent thing. There is no way I can explain it to the childless. In fact, I don't think it is possible for anyone to explain the following to the childless.

Okay, here goes. You will not tolerate a situation for your own kids that you endured as a child. All the parents reading these words nod inwardly in quiet comprehension. The rest of you will have to take it on faith. That is how I felt when the Famine Song came to my notice in May of this year.

The UEFA Cup final in Manchester did not pass without incident. Manchester saw the worst outbreak of civil disorder since the miners' strike of 1985. The rioters were supporters of Rangers Football Club. I wasn't surprised by any of this. Anyone who knows the reputation of Rangers' support knows that crowd trouble is a camp follower of their expeditions into European competition. What was new was a song that was sung by a section of the crowd in the City of Manchester Stadium. It mocked the Irish Famine and implored the target of this ditty to go home.

That the opposition on the night was Zenit St Petersburg from Russia mattered not a jot. This song was written for back home. It was intended to bait and taunt the supporters of their city rivals, Celtic. Most Celtic supporters in Glasgow can conjure up an Irish ancestor or two. My own ancestry is probably not uncommon for Glasgow-born followers of Celtic. One Irish-born parent (my father from Mayo) and a settled family in Scotland who came over during the land war evictions. My mother's grandparents were from Carlow and Donegal. All were rural, poor Catholics. All of my great grandparents were children of the Famine generation. They had held on in places like Mayo and Donegal. Just.

Not surprisingly, between such a household in the East End of Glasgow and summer vacation on Mayo's Atlantic coast, I grew up with a keen sense of Irishness. It was a proud rite of passage when the Irish embassy in London posted me my green passport with the golden harp embossed on the front. Inside, I savoured the words *saoránach d'Éirinn*. The literal English translation is "free person of Ireland". On the passport it means Irish citizen. I was indeed a citizen and not a subject of someone's hereditary good fortune. Citizen was good enough for me and it has been so ever since. One of the reasons I loved foreign travel as a young man was my affirmation at airports and borders of my Irish identity.

I have relatives with an identical genealogy in Philadelphia and in Ohio. It isn't a problem in the USA to have an Irish lineage. In fact, it is something of a social advantage. The Famine Song would never be sung to Irish Americans. Never.

With the new football season in Scotland, the Famine Song was again sung by the supporters of Glasgow Rangers. This time it was what they really wanted. They were allowed to sing it inside the stadium of their arch-rivals as their team comprehensively beat Celtic 4–2. In this hatefest, the excellent performance of the Rangers players who fully deserved their victory was a mere sideshow for the Rangers support. They had the serious business of pouring out racial hatred for those in Glasgow who remember that part of them will always, emotionally, be in Ireland.

A couple of weeks later the *Irish Times* published a letter by a Mr Dan Duggan, who had been at the game with his children. He was appalled at the anti-Irish racism given vent and fury in 2008 in a British soccer stadium. He was sickened by the Famine Song. Reading Dan Duggan's letter (Rangers and racism, *Irish Times* 10/09/2008) reminded me that I made the correct decision to take my young family out of Glasgow in the mid-1990s. The day I read Duggan's letter my son received his Junior Cert results from his Gaeilscoil here in Donegal. Like his Mayo grandfather, he is a fluent Irish speaker capable of a subtle and nuanced conversation in the first language of this Republic. In sean Dún Na nGall it is not a crime to be called Cathal. His sisters Róisín and Aislinn are also in a culturally safe place.

The Famine Song is only the most recent manifestation of Scotland's oldest racism. It is also the racism that is tolerated by the leaders of Scottish society. Although Rangers FC are currently the subject of a probation order from UEFA for discriminatory chanting at UEFA-controlled games, the club will escape any sanction from the Scottish soccer authorities for their domestic outpourings of racism towards the Irish community in Scotland. Moreover, the Scottish media tend to turn a blind eye to the racism that is all around them. The Famine is indeed over, although we Irish here in Ireland and in the global Irish diaspora continue to deal with the demographic and psychological aftermath. I did come home and it is sad that, in a very fundamental way, the city of my birth will never be home while these racists enjoy official tolerance.

A week or so after the derby match in Glasgow I was contacted by a source inside the foreign affairs department, who told me the Irish embassy in London had received many complaints following the soccer match in Glasgow in August. From my time with the *Irish Post* in London, I knew a few people I could call in the embassy. I found out that the appropriate minister in the Scottish Government didn't know of the existence of the Famine Song, never mind the import of it. The Irish Consulate in Edinburgh did bring up the issue of the Famine Song with the Scottish Government.

I dipped into the Scottish soccer debate around the Famine Song by giving an interview to Ewen Cameron of Real Radio on 16 September 2008. The very mild intervention of the Irish Consulate caused some embarrassment to a sporting establishment which had sought to deal with the Famine Song in-house. This non-confrontational approach had seen the Rangers songbook advance not an inch towards enlightenment in decades. It took a *Panorama* programme in 2005 and UEFA sanctions in 2006 for discriminatory chanting to make the singing of the original Rangers battle hymn, the Billy Boys, a banned substance inside Ibrox Park. Although it is heard regularly wherever the rougher end of the Rangers support is found, it is not heard inside Ibrox. Result.

The Famine Song was penned within the last twelve months. It was a replacement for the Billy Boys. Although marching up to their knees in Fenian blood is no longer publicly acceptable (or legal), the need to bait and taunt those of Irish descent is still a deep-seated need probably best dealt with by a psychotherapist. After this particular news cycle we know this much: the Famine Song – sung publicly in a soccer stadium in Scotland – is likely to lead to the singer's arrest for a racial breach of the peace. Result.

Here in Donegal it isn't a crime to be Irish anymore. My children are citizens of a republic and in times to come one of them may even be elected president. That is why, when I hear the laughter of my children outside in the garden, I know that their mother and I acted in their best interests when they were too young to know that they were the objects of hatred for so many where they were born. Their laughter is the best antidote to the hatred and bile that created the Famine Song.

The anger that reveals impotence

18 September 2008

Racists are not happy when their victims will not be quiet and accept their allotted role as lesser beings. In the Deep South of the United States, the "uppity nigger" was something that could not be allowed by right-thinking white folks. Soon, those folks may be ruled by their worst nightmare. I hope that comes to pass.

I have the facility of allowing or not allowing comments onto this site. The victim of racism usually doesn't have the luxury of this power. Where the comments have been non-abusive and non-threatening I have approved them. People are free not to agree with me as I reserve the right to disagree with them. However, that liberal attitude to a lively debate is a red rag to a racist bull. The people who have objected to my opposition to the Famine Song do not believe I have the right to object. That is what the Famine Song is all about; it reflects the nineteenth-century *Punch* cartoon view that Victorian Britain had of Irish people. Probably only among the rougher elements of Rangers supporters do those attitudes to Irish people still persist. Like the poor white trash of America when they see successful African-Americans, they long for the days when the blacks knew their place.

The Irish of the global Gaeltacht are no longer Britain's victims. We are a success story of the third wave of the infosphere and the de-massified media. Alvin Toffler could have written the script for this new Irish diaspora. The Rangers supporters who sing the Famine Song with such gusto hark back to an old culture of the certainties of the British Empire, where the Irish had no choice but to know their place. In that world the community that supported Rangers had a few more crumbs from the imperial table. A few extra crumbs were all that it took. They were not the bottom of the pile in Clydeside in the old days. Rangers Football Club throughout most of the twentieth century did not field players who were known to be Catholics. Recently, a Rangers player from the 1960s, Sandy Jardine, said when he arrived at the club in 1964 there were no Catholics at the club, not even in the backroom staff. It wasn't a written policy, but that is how the place operated. Everyone knew, everyone understood. That was the emotional contract with the paying public. The world tilted slightly in 1989 when Rangers, under a new management team, signed an ex-Celtic player, Maurice Johnston, who is a Catholic.

Since then, many Rangers players have been Catholics. These players have been from France, Italy and Spain as well as, of course, from Scotland. Their religion has not been an issue. Rangers' first Catholic captain was Italian Lorenzo Amoruso. The Rangers supporters took him to their hearts. His religion wasn't an issue, nor, of course, should it have been. Amoruso embodied what was at the core of the Ibrox psychosis. That Lorenzo Amoruso was a Catholic was, at the end of the day, no big deal. What their captain could not be was an Irish Catholic. For a player to be able to say he is a Rangers player and Republic of Ireland international is simply an appalling vista for the hordes who lustily belt out the Famine Song. There are Catholics in Scotland of Italian descent just as there are Catholics of Irish descent. The Ibrox hatred is aimed at the latter. In my writings in the *Irish Post* in the 1990s I made this point again and again. This is about ethnicity and nationality in Glasgow, not about religion.

Rangers Football Club issued a statement saying that if their fans sing the Famine Song at a match then they are in danger of being arrested for a racial breach of the peace. This was the advice Rangers received from the Scottish police. So, the police think this song is racist.

When Rangers was formed in 1872, Britain was the world's unrivalled global superpower. It is hard to imagine that now. Within this archipelago the Catholic Irish were clearly the first of many victims of that empire. That is why Irish people have a natural affinity with so many other peoples also forced to live under the union flag. Happily, that flag is almost gone from the planet as a symbol of imperialism. Rangers as an institution grew up in the early twentieth century to be a power in the land as a focus for anti-Irish sentiment in Glasgow. To be Irish in early twentieth-century Britain, especially on the Clyde, would be analogous to how some people view British-born Muslims today. The Irish were always the enemy within for imperial Britain.

The world has moved on, but a section of the Ibrox support is still caught in that time warp. Scottish journalist Graham Spiers, himself a Rangers supporter and committed Christian, said that the Ibrox club had a white underclass attached to it. They are financially and intellectually impoverished. Spiers, who said this in a radio show just after Rangers fans had rioted in Manchester at the UEFA Cup final, has become a hate figure for the representatives of this underclass who have access to a computer. Their anger, which has poured onto soccer message boards and onto this site in the twenty-four hours since my interview on Real Radio, is a manifestation of their frustration that a culture is changing and they don't like it.

It is always a good sign when racists are angry. They are angry because they are impotent. Contented racists are a sign that the oppressor has power over the oppressed. That is no longer the case. That is why the hatred and abuse now pours into this site like toxic waste. I will only allow those comments into public view if their missives are civil, polite and capable of basic sentence structure.

Anti-Irish racism is treated as non-issue

4 October 2008
This article first appeared in the Irish Post

Over the past few weeks I have revisited the decision that my wife and I took in 1995 in Glasgow to sell up and move to Donegal. When we moved, our son Cathal was four, his sister Róisín was a baby and we'd just got news that number three was on the way. It is normal to re-evaluate such a major life decision, especially when it involves your children. Events this year in Scotland have reaffirmed that the decision was the correct one.

Since last April, the supporters of Glasgow Rangers have had a new song. To the tune of the Beach Boys' "Sloop John B", the song is aimed at members of Glasgow's Irish community who follow Celtic. The song has five verses; here is the first one:

> *I often wonder where they would have been*
> *If we hadn't have taken them in*
> *Fed them and washed them*
> *Thousands in Glasgow alone*
> *From Ireland they came*
> *Brought us nothing but trouble and shame*
> *Well, the Famine is over*
> *Why don't they go home?*

The Scottish police have advised Rangers that anyone singing this song is in danger of being arrested for a racial breach of the peace. The Irish Government's consulate in Edinburgh was involved in seeking clarification from the Scottish Government on what they were doing about this racist karaoke after letters of complaint were received by the Irish embassy in London. So far, the official response from the Scottish Government has been muted.

When the story of the Irish Government's involvement broke in Scotland, journalist Ewen Cameron interviewed me on the Real Radio football phone-in about the Irish Government's involvement. I stated my opinion that the song was racist, as well as outlining how the story had developed. In the days following that radio interview my website was deluged with racist abuse from Rangers fans. Most of it was too vile to be approved for viewing. Most of it, however, was simply ungrammatical.

The Famine Song is only the most recent manifestation of Scotland's oldest racism. Moreover, it is tolerated by the leaders of Scottish society. Although Rangers FC are currently the subject of a probation order from UEFA for "discriminatory chanting" during European games, the club will probably escape any sanction from the Scottish soccer authorities for these domestic outpourings of racism towards the Irish community in Scotland by a section of their supporters. At the recent home game against Motherwell, the Rangers Football Club distributed copies of a club statement to fans going into Ibrox stadium. The statement warned the reader that the singing of the Famine Song could lead to the singer being arrested. The statement from Rangers did not condemn the song. During the game it was defiantly belted out by a large section of the crowd. There were no reports of any arrests.

This all takes place against a background of official inaction by organisations in Scotland tasked and funded to tackle racism in soccer. One such organisation, Show Racism the Red Card (SRTRC), has not publicly condemned the song despite SRTRC writing to complainants in May that the song was, in the organisation's opinion, racist. Piara Powar, national director of Kick It Out, an English-based organisation, welcomed the intervention of the Irish Government in the Famine Song controversy.

"This sort of government-to-government action is what we need because it takes it out of the hands of the football authorities," said Powar. "This is a matter of ethnic and national identity and it is appropriate that the Irish Government should have become involved on behalf of its citizens."

Matthew Collins, a journalist for the anti-fascist magazine *Searchlight*, said: "In my opinion, the song is racist as it is aimed at and about a particular section of society that has its own distinct language, ethnicity and cultural heritage. The song has a nasty, vile and intolerable content, rather like the morons who sing it."

George Galloway MP, himself born in Dundee of Irish descent, was unequivocal about the Famine Song when asked what the Scottish football authorities should do about it being sung inside soccer stadia: "There should be a zero tolerance approach. Imagine if it was 'The Holocaust is over' or 'Slavery is over'. There would rightly be an outraged reaction from the authorities. There should be now."

The Scottish media have historically turned a blind eye to the anti-Irish racism that is all around them, or they subsume it under the handy catch-all term "sectarianism", despite the fact that Scots of Italian Catholic parentage have largely escaped the discrimination and abuse heaped onto the Irish for generations in Scotland. I can make a John McCain defence on behalf of my fellow journalists in Scotland; it isn't that they don't care about anti-Irish racism in Scotland, it's just that they don't get it.

On Monday 22 September 2008, in his column for the *Daily Record*, sports journalist and BBC broadcaster James Traynor dismissed the Famine Song controversy thus: "So, to all those, of any religion or race, who think Scotland is such a bad, twisted place full of bigots and racists there is only one thing to say. Go. Go on, just gather up your prejudices, take your suspicions and pack your loathing of Scotland. Go find a better place to live and leave us to get on with the job of making something good of this country." That could not be clearer if it was screamed at you from the cheap seats in Ibrox Park.

Glasgow is the only major city in Britain to have received Famine refugees that has no Famine memorial. Coincidence? The Famine is indeed over, although we continue to deal with the demographic and psychological aftermath here in Ireland and in the worldwide diaspora. Recently, my son received his Junior Certificate results from his Gaeilscoil, a real milestone in our time here in Donegal. In sean Dún Na nGall it is not a crime to be called Cathal. His sisters Róisín and Aislinn are also in a culturally safe place. I now know that I did come home and I am daily convinced that it was the correct move for my family and for myself. However, it is sad that, in a very fundamental way, the city of my birth will never be home to me while these vile racists enjoy official tolerance.

Politician writes to
Rangers about Famine Song

14 October 2008

Last week, Alan Shatter TD submitted a Dáil question to Foreign Minister Micheál Martin about the Famine Song controversy in Scotland. The Minister stated: "In common with the vast majority of people in Britain and Ireland, I condemn the singing of songs or other actions which promote or encourage racism, sectarianism or xenophobia of any kind."

I spoke with Deputy Shatter last week and he confirmed to me that he had also written directly to Rangers Football Club to express his concern about this "anti-Irish chanting", indulged in by thousands of Rangers fans regularly. He had taken this action after being contacted by a constituent who had attended the Celtic v. Rangers match on 31 August. Shatter's written question was answered on 9 October, the day of Rangers Football Club's AGM in Glasgow. Sir David Murray, the owner of Rangers, called on Rangers supporters who engage in "sectarian bile" to cease their activity. He also stated that he would be meeting with First Minister Alex Salmond to defend the club's good name.

Coinciding with the AGM, the Scottish Football Association (SFA) held a high-level press conference about its continued attempts to stamp out anti-social behaviour, sectarianism and racism at Scottish soccer stadia. Chief Executive Gordon Smith stated that it would be inappropriate to punish clubs for the behaviour of their fans: "The clubs are doing everything they can, it would be unfair to punish them." A Scottish Premier League spokesperson told me that the SPL had a series of sanctions in place against clubs if their fans behaved in a racist manner. Neither David Murray nor ex-Rangers player Gordon Smith mentioned the Famine Song.

The main organisation in Scotland dedicated to eliminating racism in football is Show Racism the Red Card (SRTRC). Last week on its website, SRTRC, partly funded by the SFA, stated for the first time that the Famine Song was, in the organisation's opinion, racist.

Alasdair Allan, the Scottish National Party MSP for Na h-Eileanan an Iar (Western Isles), said: "The sentiments in this song are unquestionably anti-Irish and racist. The overwhelming majority of people here would say that there is no room in Scotland for this song."

In a parallel universe

15 October 2008

In a parallel universe there is an ice hockey match in Canada. One club draws its support and its narrative from the thousands of Scots who left Scotland during the Highland Clearances. The other club is their bitter rival and their support is largely drawn from the English ascendancy in Canada.

The Toronto Royals are Canada's establishment club; the religious ethos of the club has always been Anglican and their ex-players and managers populate the upper echelons of Canadian ice hockey. Until 1989 they did not hire any player who had a Scottish background, especially if the player had gone to a faith school where the Highland Free Presbyterian ethos was extant.

The Scottish team has been in the recent ascendancy in matters ice hockey. They are the current champions. This is unacceptable for the followers of the Toronto Royals and their owner, Dick Thatcher. It hurts their pride to see the Winnipeg Gaels becoming the main power in the land. Moreover, in the global marketplace for sporting merchandise the current interest in Scottish products has seen the Winnipeg Gaels become a global brand. They are now more financially powerful than the Toronto Royals. These "immigrants" with their tartan tops and tourist shop bagpipes are so proud of their heritage – who do they think they are? These McDonalds and Camerons are always wailing on about evictions and coffin ships.

Up strikes a song informing the synthetic Highlanders of Manitoba that the Clearances are over, why don't you go home? That night, a young lad in the tartan top of the Winnipeg Gaels is set upon. He is called a Jacobite bastard. He is kicked to death. Supporters of the Winnipeg Gaels try and get the issue raised on phone-in broadcast programmes and in newspapers. A well-known Toronto columnist says that if Canada is such a bad place then people are free to leave. It is, after all, only a song. The assistant coach of the Winnipeg Gaels, ex-team captain, Willie Munro, a Skye man, is attacked in the street in Toronto and beaten unconscious.

The Scottish embassy (it is a parallel universe so we can make Scotland an independent nation!) is contacted by a Scottish passport holder in Manitoba. The Scottish citizen complains about the anti-Scottish racism of the song that has, in the Canadian media, been treated as sporting rivalry and banter. The Scottish ambassador delegates the job to his cultural attaché. This leaks to the media and there is outrage at this interference in Canadian affairs. The Toronto Royals CEO, Godfrey Soames, issues a statement warning the club's supporters that they could be vulnerable to arrest if they sing the Clearance Song. The club statement does not condemn the song as anti-Scottish or racist and Soames is not challenged about this by the Toronto-based ice hockey journalists.

Later on, a member of the Scottish Parliament is contacted by a constituent. The person had been visiting family in Manitoba and had gone to the hockey match in Winnipeg. The Gaels were playing the Toronto Royals. He was appalled at this humorous deriding of the Clearances and those that it deposited in Canada in the nineteenth century. The Scottish politician raises the issue in Edinburgh with the Scottish Foreign Minister.

The Canadian-born journalist in Scotland who has been working on this story is pilloried with abuse from Canada. Canadian racists inform him that he is a pretend Scotsman – "We're glad you went home, kilt-wearing trailer trash!" The journalist contacts the Canadian ice hockey authorities, who have a mission statement to stamp out racism. The Ice Hockey Federation is happy; they state on their website that racist chanting at Inuit players has markedly decreased in recent years. The journalist repeatedly contacts the Ice Hockey Federation and the Canadian Ice Hockey Players' Union for comments on the Clearance Song.

He also tries for and gets a statement about the decision of Canadian-born Lachlan MacDonald to elect to play for Scotland in the upcoming Ice Hockey World Cup. Lachlan MacDonald, a Manitoba lad, is booed in every hockey stadium in Canada. He is referred to as a traitor by sports journalists. It is rumoured that he is considering moving clubs and going to play in the USA ice hockey league to escape this racist abuse. The Scotland-based journalist does a tour of various locked doors in Canada and can only report not available for comment. Finally, the anti-racism charity Let's Kick Racism Out of the Rink updates its website to say that the Clearance Song is, in their opinion, racist.

Back home in Scotland, people reading about the Clearance Song are dismayed that such attitudes exist in the twenty-first century. Official inaction against the supporters of the Toronto Royals continues and they, defiantly, belt out the Clearance Song. In the age of digital twenty-four-hour media, the image of Canada as a modern, pluralist, tolerant society suffers badly.

Of course, all of the foregoing is very, very wide of the mark; Canada is the gold standard for how to make a multicultural society work. It is the antithesis of its large dysfunctional neighbour to the south. I did say it was a parallel universe. The analogy, though, is firm enough. The Scottish embassy had every right to raise the matter and, indeed, a duty to the Scottish citizen domiciled in Canada. No right-thinking person could come to any other conclusion than that the Clearance Song was racist and those supporters of the Toronto Royals who repeatedly sang it were themselves racists.

Show hypocrisy the red card

22 October 2008

As a journalist, you know you're doing your job when people aren't pleased to see you. My family are pleased to see me, and my friends welcome me into their homes, so I don't take it personally when people don't want to see my press card. It's only business; it isn't personal.

Billy Singh of Show Racism the Red Card (SRTRC) wasn't pleased to see me at Tynecastle last Friday. It's okay, Billy, this is business, nothing personal. I had, since mid-September, been trying to get an interview, a comment even, from him. I had spoken on the phone with two of his colleagues. I wanted SRTRC's view on the Famine Song. Many people considered the song racist and it was sung at soccer grounds by Rangers fans.

The nice people at SRTRC told me that Billy was dealing with the issue and that I would have to deal with him. I left my number but got no reply. I had to go to print in the *Irish Post* on Friday 1 October with SRTRC having made no public statement about the Famine Song. Later that day, SRTRC made a statement via its website that anyone singing the song could be liable to arrest for a racial breach of the peace. This statement was, well, very similar to the statement released by the Ibrox club in late September.

At this stage I felt like one of the journalists piecing together the sequencing of the Northern Ireland Peace Process. Who was writing statements for whom? Still no call from Billy. Finally on Monday 6 October, STRC made a public statement on the website that, in their opinion, the Famine Song was racist. Phew!

I knew several Irish community organisations had approached SRTRC in May to complain about the Famine Song. Still my phone didn't ring. A journalist who works at the Scottish Parliament told me there was a charity football match due to be played between a SRTRC select and MSPs at Hearts' ground, Tynecastle. No-brainer. A few clicks on the Aer Lingus website and I was good to go.

It is fair to say Billy was surprised to see me turn up in Tynecastle as the game was about to start. I introduced myself and showed him my press card. I told him I was researching a piece on the Famine Song. I asked him why SRTRC had taken so long to state publicly that the Famine Song was racist. Billy said: "We have always considered the Famine Song to be racist. It brings nationality into it; it is racist and it is wrong."

I asked Billy why, having been petitioned by Irish community groups in May, his organisation had only made a public statement two weeks before our conversation. Billy could not answer my question, but conceded that the 6 October statement on the SRTRC website was the first public pronouncement by the organisation on the Famine Song. Billy said SRTRC was working behind the scenes with Rangers and the Rangers supporters' organisations. He went onto the field of play and slotted in at right back. He did very well. As I watched, the Red Card

Select XI confirmed to the MSPs that they would never have made it as footballers. I stopped counting the score after five to the Red Card.

I chatted with Red Card manager for the day, Lex Gold, a very amiable man. He explained to me that the SPL did not have a songbook of banned songs and he, publicly, could not have an opinion on the Famine Song as he might be the guy to punish an SPL club if it was deemed to be negligent in tackling racism among its own supporters. There was, of course, a corollary to this. If the SPL deemed the club in question was doing everything possible to eradicate the illegal behaviour of its fans, then the SPL would not punish the club. He agreed with me that, in a situation where the club could not be found to be negligent in tackling racism by its fans, but racist behaviour persisted, then it was a matter for the police, not the SPL.

I also interviewed SFA boss Gordon Smith. The ex-Rangers man stated that the SFA could not have a public view on the Famine Song as the SFA was, in effect, the court of appeal of SPL clubs. If the SPL punished a club and the club thought this unjust or unfair then the club could appeal to the SFA. Subsequently, Smith explained, the SFA could not have a public view on the Famine Song for that reason. I also asked the SFA chief about the treatment of young James McCarthy, who had decided to play for the Republic of Ireland. Smith was particularly adamant McCarthy should be left alone: "It is his decision; it was his decision to make. He should be left alone."

In fairness, he couldn't have been clearer or more unequivocal. People should leave young James McCarthy alone and respect his decision to play for Ireland. That was from the guy at the top of Scottish soccer. He had just come off the field where he had scored the goal of the match, a twenty-yard curler, with the outside of his right foot. Smith's goal was an absolute cracker, even topping Chic Charnley's swerving shot which was also from outside of the box. As the Red Card team celebrated, Gary MacKay started to sing to the MSPs: "Are you the House of Commons in disguise?"

There is nothing wrong with rubbing it in to your defeated opponents, nothing at all. Everyone who assembled in Tynecastle that day said racism could not be included in any song or chant in soccer. Agreed.

I had been concerned that following on from Ally Ross's piece in the *Sun*, which attacked James McCarthy's decision to elect to play for Ireland instead of the country of his birth, he would be the victim of racist abuse. I had been in phone contact with the club secretary, Scott Struthers, the week before I travelled to Scotland and I was impressed with the vehemence with which he objected to the attacks on James in the media. Moreover, he told me that everyone in the club knew that James would declare for Ireland. He explained to me that following on from the Ally Ross piece, James was not speaking to the media. This I fully understood.

I attended the Hamilton v. St Mirren match the following day at New Douglas Park. I called Struthers the day before on my way back to Glasgow from Tynecastle. Scott was surprised that James had not been in touch, but it was absolutely no problem on my part. I told him of my intention, as a journalist, to attend the next Hamilton match and sit in the away end.

James McCarthy was subjected to sustained racist abuse in the second half from St Mirren fans. Every touch of the ball was booed. In the second half, Hamilton were attacking the away end. Each time McCarthy was on the ball for any length of time some chant or other would be struck up. "Plastic Paddy" was the main one. On the scale of racist chanting this wasn't up there with the shameful treatment of Mark Walters by Celtic fans in the 1980s. However, it was sustained throughout the second half. There was a vociferous minority of St Mirren fans at the back of the away end where I was sitting. Every touch of the ball was booed, from the time I took my seat with a few minutes played, right through to the final whistle.

In the first half he was the only Hamilton player booed by the St Mirren fans. In the second half, as Hamilton chased the equaliser, James McCarthy was regularly on the ball charging from midfield towards the St Mirren goal. On each occasion the chant of "There's only one Plastic Paddy!" struck up from the hard core of St Mirren fans. After the match, I went down behind the goals and introduced myself to a senior police officer. I showed him my press card and told him that I was in touch with Scott Struthers, the Hamilton club secretary, and that he was expecting me.

As we walked around to the tunnel area I asked the police officer if he had heard the abuse directed at young James McCarthy. "Yeah, he gets a bit of stick doesn't he?" stated the officer, with a slight giggle. Little chance of this law enforcer approaching the match delegate through the appropriate channels, I thought. After several phone calls and emails, I got to meet Scott Struthers. Lex Gold had spoken of him in high terms and I had already made, as one does, an assessment of the disembodied person I was communicating with. He is a fine man, with only the best interests of James McCarthy at heart.

He was willing to go on the record about the booing. He declared that he was "disappointed" at the conduct of the St Mirren fans towards James. I was led into the press box, where the rest of the media were preparing words and images of the soccer match we had all just witnessed. When I was asked what *blatt* I was working for, a couple of the pack were interested in the piece I was researching.

One sports journalist, who I won't name to save his blushes, said to me: "This PC thing has gone mad, hasn't it?" I thought of the event I had attended the previous day. I countered with: "When is anti-racism political correctness? Surely it is beyond debate that racism is a social evil and that it should be confronted at every opportunity?"

"Yeah, but James McCarthy is white and Scottish so it can't be racist." This, I suspected, was what he thought to be a winning polemical point. "Well, racism isn't necessarily a matter of skin colour, although of course it can be," I replied. "FIFA and UEFA are very clear that racism can be about nationality, citizenship or ethnic heritage. The abuse aimed at James McCarthy was specifically about his Irishness and his decision to declare for the Republic of Ireland. Hence the abuse was racist." His answer was a mumbled "Yeah, suppose …"

I considered that if this was typical of the level of awareness of such issues in the pressroom, what chance had the supporters in the cheap seats? Scott Struthers then brought James out to be interviewed by me. The first thing that strikes you about the young Irish midfielder is that he is young. I was standing in front of him outside the pressroom at New Douglas Park and thinking this was a boy doing a man's job. It wasn't the time or the place to have a relaxed chat with a hassled seventeen-year-old about national identity, so my questions were to the point.

"Why did you pick Ireland, James?"

"When I was young, when I was a kid, I would always watch the Ireland matches on the telly."

For a fifty-year-old to hear a lad of seventeen hark back to the days of his innocence made me smile, but it was a clear answer from the lad. He felt drawn to Ireland. He qualifies through his mother's side. Donegal people. His uncle, Hugh Coyle, stated quite clearly in a piece in that day's *Sun* that James was Irish on both sides of his family. In qualifying to play for Ireland, he was also entitled to legal citizenship.

"You will need to get yourself one of these for your travels," I told him, as I brandished my Irish passport. His smile said it all. James McCarthy is for the wearing of the green. He told me: "The Irish set-up has been great." He said that in a recent 2–2 draw with Portugal, his midfield partner was Owen Garvan of Ipswich Town and he hoped they could strike up a partnership together. I told him that he would need to learn the words of "Amhrán na bhFiann" [the Irish national anthem]. He promised he would. I asked him if he could hear the abuse from the St Mirren fans: "Yeah, I heard it, but I just keep my head down and try and block it out."

James McCarthy is a lovely young lad, polite and well mannered. As I left New Douglas Park I hoped that the fans of all Scottish clubs would heed the words of Gordon Smith and leave the kid alone. The following day not one of the Sunday papers covering the match mentioned the booing of James McCarthy. There is no doubt anyone in New Douglas Park that day would have known he was booed every time he got a touch of the ball. They may not have heard the chants from the knot of St Mirren fans up at the back of the away end, but almost the entire away end was booing when James was on the ball.

There was no play-related reason to boo him, so they would have had to discount the fact that he was being booed in order not to comment on it. So there it was, it didn't happen. Within twenty-four hours of the Show Racism the Red Card football match and the fine words, here was racist abuse and not a word in the papers. The next day, I was on my way to the airport when a journalist colleague in Dublin called to say that there had been a match report on the Hamilton official club website which had mentioned the racist abuse of James McCarthy by a section of the St Mirren fans.

Luckily, he had printed the screen because a short time later the report was amended and the reference to "racist abuse" excised. I called Scott Struthers to ascertain what had happened. He confirmed there had indeed been such a match report on the club site, but it had been altered. I asked him why and he said it was because there had been no abuse.

"Sorry, Scott, but I have you on record saying that you were disappointed at the booing of him every time he touched the ball."

"Yes," the club secretary replied, "but there wasn't any racist abuse of James." I heard the unmistakable sound of goalposts being moved. I reminded Scott I'd personally told him after the game about the chants. "Yes, but it was only you who heard them," he said. "There was no report by the stewards or the police." I thought of the policeman who took me around to the tunnel. I thanked Scott for taking my call and for all the hospitality and help he had afforded me on the match day, and before, in facilitating my work.

I remain of the opinion that Scott Struthers is a fine man. He told me

James had given an extensive and exclusive interview to the *Advertiser* that week and he was no longer speaking to the press. I got through to Andy McGilvray, who covers the 'Accies' home games at New Douglas Park. I told him who I was and about the conversation I had just had with Scott Struthers.

"That's nonsense, I heard it!" I asked Andy where in the ground he was. "I was in the main stand, right in the middle," he said.

"Like, above the tunnel area?"

"Yeah."

"And you heard the 'Plastic Paddy' stuff?"

"Yes, everybody heard it."

I asked if I could go on the record with this conversation and he agreed. I thanked him and hung up. My cell phone immediately went off in my hand again; it was my colleague in Dublin. He was intrigued by the censored match report between, let's face it, two not very unimportant Scottish soccer teams. He had gone onto a message board for St Mirren fans and there had been reports of phone calls made to the Paisley club by St Mirren fans about the original Hamilton match report. A complaint from St Mirren to Hamilton seemed a likely explanation for the removal of the original report.

I called St Mirren and asked to speak to the press officer. I was told that he was on vacation. Okay, could I speak to someone else? General manager Brian Caldwell took my call. He denied there had been any racist abuse of James McCarthy. I told him I heard the abuse and I had been in the away end. He countered that he had also been in the away end and had heard nothing. He asked me what I was doing in the away end with the St Mirren fans.

I told him bluntly that following on from the Ally Ross piece in the *Sun* and the Real Radio football phone-in, I feared James McCarthy might be the target of anti-Irish racism because of his decision to play for the Republic of Ireland. "So you went there looking for it?" accused the St Mirren general manager. Well yes, Mr Caldwell, I'm a journalist. I was there checking out a story. It is what journalists are supposed to do. Journalists find stories and then report them. I admitted it was a small minority of the St Mirren fans subjecting James to the abuse. Mr Caldwell then said that if it was only a small minority then it wasn't a story. This, I told him, was slightly different from "it didn't happen at all". Silence. At that stage it seemed almost impolite to tell him a journalist from the local paper sitting in the main stand could hear the racist abuse of James McCarthy that he, sitting in the same stand as the

St Mirren fans, claimed he could not hear. I thanked him for taking my call.

I am back home in Ireland now and I can reflect that in the space of four days I attended an event dedicated to eradicating racism from the game in Scotland, a soccer game where an Irish kid received racist abuse and found out, by looking at the Sunday papers, that it didn't make it into a single match report. Moreover, there is a hesitance in Scotland to call what happened to James McCarthy racism. You know you're doing your job as a journalist when you ask questions that people don't want to answer.

Famine Song gets the red card

15 November 2008
This article first appeared in the Irish Post

The large electronic screens at Ibrox Park told those among the crowd who had the ability to discern that there was a new dispensation in town. The supporters of Rangers Football Club had a special message from their club as they took their seats to watch the match against Hamilton Academical – if they sang the Famine Song they were liable to be arrested.

The club issued the statement after consultation with the police and throughout the match the crowd sat in quiet obedience. But the real message, if not up in lights, was clear enough; the Irish were no longer fair game for those who inhabited the cheap seats at Rangers' home ground and the Ibrox crowd knew it.

James McCarthy, the young Irish midfielder for Hamilton who had received sustained racist abuse from Rangers fans the Saturday before in the SPL at New Douglas Park, was allowed to go about his job that night without being told to go home to Ireland. After the match, I sent a text message to a senior member of staff at Hamilton Academical. I told him we should be thankful the game had passed off quietly and his reply was: "I got the impression that the fans were too terrified to sing." This is progress. If it takes little electronic reminders to Rangers fans not to indulge in racist singing because they are at risk of arrest then so be it – the hope is that one day such warnings will not be required. They are, at the moment.

The "self-policing" initiative brought in by Rangers supporters' organisations obviously did not include forbidding grown men racially abusing a seventeen-year-old kid who plays his international football for the Republic of Ireland, and so if self-policing fails, real policing is required. As it turned out, all that was needed was to remind the Rangers support that the Famine Song was, in the opinion of the police, illegal.

When social historians come to trace Scotland's journey into multicultural modernity they will spend some time on the significance of the Famine Song controversy. I am certainly convinced that the Famine Song represents the old Scotland – a Scotland that was a reliable component part of the empire where the Irish were despised outsiders. Jock could be trusted, but Paddy had to be watched. As with any new dispensation there are those who will hanker after the old certainties. There are elderly people in Alabama today who tell their grandchildren that things were better when the blacks were at the back of the bus. Now, the USA has its first African-American president and you will note that the sky has not fallen in.

The Glasgow of my childhood in the 1960s was a city that practised social exclusion against Scotland's largest ethnic minority – education was the escape route. In 1990 I qualified as a social worker and took up my first position a few weeks after being on active service in Italy with Jack's Army. You only get one chance to make a first impression – unfortunately my tales of Italia '90 were, at best, sniffed at by some of the less broadminded of my colleagues.

"Why don't you support Scotland?"

"Because I'm Irish."

"No, you're not."

"Wanna see my passport? It is a lovely green colour. What does your Scottish passport look like?"

Yes, all very childish, but there is a greater truth at the heart of the vignette. This, I realised, was not a confident culture. Beaten, bribed, annexed, demoralised and Balmoralised, these Scottish people didn't take kindly to having a reminder around that if they paid the entrance fee they too could be among the community of free nations and not someone else's province. As I recall, it was mainly the administrative staff who were least happy to have a culturally confident Irish Glaswegian among them. My qualified colleagues had no problem with my identity regardless of their own background. In the end it was a matter of education. Confident cultures and confident people do not feel the need to abuse or denigrate those among them who are by race, creed, nationality or citizenship different. Graham Spiers, the Scottish journalist at *The Times*, who has written extensively about the Famine Song mindset, stated recently that the answer to the Rangers problem in Scottish society was "education, education, education".

The Famine Song controversy has been a clash of rights versus racism. In the old Scotland the idea of the mere Irish having rights was as stupid as black people being at the front of the bus before Rosa Parks said "Enough!" Racism is, in contemporary Scotland, not only socially acceptable, it is also illegal. So the Famine Song had to be defended by those who sang it with a denial that the song was racist.

David Edgar of the Rangers Supporters Trust said on *Radio 5 Live* that the Famine Song was "a rather tasteless chant", but he dismissed the idea that the Famine Song was racist as "nonsense". Belatedly, the campaigning organisation Show Racism the Red Card publicly stated last month on its website that the Famine Song was racist. The police advised Rangers in September that singing the song could put singers at risk of arrest for a racial breach of the peace. The Famine Song is racist – so the debate on that should be closed. This controversy ensued because the denigration of the Irish in the west of Scotland is in the societal DNA of the old Scotland of the British Empire. The empire is over, and now only the trailer trash of that empire remains to vent their hatred of those who once were that empire's victims.

Graham Spiers stated in the aftermath of the Manchester riots in May that "a white underclass has attached itself to Rangers". Moreover, the *Times* journalist was of the opinion that "there is a social poison at the heart of the club".

Ironically, it has been the involvement of the Irish in Ireland and our elected representatives that has seen this issue dealt with by the appropriate authorities in Scotland. Several TDs have raised the Famine Song issue in the Dáil with Foreign Affairs Minister Micheál Martin. Alan Shatter TD wrote to the Ibrox club in early October about the Famine Song – I checked with his office a few weeks later and was told that he had yet to receive a reply to his letter.

The Famine Song was written to take the place of the Billy Boys in the Rangers unofficial songbook. The Billy Boys, to the tune of "Marching Through Georgia", is a song that has been roared in hatred at the Glasgow Irish Untermensch for generations. The Billy Boys is now gone from soccer stadia in Scotland because of the intervention of UEFA in 2006. It is appropriate to use the lexicon of the Nazis; the song celebrates the street gang formed by Billy Fullerton – Fullerton was one of Mosley's Blackshirts and formed a chapter of the Ku Klux Klan in Glasgow in the 1920s. In the new paradigm of rights and respect, the old culture of the Billy Boys and the Famine Song has no place in Scotland. If it is required for a while that such basic tenets of human decency need to be displayed on large screens in big writing, if not big words, at Ibrox Park, then so be it.

Rangers beat Hamilton 2–0 but the main event was that the Famine Song was not sung. Now that is a result I can celebrate.

An important visitor

4 December 2008

Sociologists have a term for what an outsider does to a society just by being there. The stranger conducts a "common sense inventory"; this is not a conscious act, but because the outsider has not been socialised into that system he or she has the effect of making everyone else there consider what the accepted wisdom is.

Eoin Ryan, the Fianna Fáil MEP from Dublin, caused official Scotland to carry out a common sense inventory last Thursday in Scotland. I was there to witness the event. Ryan had raised the issue of anti-Irish racism in Scotland, manifested by the singing of the Famine Song by Rangers supporters. The MEP from the governing Fianna Fáil party took up the issue in early November and raised it in the European Parliament, where his contribution was heard by SNP MEP Alyn Smith. The Scottish nationalist decided to invite Ryan to Scotland to show him around. I was alerted to this day out from Brussels by a journalist colleague in Scotland.

Ryan's impending visit was picked up by *Irish Independent* political correspondent Aine Kerr and he was interviewed on RTÉ's *Drivetime* radio show by Mary Wilson. Wilson persistently used the term "sectarianism", whereas Ryan stuck to his guns; this was an issue about racism in sport and the Famine Song was racism against the Irish in Scotland. I called Ryan the following day at his office in Brussels. He joked with me as he described the "fan mail" he had received that morning from people who, let's just say, don't have a problem with the Famine Song. I empathised, telling him it sounded like the toxic waste that flows into my website most days. The toxic sludge produced by the Ibrox belief system.

When I called back to check on his itinerary for the day, an office assistant said that I should liaise directly with Dave Harmon, the press guy for the Fianna Fáil group in the European Parliament. Over the next few days, Dave and I were in regular contact about which papers I should file to when the day was over. He was happy to have a print journalist in attendance who knew the story. He had read my stuff about the Famine Song controversy in the *Sunday Tribune*.

We originally thought that the entire day was to be at the Scottish Parliament where Eoin would meet the appropriate stakeholders and the Scottish Government Minister Fergus Ewing. I arranged through a contact to get myself press accreditation for the day at the Scottish Parliament. I flew to Glasgow on the Wednesday night, ready to be in Edinburgh to meet the Irish MEP at the Scottish Parliament.

When I arrived at Glasgow airport my cell phone had a message from my contact in the Scottish Parliament. The day – in the main – would be held in Glasgow. Dave phoned me early Thursday morning to tell me what I already knew. The day would start with a meeting at 11 a.m. at the City Chambers. I agreed to meet Dave there. I was there for 10.30 a.m. and showed my press card. I got a pass to the councillors' corridor. This was, I thought, Glasgow's West Wing.

For all the derision of local government in Glasgow, the City Chambers is hugely impressive. How much more impressive would it have been when it first opened in 1883? Built at a cost of £500,000 in 1883 prices, the cost today would be many millions of pounds. I thought of the Irish of the period, Famine survivors being awed by this building and the people who controlled it. This is the historical moment when the *Punch* cartoons were depicting Irish people as half-ape, half-human.

The first people Eoin Ryan was to meet were people with responsibility for crowd control at football matches including, of course, the police. The guy representing Glasgow's finest was Inspector Drew Innes. His job title is Operational Planning G Division. He is the top cop covering policing operations for Ibrox and Hampden and an instantly likeable, straight-talking cop. So I asked him in terms of the Famine Song which laws, possibly, were being broken. He didn't miss a beat: Section 74 of the Criminal Justice (Scotland) Act 2003.

I asked Drew what that law said: "There is an offence of breach of the peace by racial prejudice," he replied. I then asked about the warning on the Ibrox screens last month at the cup game with Hamilton 'Accies. Drew looked to the ceiling. "You want me to put the notebook away, Drew? We can go off the record," I offered. "No, it's fine, no problem," he said.

I had reported on the warning to the Rangers supporters at the Rangers v. Hamilton game, and my initial understanding was that it had been a police warning put up on the club's screens. "No, it was a club statement after they had consulted with us," he told me. It was clear from his demeanour that there had been something of a mini-drama behind the screens at Ibrox *apropos* this statement on the Famine Song being sung inside the stadium. Our conversation then drifted to what the Famine meant for the Irish collective psyche and how, on TV, there had been a couple of major events on RTÉ about the Famine and what it meant for modern Ireland. I remarked that whoever wrote this ditty and the chaps who belted it out couldn't have grasped the synchronicity of using the events of 1847 to bait people of Irish descent in Glasgow in 2008. He took it on board.

"Bad timing, then?"

"Very bad timing, Drew."

Other people were filing into the room. I thanked Drew and before I could go and speak to anyone else he handed me his card and offered me his hand. "Keep in touch, it would be good to know how people are feeling about this in Ireland, the level of feeling," he said. I walked over to some people, one of whom introduced himself as David Bell of the Scottish Government. I showed Mr Bell my press card and told him I was covering the day for the *Irish Post* and titles in Ireland.

"You do realise that these are private meetings?" said the guy from the government. I was still processing the import of what he had just said to the Fourth Estate when my cell phone rang. It was Dave Harmon. He was downstairs and it sounded urgent. I bounced down the palatial stairs and finally met with the guy I had been speaking to on the phone for days. "Listen, the Scots are really, really edgy about this whole thing. They've even freaked that I have invited the TV." I didn't believe, initially, what was unfolding. "Listen," Dave said, "I'll give you a full brief when we come out of the meetings."

A cameraman and another guy were coming down the stairs. The guy without the camera introduced himself as David Henderson of *Reporting Scotland*. He also thought it, at best, iffy that there was to be no access for the media. The last time I was in Scotland I used the time-honoured journalistic technique of door-stepping. This time I employed another technique: the grab. I initially wanted down in the main area to see who was attending. That's when I saw Billy Singh of Show Racism the Red Card.

"Hello, Billy."

He had been surprised at Tynecastle, but perhaps this time he was half-expecting to see the guy from the *Irish Post*. "I read your piece," he smiled. "And?" I asked. "It was honest, I'll give you that. It was fair comment."

"I always try to be that in my work, Billy, then people have no grumbles with you."

I asked him for his mobile phone number: "I don't give out my mobile number."

"Not even to the media? You have to deal with the media."

"No, contact the office if you want to get hold of me," he responded. Remember, dear reader, I door-stepped the same chap because my calls weren't returned from SRTRC's office, but it isn't personal, it is only business. I offered him my mobile number. He keyed the number in "And Phil ..." He hesitated. "I'll put you in as Comrade Phil," he joked. In the end he keyed in Phil Journo. That works for me, I thought.

What Billy didn't know was that I already had his mobile number, but I wanted to see his reaction to the guy from the *Irish Post* asking for it. I went back upstairs with my backstage pass to where the meeting was about to take place. The big doors were closed and the meeting, including a working lunch, was planned to last two hours. One of them, I thought, would have to go to the toilet. After about thirty-five minutes, out came a young bearded chap in a checked waistcoat who introduced himself: "Hello, I'm Grant Baskerville, the press officer to Alyn Smith."

I resisted any observations about being a newshound, as, even by his young age, he would have heard them all several times over. This was an important lad in the proceedings. It was Alyn Smith MEP who had responded to Eoin Ryan's statement in the European Parliament by inviting the Irish politician over. I showed him my press card and told him the titles I would be filing to. Young Baskerville then blurted out: "We're not sweeping anything under the carpet in there." It sounded like someone protesting just a bit too loudly. I smiled and walked away.

There was nothing to do but await a grab and I didn't have to wait for long. Another straight-talking man from the world of law enforcement who gave me some copy emerged. Derek Kirkwood is the head of security for the SFA. I did the grab; I asked him who he was and how the meeting was going. He didn't hesitate: "It is a very positive meeting. Hopefully Mr Ryan will have a greater understanding of the level of work that we in the SFA have done, together with others, in combating racism in Scottish football." Here was someone in Scottish football that could use the R-word and not burst into flames. Respect.

When the meeting broke up I got the quote I needed from Eoin Ryan. He made all the right noises and used the R-word himself. Dave Harmon thought it better that I go ahead and file for the next news day, as the trip to Edinburgh was "just to shake the minister's hand". It was a good call. I went and filed my copy to the *Irish Post* and various Irish titles. My work done, I sent a text to Billy Singh to wish him the best with his "work behind the scenes". He replied back: "Rangers fan convicted for singing 'Famine Song'." I responded: "Hopefully this is the beginning of the end of this issue. Scotland is better than the 'Famine Song'."

The next day, the *Herald* was the only Scottish paper I could find that had any coverage of the visit. The *Herald* piece, by Robbie Dinwoodie, was clearly on message: "Anti-sectarian campaign backed by MEP". Nothing to see here, move along now.

Although I was assured by young Baskerville that nothing was "being swept under the carpet", it was notable that not a single organisation representing the Irish community in Scotland was present that day in the City Chambers. Can you imagine, say, a member of the Israeli Knesset visiting a country, as a guest of its government, where there had been a worrying upsurge in anti-semitism to see what the government was doing about the problem, and not being introduced to the local Jewish community's representatives? That, in contemporary Scotland, is just common sense.

Forbidden word, hidden truth

12 December 2008

Words are important. Well, you would expect a journalist and author to believe that. Words condition the response. Words have baggage. Words are never, ever neutral. Never.

I have been thinking about this increasingly since Eoin Ryan's visit to Scotland. The visit was arranged after Alyn Smith MEP heard Ryan raise the issue of the Famine Song controversy in the European Parliament. Ryan was very precise in the use of his language when raising the issue; this was a problem of racism and, to further press home that point, Ryan had flagged up his long-standing interest in combating racism in football across Europe. Ryan, who is one of the authors of a key European report on football in Europe, told the press before his visit to Scotland that he was heavily involved in the EU white paper on sport. The Dublin

MEP stated that one of the major aims of the white paper was to eliminate racism in sport in Europe, and in particular at football stadia.

When Ryan was interviewed on RTÉ's *Drivetime* radio programme
by anchor Mary Wilson, she persistently used the term "sectarianism"
when describing the Famine Song. Ryan was too gallant to correct the
RTÉ lady. However, he continued to use the term "racism" as opposed
to the inappropriate "sectarianism".

Alyn Smith's press officer is Grant Baskerville; he handled the PR for
Ryan's trip. This is the press release he sent out:

ATTENTION: NEWS DESKS

*SCOTS & IRISH MEPS IN ANTI-SECTARIAN
PROGRAMME   HOSTED   BY   SCOTTISH
GOVERNMENT*

*Alyn Smith SNP Member of the European Parliament for
Scotland will tomorrow (Thursday) welcome his Irish coun-
terpart, Fine Fail* [sic] *MEP Eoin Ryan to Scotland for
top level talks with the Scottish Football Association, Sport
Scotland and a host of anti-sectarian charities in Glasgow.
The pair will then travel to Edinburgh to meet with Minister
for Community Safety Fergus Ewing MSP at Holyrood.*

*The programme has been organised by the Scottish
Government, and comes in the wake of Mr Ryan raising the
issue of sectarianism in the European Parliament last week in
Strasbourg, whereupon Mr Smith invited him to Scotland. The
programme will highlight the ongoing work that is taking place
by charities, clubs and the Scottish Government to combat the
issue and explore EU avenues of support for these efforts.*

*Alyn Smith said: "We have a full day in store that covers
everything from grassroots to Government Ministers. Eoin is a
friend of Scotland, and I am sure that he will be thoroughly
impressed with the measures that are being taken by all parties involved, and I'm grateful to the Scottish Government
for putting such an impressive programme together so quickly.*

*"In Scotland, key organisations such as Nil by Mouth and
Show Racism the Red Card work hand in hand with the
Scottish Government, Scottish FA and most importantly the
clubs themselves to tackle sectarianism.*

"The Scottish Government are showing real leadership on this issue through a variety of initiatives and funding programmes.

"We have a strong history and commitment of tackling issues like this head on, but we can never be complacent. The sad reality is that when a vocal minority, on any side, behave in an unacceptable manner, it not only reflects poorly on their club, but also their city and their country. We must not allow them to tarnish Scotland's reputation in Europe."

ENDS

Eoin Ryan MEP was invited to Scotland to see the sterling work being done on the ground by voluntary bodies and public agencies. However, the concern about the racist abuse being directed against the Irish community in Scotland suddenly became anti-sectarianism. This isn't mere semantics. This goes to the heart of the matter of the denial of the existence of the Irish in Scotland as a distinct people. This is bizarre given the import the Famine Song, which is telling people to go home to Ireland. Clearly, anyone whose home is Ireland is, *ipso facto*, Irish.

It is a logic I cannot argue with, hence these words are blinking to life in Donegal, not Glasgow. However, the same people who would sing the Famine Song and taunt those of Irish descent that they should go home to Ireland sneer at the very idea that people born in Scotland can consider themselves Irish, even when they travel on Irish passports and have legally verifiable links to Ireland.

I recently attended a St Patrick's Day organising committee meeting in Glasgow. I saw some old friends from my time as a teacher with Conradh Na Gaeilge and met some new friends. I told them, although I couldn't know their personal circumstances, that I didn't know why they were still in Scotland as the Famine Song surely had crystallised the low esteem in which Ireland and the Irish were still held. No one had an answer for me. I wish all of them well. They have a huge boulder to push up the hill of anti-Irish sentiment in Scotland, that's for sure.

The sectarianism-not-racism proponents in Scotland implicitly state that there is no Irish community in Scotland. The facilitator of Eoin Ryan's fact-finding mission to Scotland was the Scottish Government's equality unit. These equal opportunities folk wanted no media around, but I'm kinda persistent. Just before the big doors were closing and I was about to be ejected, I spoke briefly with Dave Harmon, Eoin's press secretary. I had one chance to put this into his head: "Dave, the words being used here are crucial; this is Derry/Londonderry – they're using sectarian, the word to be used is racism."

In Eoin Ryan's final quote to me that day he acknowledged that some people wanted to call the Famine Song controversy an issue of sectarianism, while others wished to call it racism. Whether you call it sectarianism or racism you have to stand up to it. The trip and how it was reported, or not reported, crystallised for me the essence of the words used in this controversy and what they mean. My work on the issue has clearly thrown up a clear demarcation between those who would characterise the Famine Song sectarian and those who would view it as a manifestation of racism.

Since the Famine Song controversy broke here in Ireland in September, people in the Irish media have largely viewed the Famine Song as a manifestation of anti-Irish racism. Not surprisingly, Irish people in Scotland consider the Famine Song racist. The police consider the song to be an arrestable offence under Section 74 of the Criminal Justice (Scotland) Act 2003, in that singing the Famine Song is likely to cause a breach of the peace aggravated by racial prejudice. Show Racism the Red Card, as of 6 October, consider the Famine Song to be racist.

Most reasonable, objective people viewing this controversy would consider the Famine Song racist. In Ireland, it is definitely considered racist and anti-Irish. The issue was raised by several TDs in Dáil Éireann. Alan Shatter, his party colleague Michael Ring (Fine Gael), Tommy Broughan (Labour) and Joe McHugh (Fine Gael) have all asked questions of Foreign Minister Micheál Martin about the Famine Song.

They all received fairly standard civil service replies to their written questions, explaining that the Irish Consulate in Edinburgh was doing a wonderful job. It was clear from the civil servant who drafted the answers that he or she didn't understand the issue. Despite being asked by all of these Dáil Deputies about racism in Scotland directed towards the Irish community, they received stock answers about great moves in Scotland to combat sectarianism. If these parliamentary questions prove little else it's that the Department of Foreign Affairs currently does not consider the Famine Song a manifestation of racism. Given the influence of revisionism within the Dublin state over the last thirty years this should really come as no surprise to anyone.

There was another political development from Mayo; a man in Achill contacted Marian Harkin MEP. Ironically, Achill is one of the few places where people had a fighting chance of surviving the Famine because the sea provided food to the island folk in those dark years. Ms Harkin has developed a reputation for tackling various issues of discrimination and equality during her time as an MEP. As a member of the European Parliament she sought a European route to deal with the Famine Song. She contacted UEFA *apropos* the Famine Song on 10 November, writing directly to Michel Platini. Her letter to the UEFA President stated that she was concerned about reports of "racist chants from the Rangers supporters". She wanted to know what UEFA could do about this as she was concerned that such racism could "escalate out of control".

The reply from UEFA's Peter Limacher, head of disciplinary services, on 20 November was prompt and concise. Limacher stated that as it was a domestic match that was being complained about it was a matter for the Scottish football authorities. To this end, Ms Harkin's letter was passed on to the relevant Scottish bodies. One wonders if Marian Harkin MEP will receive a similar letter from Scotland to that which Tommy Broughan received from Gordon Smith.

"'Famine Song'? Racism? Rangers? Yes, we have a big problem with Celtic and Rangers and sectarianism ..."

Enclosed with the letter to Marian Harkin from UEFA was a copy of the judgement in 2006 about the behaviour of Rangers supporters in Spain at the Villarreal game. It was, perhaps, a diplomatic UEFA way of saying to the Irish MEP: "Look, we know there is a problem here. We believe you, we have taken action against Rangers in the past and we will be ready for them next time."

It was, of course, UEFA which put the Billy Boys on a list of banned songs. After I had received copies of this correspondence between Marian Harkin and UEFA I interviewed Marian to further explore the issue with her. I put the question to her that the song was, according to those in Scotland who defended it, merely a manifestation of ironic humour, satirising a mawkish pretend Irishness of some Celtic fans. "No, no, this is horrible stuff, vile, utterly vile," she responded. Of those who wrote the Famine Song and sing the first few lines at football matches, her opinions were equally unequivocal: "Their intentions are very clear to me. They wish to diminish people."

It is highly unlikely that anyone in County Mayo would view the Famine Song as humour. "We're from Mayo, God help us!" was the strapline of the Famine story in the grim years of the Irish holocaust. At least, however, the Famine Song issue is now on the Irish political radar.

I commented to Matt Cooper of Today FM's *The Last Word* that the story of the Famine Song wasn't just about the song itself but the official inaction in Scotland at a sporting and political level that had, quite understandably, led those who sang it to consider that they could do so with impunity. Slowly, that political inaction is being chipped away.

The Famine Song suggested that the Irish community in Scotland should "go home". Wriggling on the hook of public scrutiny and facing police action, those who initially sought to defend it dismissed those who condemned the song for its racist content as missing the point that the song was merely "banter".

The Famine Song controversy has, I believe, served the public good. It has stripped bare the nature of the Ibrox belief system. When the issue was presented as one of sectarianism, Rangers apologists could look at the number of Catholics signed by Rangers since 1989, a Catholic captain and a Catholic manager. That was progress. However, the ban on Catholics playing for Rangers was only ever a handy way of excluding the Irish Catholics despised by the Rangers subculture. Hatred of the native Irish Catholics and their descendants was what defined the Rangers subculture.

At time of writing, one of the Queen's loyal underclass is on remand; at Kilmarnock Sheriff Court the week before Eoin Ryan's visit to Scotland, a 20-year-old Rangers fan was found guilty of committing a breach of the peace – aggravated by religious and racial prejudice – during Rangers' 4–0 victory over Killie on 9 November. The fan was arrested at Rugby Park for singing the chorus of the Famine Song. Sheriff Iona McDonald stated that singing just the chorus was racist. "That, in itself, is a racist sentiment," said Sheriff McDonald. Result!

I started writing and broadcasting about the Famine Song in September. I largely did so because those in Scotland who have sports columns did not seem to grasp the importance of the issue. Hopefully the courts will deal with this issue now, as and when required. As for the soccer authorities in Scotland, they have failed to act. UEFA know of the Famine Song and when Rangers are in European competition next season the Ibrox club can expect a far different response from Europe's governing body than they've had so far from the men running Scottish football.

Groundhog Day at Celtic Park

22 February 2009

I was discussing this story with the news editor of the *Irish Post* this week. As ever when journalist and editor discuss a piece, the question from the editor is always, what is the peg? I didn't have to think

too much about that one. I immediately said: Groundhog Day at
Celtic Park.

That was my initial feeling. It felt like the first few days of September
last year when I had reported on the singing, by Rangers fans, of the
now infamous Famine Song at Celtic Park. Most of you will know
that, following on from that soccer match in Glasgow, the Famine
Song controversy became a matter of inter-governmental communication between the Republic of Ireland and the devolved assembly in
Edinburgh.

I thought we had all heard the last of it. I was wrong. Rangers were
back at the home of their rivals this month for the first time since 31
August 2008. This time, just as in August, the Famine Song, the racist
anthem that has replaced the Billy Boys as the main signature tune of
the Rangers support, was heard by almost everyone in the stadium and
by anyone watching the match on television.

The Famine Song was heard loud and clear several times throughout
the match by almost everyone. What was not lost on many in the Irish
community in Scotland, and here in Ireland, was the way the story
was covered in Scotland. Ewan Murray writing in the *Guardian* and
Graham Spiers in *The Times* mentioned the singing of the Famine Song
in their match reports. Match reports in the Scottish papers didn't have
a mention of the behaviour of the Rangers fans at Celtic Park that day.
This is very similar to what happened in the reportage of the Old Firm
match at Celtic Park last August.

There was, however, one important difference from 31 August. The
SPL match delegate, Alan Dick, made reference to the singing of the
Famine Song. In August, the SPL match delegate was ex-Scotland manager Craig Brown. In that match report the song wasn't mentioned.
Brown himself was embarrassed some years back when a tabloid newspaper received a tape recording of a voice message he left on his girl-
friend's answering machine. After a Rangers victory over Celtic, he sang
the Billy Boys. Brown stated, in his defence, that he had done it as a
joke. This song is now banned by UEFA. Many think that, as nature
abhors a vacuum, the banning of the Billy Boys by UEFA and then by
the SPL, created the need for a new anthem that articulated the Rangers
belief system.

Following on from this recent performance of the Famine Song there
was a swift reaction from representatives of Glasgow's Irish community.
The Garngad Irish Heritage Group spokesperson said: "The sad fact
about this ongoing racist abuse is not the half-educated racist morons

who sing it, it is the deafening silence from the Scottish establishment, from the SNP Government right through to the media, whose silence on this serious issue makes them just as guilty as the perpetrators."

One Scotland, Many Cultures is a popular slogan from this SNP Government. It should have in brackets (unless you are of Irish descent). Scotland's shame is not sectarianism; Scotland's shame is anti-Irish racism.

Kieron Brady, ex-Sunderland and Republic of Ireland international, who has worked extensively in the anti-racism field, said: "When you look at the history of the 'Famine Song' and the persistence in airing it and its alternative adaptations for James McCarthy and Aiden McGeady, there has to be some action which gives Rangers an incentive to ensure this anti-Irish racism is removed completely from the song sheet."

My own view is that the threat of police action is in many ways futile *vis-à-vis* acting as a worthwhile and indefinite deterrent. What would be welcome from Rangers FC is a statement that all who hold anti-Irish attitudes are not welcome at Ibrox Park. Such statements have been issued by various other clubs in light of racist incidents. I would refrain from second-guessing any potential SPL sanctions.

I then asked Kieron about the "self-policing" that had been announced by the Rangers supporters' organisation: "I think such initiatives *per se* are positive but only if strenuous efforts are made to marginalise and mute those who are motivated by self-interest and intolerance. It would be encouraging if a collective of supporters felt empowered enough to introduce measures which could rid the support of the racist element. In a similar vein to any club statement, it would be encouraging if such a collective made a statement saying that those with anti-Irish attitudes were no longer welcome within the ranks of the support."

I put to Kieron the view that the Famine Song was merely a bit of ironic banter: "The concept of inviting or telling immigrant groups to 'go home' is a mainstay of global racist mantra," he said. "Ergo, it is erroneous to label it as 'banter'. The Irish community in Scotland, just like the Indian and Pakistani communities, for example, have the right to celebrate their culture and heritage and likewise have the right not to be discriminated against. These are fundamental and key cornerstones of equality."

The fact that the singing of the Famine Song was included in the match delegate's report made sure that the story did break into the Scottish sports pages on the Tuesday after the Sunday match. It was also discussed on *Radio Scotland*. In the radio broadcast anchored by the

BBC's Richard Gordon, *Daily Record* journalist Keith Jackson made a defence of those singing the Famine Song and, effectively, blamed the Celtic fans for the fact that the song was sung that day at Celtic Park. At the start of the match some Celtic supporters unfurled a banner with the statement that Celtic FC had been born out of famine and oppression.

"I can't pretend to be outraged or mock some kind of horror at the 'Famine Song'," the *Daily Record* journalist said. "The lines that are sung at a football match, to me it has just got silly. People want to point score and to get people into trouble." Keith Jackson stated some bemusement at the presence of police officers pointing video cameras. Perhaps it had something to do with the fact that singing the Famine Song is, in Scotland, illegal. Jackson may be unaware of the court case in November at Kilmarnock Sheriff Court when a Rangers supporter was convicted for, yes, you guessed it, singing the Famine Song. When I covered MEP Eoin Ryan's visit to Scotland the week of the Kilmarnock case, I met with a senior police officer in charge of operational planning for Ibrox and Hampden. This was a serious no-nonsense cop and he was very clear that singing the Famine Song in a soccer stadium was illegal. He even told me the law, the section, and the subsection.

Several months on, a senior journalist like Keith Jackson is still treating the Famine Song issue as political correctness gone too far. I went back to Kieron Brady for his analysis of Keith Jackson's thoughts on the Famine Song. After listening to the BBC podcast, the ex-Republic of Ireland international and anti-racism campaigner was trenchant in his criticism of the *Daily Record* journalist: "Keith Jackson's assertion that the banner unveiled by a section of Celtic fans is in some way inviting the 'Famine Song' is fundamentally flawed, bordering on the most warped logic," he said.

"A basic right relating to equality is the right to overtly and openly illustrate a pride in identity allied with the right not to be discriminated against for the same reason. If this logic was applied across the board we would have racism and sectarianism as well as other forms of intolerance not only commonplace in sporting stadia, but throughout society.

"If Tottenham fans of Jewish extraction or of the Jewish faith were to illustrate a pride in their identity would this give *carte blanche* for supporters of other clubs to engage in anti-semitism? I very much doubt that the media, Tottenham Hotspur FC or the English FA would tolerate such behaviours. Additionally," he continued, "his assertion that Scotland has 'cleaned up its act' is fantasy. I spoke with a former colleague at Show Racism the Red Card Scotland and I am also aware of the thoughts at Kick It Out, with all in unison that the 'Famine Song' and how it has been sustained for almost a year is the worst racism in British football stadia for many, many years. When you look at the persistent anti-Irish abuse meted out to Aiden McGeady and James McCarthy, there is recognition that Scotland has a unique problem with anti-Irish racism, and what is arguably more shameful is that in relation to the racist abuse of both players, much of it has been engendered by anti-Irish racists in the Scottish media.

"Throughout mainland Europe, anti-racist bodies look at England as a positive model regarding eradicating racism from footballing environs. Of course, this does not mean that offensive and insensitive expressions have been absented completely. We only have to look at the despicable abuse of Sol Campbell several months ago to witness that, on occasions, reprehensible expressions can rear their ugly head.

"Likewise in mainland Europe, particularly in the east of the continent, there is much work to be done to ensure that vocal and visual expression is kept within the parameters of football, or at the very least is not based around prejudice. I would agree with his assertion that there has to be more of an even-handed approach. That would mean that the Irish community is entitled equality in relation to the right not to be discriminated against. Admittedly, this concept may seem foreign to certain elements in Scotland, including some in the Fourth Estate, but anti-racism only has credibility when it operates from a platform of equality and ensures there is no hierarchy, whether that is based around the victimised group or indeed the perpetrator. What this means, effectively, is that that the Irish community, the Jewish community or the African or Caribbean communities being asked to go home is equally abhorrent and equally racist. Referring to a tragedy such as An Gorta Mór only makes it all the more reprehensible, in the same way as alluding to the Holocaust or slavery may in particular be offensive to the aforementioned communities. On that note, measures have to be introduced to address all forms of anti-Irish racism in the same way they would address other forms of racism, or indeed other forms of intolerance."

He added: "On his last point about potential sanctions, I would be inclined to agree in that the chances of a points deduction is negligible. This is not only an unwanted sanction in Scotland for clubs but throughout Europe national associations have reservations about such sanctions being imposed."

Rangers supporters' organisations themselves, in as much as they made statements on this reappearance of the Famine Song, were dismissive of the criticism that the song was a manifestation of anti-Irish racism. The Rangers Supporters Trust concentrated its response on the author of the match delegate's report. They questioned the impartiality and the integrity of Alan Dick. Rangers Media, another fan group, dismissed the entire episode by looking back into the history of the two Glasgow clubs, with an article on their website headlined: "The 'Famine Song' – surely something to celebrate?" The article looked at the events at a Celtic v. Rangers match in April 1909, recounting a Scottish Cup replay at Hampden that ended in a riot with 50 police officers injured.

The article stated: "Now that happened exactly one hundred years ago this spring. I think it is fair to say we've moved on a fair bit from then. So why is the media reaction to what is reported to have been sung on Sunday so strangely out of kilter with reality? I've yet to see the statistics for arrests on Sunday but I'd be astonished if more than twenty were made during the entire match, inside and outside the ground. There certainly wasn't a riot, despite the poor performance from both teams, I'd hate to see the reaction if there ever was. Some people might have sung a song that doesn't slander anyone. Isn't it great that this is all we're talking about, look how far we've come." Rangers supporters of 1909 and 2009 are, of course, products of a radically different society. What they do share is a hatred of the Irish and any expression of Irishness. This dismissal of the racist Famine Song as "no big deal" is identical in content and tone to Keith Jackson's opinions on the BBC podcast.

When Eoin Ryan MEP visited Scotland in November as a guest of the Scottish Government, the objective of the trip was to show the Irish politician the excellent work being done at grassroots level in tackling racism in Scottish football. I was the only print journalist present that day to cover the event at Glasgow City Chambers. One of the organisations invited to meet Ryan that day was Show Racism the Red Card (SRTRC). Readers will know that SRTRC was petitioned by Irish community organisations in May last year after the Famine Song was sung at Celtic Park during an SPL match. Despite conceding in these meetings that the Famine Song was racist, it took SRTRC until October to state that on its website. This week, I tried in vain to gain any response from the Scottish office of SRTRC. I finally called the English office and was given the mobile phone number of one of their Scottish workers, Tommy Breslin. Tommy was surprised to take a call from a journalist. It isn't his role, but no one else was, so to speak, at home. I explained why I was calling. It was, essentially, the same conversation I had had with Tommy in October – remember, this is Groundhog Day.

I have never met Tommy, but he seems a very decent sort of man. He agreed to pass my request for a statement on to SRTRC Scottish co-ordinator Billy Singh. Before calling Tommy I had tried to get Billy on his mobile over several days but his phone seemed to be off. I had a deadline to make for the *Irish Post* so in the end I had to go to another organisation that works against racism in soccer for a statement to make the story stronger. As in October, I called the organisation Kick It Out! Groundhog Day. Kick It Out doesn't seem to suffer from any shyness problems when it comes to dealing with the anti-Irish racism of some Rangers fans. Danny Lynch, a spokesperson for the organisation, made this statement: "Recent efforts to eliminate offensive singing and chanting from Old Firm games need to be reinforced if the situation does not improve quickly. The singing by Rangers fans of songs such as the Famine Song, which invites second-generation Irish people to go back home, is clearly racist. If the club cannot persuade fans to refrain from singing such offensive songs, then the SPL will need to take action."

Why couldn't SRTRC make such a statement? When Jason Scotland was racially abused in 2007 by Motherwell fans, the response of SRTRC and, indeed, sports journalists in Scotland was swift and appropriate. Since then, Noel Hunt of Dundee United, Aiden McGeady of Celtic and James McCarthy of Hamilton Academical have been on the receiving end of anti-Irish racist abuse from opposition fans. Sadly, the organisation that is supposed to work against racism in Scottish football seems somewhat compromised when the victim of the racist abuse holds an Irish passport.

The SPL board will consider Alan Dick's match report at the next meeting in March. Rangers, who have already received a warning from the SPL for similar behaviour from fans, could face a fine or points deduction. A points deduction by the SPL is unlikely. However, this season action has been taken against clubs in Europe for the behaviour of their fans. Paris Saint-Germain were banned from this season's French League Cup after unveiling an offensive banner, but were later reinstated on appeal in a civic court. Botev Plovdiv were deducted points in the Bulgarian top flight, again for a banner that was deemed racist. They also had to play a subsequent game behind closed doors. It is worth noting that this club, like Rangers, has had a recent history of hooligan problems. Last season, Botev Plovdiv were forced to play more than one game behind closed doors because of hooliganism. This will be a real test for the SPL. It is time for Lex Gold and his organisation to walk the walk. If Rangers fans think they can act with impunity then they certainly will. Just ask the good people of Manchester.

Blowing the whistle

26 March 2009

Kieron Brady, the Scottish-born ex-Republic of Ireland international, today launched an attack on those tasked with eradicating racism in Scottish soccer. Brady, himself an anti-racist educationalist, called on Irish players in Scotland to disassociate themselves from anti-racist publicity campaigns.

"In light of the inaction of certain bodies to comprehensively challenge the ongoing anti-Irish racism in Scotland I would ask Irish players to disassociate themselves from the Show Racism the Red Card organisation until such time as more efforts are seen to be made in relation to this ongoing racism in Scotland," said Brady. "James McCarthy and Aiden McGeady, two Scottish-born Irish internationalists, are being compelled to endure anti-Irish racism almost on a weekly basis in stadia in Scotland, and in three Show Racism the Red Card publications since last June this has not been alluded to, nor has the racist 'Famine Song'."

He continued: "The absence of any reference let alone condemnation is staggering and is more and more becoming an illustration of anti-Irish racism not being viewed with any merited consideration. The fact that SRTRC Scotland has been discourteous in refusing to pass comment on this issue in a worthwhile manner, despite requests, as well as the impolite refusal to engage in further dialogue with Irish community representatives after their meeting last May, has also been contributory to this request. As the first Scottish-born player to decide to play for Ireland when still in his mid-teens as far as I know, as well as all three of our Irish ancestral homelands being in and around Cloughaneely, Gweedore and the Rosses, I have an interest in both James and Aiden, as well as being someone who has five years of experience in the area of anti-racism and equality."

Brady was an employee of SRTRC in England and has persistently claimed since his resignation last year from the organisation that it was unwilling to tackle the issue of anti-Irish racism in Scottish soccer. He pointed to the fact that a recently launched anti-racism DVD by SRTRC included no interviews with Irish players in Scotland. Billy Singh, campaign coordinator for SRTRC, denied that the omission of Aiden McGeady and James McCarthy from the DVD was an indicator of the organisation's weakness on the issue of anti-Irish racism in Scottish soccer. The DVD featured interviews from Thierry Henry, Rio Ferdinand and Scottish players Barry Ferguson and Stephen McManus. Brady also pointed out that SRTRC made no mention of the Famine Song controversy in the organisation's newsletter last month. SRTRC did state on its website last year that it considered the song racist. However, that statement was removed when the organisation's website was redesigned.

Ged Grebby, the chief executive of SRTRC, responded to Brady's claims: "I admit we were slow on the 'Famine Song' issue, but that was purely pressure of work in Scotland. We are working behind the scenes with Rangers FC about the 'Famine Song'. We have revamped our website and we will put right the fact that our statement on the 'Famine Song' was lost from the site. The song is racist, it is anti-Irish, and we have said so and will continue to say so." Grebby pointed out that SRTRC had a long association with Irish soccer players, including Niall Quinn as patron. "We employ John Anderson, ex-West Brom and Republic of Ireland international," he said. "John uses his experiences as a young Dublin kid in Birmingham in the 1970s as a way of engaging with youth around Islamophobia issues."

Preventing further offence

20 June 2009

It was only a few evenings ago that I was compelled, reluctantly, to reconsider the Famine Song issue. RTÉ was reshowing the brilliant *Where Was Your Family During The Famine?* The programme uses three Irish TV celebrities to trace their family history in the Famine period.

Most of the programme I found fascinating and very well done. The final part, where my friend John Waters finds documentary proof that his great-grand-uncle died of starvation in a Sligo parish, I found very difficult to watch. Very difficult. Towards the end of the piece, John stood in the graveyard where some of his people were dumped in an unmarked grave under Ben Bulben in County Sligo. "This mountain looked down on these people with more compassion than did the British authorities during those times," he said.

As my father is from Mayo and his mother's people are only found in that county, the Famine was always something in the background of our family's story. Last year, with the help of the Mayo Family Research Centre, I found that a brother of my maternal great-grandfather in Mayo had been born in 1845 but had not been in the family Census in the same modest abode in 1851. The strong possibility – the genealogist said – was that he had died as a toddler in the Famine. This is my grandmother's uncle, hardly ancient ancestry. My grandmother, of course, did not know him as he died before she was born. As John Waters said of his own great grand-uncle, "What we have here is a crime, multiplied by a million, and it was a crime. For that is what it is." My great-grand-uncle has no grave – there were mass graves – there are mass graves – all over this island. A reasonable person might ask what type of mind makes mocking and humour out of such a tragedy. I think I know.

My last day job in Glasgow in the 1990s before I relocated to Donegal was with the city council. I worked in the social work department and, in the main, I carried out the tasks of a probation officer, although in Scotland no one actually held that title. The bulk of my work with probationers was rather prosaic one-to-one casework. The legislation empowering the supervising officer states that he/she should assist and control the offender. Most of the assist part was simple enough social work that would be recognisable under general welfare work. However, they're under a probation order from the courts as an alternative to custody. This is the control part. The offender's behaviour and attitudes have to be addressed or they will be back up in front of the courts again and again. I particularly enjoyed working with these offenders in a group work setting. Often we would use a tool like an educational video to tease out why they had got to where they were. Remember, these are lives that are not going well. If your life is going well you are not processed through the courts and you are not subject to a probation order.

I was thinking of this when I read of the failure of the appeal of William Walls. First, Mr Walls has been processed by the courts and has been found guilty. Part of his offending behaviour was to sing the Famine Song at Rugby Park, Kilmarnock's ground, last year. Walls, of Craigend, Glasgow, was put on probation for eighteen months and given a two-year football banning order at Kilmarnock Sheriff Court. He will now begin a period of probation under the direction of a supervising officer as directed by the court. I don't know him and intend him no ill-will. I hope he emerges from his period of probation a more useful member of society. I have the same feeling about him as many of the hundreds of young men who were directed to me from the Glasgow courts in the 1990s; as you look at the pinched, unhealthy face across the interview table from you it's clear that this is a life that isn't going well. Sometimes that offending is the result of an addiction which leads the person into trouble. However, it can also come from delinquent values, from a disordered worldview.

The singing of the Famine Song is a race-hate crime. Considering the Famine Song, Lord Carloway found: "The court does not consider that the lyrics of this refrain bear any reasonable comparison to those of 'Flower Of Scotland' or, indeed, 'God Save The Queen'. Rather, they are racist in calling upon people native to Scotland to leave the country because of their racial origins. This is a sentiment which … many persons will find offensive." Game, set and match. The Famine Song is racist. Hopefully Scottish soccer stadia will not hear this anti-Irish racist dirge again. Should that not prove to be the case then the full rigours of the law will have to be utilised. If any of these offenders find themselves subject to a probation order because of the Famine Song then I have a DVD of the RTÉ programme that I would be happy to lend to one of my old colleagues in the department. Like all social problems, from obesity to suicide, we all have a part to play.

Journalism has a crucial role in guarding against writing a permission slip for racists. James Traynor wrote in the *Daily Record* about what not to do if you wish to discourage racist chanting at soccer stadia, in an article titled *Isn't there enough to worry about without beating ourselves up over a line in a song?* The piece is not without merit. It would be a useful teaching aid on a journalism course, but not as an example of best practice. When one observes these attitudes on the streets of Glasgow it is clear that the opinion-formers of Scottish football should be aware of their influence for good and ill. Mr Traynor could join Graham Spiers and be part of the solution. I trust Mr Traynor will revisit this issue and, after a period of mature reflection, condemn the racist Famine Song. Hopefully his colleague Keith Jackson will do likewise. Thankfully Lord Carloway and his eminent colleagues disagreed with Mr Traynor.

The judges concluded that Mr Walls, in singing the Famine Song, caused offence, caused hurt and broke the law. This is probably not the best way to use up your fifteen minutes of fame. A person like Mr Walls, in so many ways, needs education, education, education. Sadly, departmental budgets would not fund a trip to the mass graves of the west of Ireland, where he could see the reality of his humour. I wish Mr Walls and his supervising officer well in the next eighteen months. They both have work to do.

Lawwell unhappy about inaction on Famine Song

27 October 2009

Members of Show Racism the Red Card were taken to task by a tetchy Celtic Chief Executive, Peter Lawwell, at New Douglas Park after the match between Hamilton Academical and Celtic on Sunday 25 October.

Show Racism the Red Card workers Tommy Breslin and Elio Ajmone were introduced to the Celtic CEO by local MSP Michael McMahon. The conversation was initially friendly, focusing on Celtic's Somalian starlet Islam Feruz and the new video from SRTRC, *Combating Islamophobia*. Then Peter Lawwell asked the SRTRC men what their organisation was going to do about the singing of the Famine Song by Rangers fans and the taunting of Celtic's Irish players. Lawwell's tone became tetchy to say the least as he explained the pain and offence caused by the Famine Song and the abuse of Celtic's Irish players by the fans of other clubs in Scotland. Sources in the room at New Douglas Park said the charity workers were taken aback by the vehemence of the Celtic CEO. Michael McMahon MSP, who was in attendance, confirmed the details of the conversation that had taken place at New Douglas Park, as did SRTRC worker Elio Ajomne.

Earlier in the afternoon, the Bellshill MSP and leading member of the Irish community in Scotland, who was at New Douglas Park as a guest of SRTRC, asked the charity workers if they had attended the match at Ibrox the previous day between Rangers and Hibs. They said they had. When asked by McMahon if they heard the Famine Song being sung by Rangers supporters after Irishman Anthony Stokes scored for Hibernian, they said they didn't hear the controversial song. Michael McMahon expressed surprise at this as he had been contacted by constituents complaining that they heard the racist song while watching the game on TV.

Elio Ajmone is originally from Turin, Italy, and has a background in the UK of working with asylum seekers. He was recently appointed to work for SRTRC after the charity received extra funding from the

Scottish Government. He told me: "This is only my eighth week in post. My job is to create a new strand in Show Racism the Red Card's work in combating sectarian prejudice." When asked to characterise the taunting of Irish player Aiden McGeady, Elio stated: "This is a racist issue." When put to him that the taunting and abuse aimed at McGeady for playing for the Republic of Ireland was seen by the Irish community as anti-Irish racism, he replied: "No, that is a fair comment."

SRTRC national director, Ged Grebby, defended his organisation's work in Scotland, firstly by pointing out that the charity received no money from Scottish football. On the racist abuse of Aiden McGeady, he said: "We have spoken out on the racist abuse that Aiden McGeady receives from football fans. Tommy Breslin, for example, gave a statement to the *Paisley Daily Express* on 3 March 2008 after Aiden was racially abused by St Mirren fans. We are aware that anti-Irish racism is being used by Rangers supporters in a sectarian manner. We are planning a campaign called Show Bigotry the Red Card! We have written to Aiden McGeady to take part and we hope that he will."

Michael McMahon MSP later said: "The problem I have always had with the anti-sectarianism campaign of successive Scottish administrations has been the lack of clarity about the difference between sectarianism and racism. It is an easy get-out for the government, the football authorities and anti-racist organisations like Show Racism the Red Card to label the 'Famine Song' as sectarian abuse and treat it as just another manifestation of religious division rather than deal with it for what it is. The chant has already been identified in the Scottish courts as racist but it would seem that to deal with it as such presents too much of a challenge for the authorities, who find it much easier to see issues between Celtic and Rangers as two sides of the same coin. They are not. Each club has its own problems with its fans but this particular problem is one of anti-Irish racism and has to be dealt with for what it is." Neither Peter Lawwell nor Celtic FC was prepared to make any comment on the matter.

A day to remember

23 May 2010

Over a thousand people came to the foot of Croagh Phádraig in Mayo last Sunday to the national Famine memorial at Murrisk. A beautifully troubling sculpture of a coffin ship is the centrepiece of the memorial gardens. Family duty kept me from attending but I hope that next year I will be there. That's my entirely truthful excuse for not attending. However, I wonder what explanation the British Government has for not sending a representative.

It did not go unnoticed that the political descendants of the people who actually caused An Gorta Mór weren't at Murrisk. A few days after the commemoration I was able to get out there myself. I walked from Westport to Murrisk and back. That is now, I am told, to be the annual Famine memorial walk. It was a shimmering day in West Mayo. Hard to imagine that only a lifetime before my grandparents were born here the term "We're from Mayo, God help us!" was in common usage in Ireland. Mayo is the Famine county.

On my way out to Murrisk I stopped by the Westport quay. On a day like it was, it's simply a crime against your soul not to sit by the lobster straps, nets and assorted paraphernalia of the men of the sea. I fished here as a boy from the quay and out in Clew Bay on a boat wonderfully named the *Seumas Mac a Dang Dang*. During the Famine years huge amounts of grain and agricultural produce were exported from this quay to Britain. There was no food shortage in this county let alone this island. The term "Famine" irks those people academically concerned with those awful years. I continue to use it because it is the generally understood term in common English usage. The authors at irishholocaust.org are quick to rebuke anyone in contact with them about the use of the word "Famine" when describing what happened to the Irish people in those years. Famine implies that the place ran out of food and people starved. The island of Ireland had plenty of food, even in the west there was field upon field producing grains and cereals. As they say on their site: "As no Jewish person would ever refer to the 'Jewish Oxygen Famine of 1939–1945', so no Irish person ought ever refer to the Irish Holocaust as a famine." Quite.

The people of Mayo starved when the county was ruled by the most powerful empire the world had ever known. Ireland was an integral part of the United Kingdom. The Ottoman Empire and the Choctaw Indians were moved to do more for the starving Irish than our rulers in London. In those horrible years the British state lost all moral authority to rule here. They never got it back. For me, this isn't a matter of historical discourse, nor should it be for anyone who is of Ireland.

Last year I found that my father's mother had an uncle who died in childhood in the Famine years. Their parish was right in the middle of Mayo's An Gorta Mór. The genealogist conjectured that it was probably a Famine-related death. He was born in 1846 and they remained in the same house in North Mayo by the time the British Census of 1851 was compiled. The family was there, but he wasn't on the list of people in the house. I have more work to do on this. Some deaths in those years were simply not recorded because there were so many of them. Officials were overwhelmed by the scale of the calamity. I recall my friend John Waters discovering that a great-grand-uncle of his had also died in childhood in his ancestral parish in South Sligo. A death notice in the local paper said that John's relative had "died of starvation". There was no money available for a proper burial. On discovering this chapter in his clan's story, my buddy from Roscommon was unequivocal: "What we have here is a crime, multiplied by a million, and it was a crime. For that is what it is." Agreed, John. The Famine, the Irish Holocaust, was a crime. Anyone thinking to make mocking, racist "humour" from that crime is beneath contempt.

The power of myth

3 January 2011

As I travel through life I am increasingly dismayed at the power of myth in human communities and the need to create legends from virtually zero evidence. People seem to need myth, especially groups of people. It appears to be the glue that holds them together through an agreed feel-good narrative. If the discernible verifiable reality doesn't fit the myth, the reality is ignored. In recognising that, I am already admitting defeat as a rationalist, as a follower of David Hume. What I am sure of is that this trade of mine should deal in reality and not in shoehorned versions of the facts, bent out of shape to fit a preconceived narrative.

The reportage of yesterday's commemoration for the sixty-six people who died in an unsafe stadium forty years ago could be Exhibit A in any trial of myth versus reality. Almost everyone said that the silent tribute for the sixty-six people who died in the Ibrox disaster was impeccably and completely respected. Ibrox, for one minute and twenty seconds, was a very, very silent place.

This wasn't in the preferred script for many in the press box. There was barely disguised glee in the Scottish tabloids in the run-up to the match with an expectation that Celtic fans would bring shame and disgrace on themselves and on Celtic. Rather than show respect to the memory of sixty-six people and their still grieving families, what some of the press pack wanted was a "Celtic Boo Bhoys shame!" headline. They didn't get that any more than they got the "Walter Triumphs Hapless Lennon!" headline, where Lennon's nationality would be juxtaposed with observations about his naiveté and his inability to organise his team against the "wily old fox". No, the Celtic fans behaved, Lennon got his tactics right and the Celtic players excelled. Therefore, the hoped-for headlines had to be binned until the next time a minute's silence could be used as a booby trap in the PR war against Celtic.

Because the reality didn't fit the bill a myth had to be created. "Coughgate" was born in a disturbed imagination and planted in the stagnant soil of a Rangers message board. Today it appeared in the column of a major daily newspaper in Scotland. Myths tend not to be ossified, but instead develop and morph as the situation demands. Now, the "orchestrated coughing" of Celtic fans yesterday in the Broomloan stand has become the "fact" that they were coughing as a code to ape the dying gasps of the crushed people in 1971.

I'm truly saddened for anyone who would think this is possible. It isn't. That there is zero evidence for this claim actually lends weight to the myth. It will now be an article of faith in the Rangers tribe. They will believe because they want to believe, because it tells them that they are intrinsically better than "that other lot". I cannot think of a more heinous insult to the memories of those sixty-six people than this. They should be sick with shame, but, of course, they won't be. Those who consider it sport to kick policemen to the ground in Manchester or urinate on war memorials in Barcelona are beyond reach on any level that appeals to human decency.

Yesterday, the Celtic fans did themselves and their club proud. Had they not I would have been quick to respond. If you doubt me, read me on this site following on from Remembrance Sunday at Falkirk in 2009. No, the silent tribute was beautifully observed by all in the stadium, irrespective of their club allegiance. To expect that over fifty thousand people can stand silently on a Glasgow day in January without a cough or a sneeze is nonsense. Moreover, how could anyone know that the coughing, which is an involuntary human activity, was confined to the Broomloan stand?

I had thought that the *Sun* might have learned a lesson since Hillsborough and Liverpool about printing such offensive rubbish in the wake of a football disaster. Clearly not. Columnist Bill Leckie's hearing was highly selective; hearing things that weren't there and then failing to notice that which was booming out only four minutes into the match. Thousands of Rangers fans were in full voice singing the Famine Song.

Singing this song is an illegal act in Scotland, established in case law by Lord Justice Carloway in June 2009 at the High Court of Justiciary. Once more it goes largely unreported, the perpetrators act with impunity and the club is not held to account by the SPL. So the following is just for you, Bill: the Famine Song is illegal, coughing is not.

Interview with Danny Boyle of the Harps Community Project

24 February 2011

I recently interviewed Danny Boyle of the Harps Community Project.

What is the Harps Community Project?

The Harps Community Project is core-funded by the Department of Foreign Affairs in Dublin through the Irish Government Emigrant Support Programme. The project aims to support the Irish community and others in Glasgow, utilising Irish cultural activities such as music, sport, language or dance to harvest opportunity and promote active citizenship. We have over sixty children involved in our music project who avail of free music lessons on a weekly basis.

I became involved with the project in September/October 2010 and realised that issues which pertain specifically to the Irish community in Scotland – such as cultural recognition, facilities for Irish elderly, an Irish Centre etc. – weren't as developed in some settings as our sister communities in England. The Harps Project now looks to engage in two settings; supporting both grassroots initiatives, such as our own music project, and working closely with cultural institutions such as Comhaltas, the GAA, Irish Dancing and Conradh Na Gaeilge on areas of mutual benefit. Examples of this would be the current and ongoing census campaign, Irish Centre proposals or pilots for Irish elderly facilities. It's important that the Irish community also engage with both local and national government to increase awareness of these specific issues but also to express our consciousness of community responsibility. It's not all about focusing exclusively on the Irish community, we also recognise our social and civic responsibility as a community group.

The Irish community have made an outstanding contribution to Scottish society, will continue to do so and, as individual or collective organisations, always work within the ethos of celebrating cultural diversity and promoting active citizenship. The Glasgow St Patrick's Week Festival reflects this sense of community and cultural celebration with everything from Nigerian dancers to Irish traditional musicians making up the content of the festival, which will be celebrated throughout the week 12–19 March, in conjunction with the project, the Glasgow Irish Heritage Group, Glasgow City Council, An Scéal, the Education Authority and Big Lottery.

What is your role within the project?
I took over the role of project manager in September/October 2010. The project works with a five-person management committee and myself as project manager. We look to engage with our network of contacts throughout the Irish community on areas of particular relevance to individual groups or the broader community.

For example, before Christmas we organised an Irish Centre development fund night. This was supported by the GAA, Comhaltas, Conradh Na Gaeilge and Ceili Dancing Club, as well as outstanding support from the broader community. This is crucial to our strategic aims *inter alia* the involvement of the broader community. It's impossible to speak to everyone individually. However, the more groups we can engage with, be that internally to promote the Irish Centre or externally to work with other BME groups or umbrella organisations, such as BEMIS (Black and Ethnic Minority Infrastructure), to target issues such as cultural/ethnic recognition or anti-racism, the better. We look to facilitate a culture of cooperation between the different Irish groups. Each individual group gave support to the night, musicians played for free, the venue was provided for free. The strongest asset we have as a community is the hard work of our volunteers and if we can harness that into strategic development then we'll address issues such as Irish centres or facilities for Irish elderly, as well as create opportunity for our youth. Following the success of the fundraising night and cross-party support in the Scottish Parliament recognising the work and culture of the Irish community, we will be meeting the Scottish Government to discuss the Irish Centre proposal.

Why did you get involved with this project?
From a young age I have been involved with the Comhaltas Ceoltoiri Eireann (Irish music) learning, participating and competing at

Fleadhanna (festivals) throughout the year. I now teach voluntarily on a weekly basis and adjudicate at fleadhs throughout Scotland, England and Ireland.

I had a brief stint with the McLaughlin School of Irish Dancing when I was younger and latterly played Gaelic football for Tir Conaill Harps GAA club in Glasgow. I've always been aware and proud of my Irish heritage. I worked as a development officer for BEMIS before taking the post with the project so I had a good measure of personal and professional experience in the voluntary sector as well as being aware of issues which affect the Irish community in Scotland. I'm in a very fortunate position where my work is also something I feel passionately about and have always been involved in some capacity.

Some would say that the idea of a distinctive Irish community within Scotland in 2011 is a fiction; that the Irish people who settled in Scotland over a hundred years ago have totally assimilated and that who you style as the "Irish community" are indistinguishable culturally from the rest of Scotland. What is your response to people who hold that view?
It's not within the interest of Scottish society to see immigrant communities assimilate into Scotland. People should feel comfortable with their own ethnic heritage. This may manifest itself through music, language, dance, faith or sport. Cultural diversity should be embraced. The Irish community is no different in this regard. Although misgivings have been expressed that Irish people should go home because the Famine is over, particularly within settings such as football matches, and that this is aimed primarily at the "Plastic Paddy" stereotyped perception of Irish identity is just plainly anti-Irish racism.

The reality is that Irish culture is alive and well. Glasgow – and beyond, of course, in Lanarkshire – is famous for the standard of its music and dancing, with world champions in both arts hailing from Glasgow and representing their city on a world stage. This is good for Glasgow and good for the community. Irish cultural initiatives run every day of the week in Glasgow and beyond supporting music, language and sport. These initiatives utilise Irish cultural activities as mechanisms for empowerment of citizens, be they of Irish background or not.

Glasgow is changing all the time, cultural diversity and active citizenship will need to be at the forefront of the development of the city. The Irish community will continue to play their part in this responsibility. Integration and assimilation are different concepts, a community should be able to integrate into society while maintaining their distinctive identity but recognising their responsibility as active citizens. The Scottish Government work through the slogan *One Scotland Many Cultures*; Irish culture has an equal part to play in this without fear of the community feeling marginalised or forced to disregard their Irish heritage in order to fit in.

If an Irish person moved here from Ireland what community life could they enjoy?

Music, sport and language are thriving. It's an exciting time to have an Irish identity in Glasgow. The pressures which affected older generations are slowly but surely waning. Although there is still anti-Irish racism and misperceptions of the Irish community around celebrating their ethnic identity, the confidence of Irish youth now manages to outshine this. Anyone arriving to Scotland now would encounter a vibrant, positive community.

This is symbolised by the fantastic work of festivals such as the Glasgow St Patrick's Festival and Coatbridge St Patrick's Festival, engaging with the local community and service providers. These festivals may not have been possible fifteen or twenty years ago. However, they're now just getting bigger, with their infrastructures developing year after year. We have GAA, Comhaltas and Conradh Na Gaeilge development officers in Scotland and this bodes well for the future of the Irish community. Although the Comhaltas and Conradh Na Gaeilge are primarily based in Greater Glasgow, there would be nothing to stop communities around the country starting up individual branches of the respective organisations if they wanted to partake in music, language or sport, Irish background or not. These groups are very much global and encourage all new membership. So, in short, anyone arriving to Glasgow would find a thriving, welcoming, confident Irish community.

What do you see as the major objectives of your project over the next five years?

Like most other groups and individuals, the financial climate is worrying. Our core funding comes from the Irish Government, which has shown great faith in the Irish community around the globe by providing opportunity to apply to the Irish Government Emigrant Abroad Support Programme. All indications are that this funding will continue to be maintained. However, naturally, we need to be meticulous in our costing, projections and aspirations. As mentioned earlier, and this can't be emphasised enough, the importance of volunteers and community activists is paramount to our future hopes, especially as funding becomes tighter across the board. I have only been in my position for five months so it's difficult to aspire to five-year plans when funding is commissioned on an annual basis. However, we always work from this basis. The project isn't about token gestures; we have highlighted and seek to assess issues which pertain to the Irish community and Scottish society in general. In the next twelve months we'll be looking to build on our positive relations within our community, outreach to other community organisations and continue to engage positively with local, national government and service providers.

Do you believe that Celtic FC is a legitimate expression of an Irish identity in Scotland?
The history of Celtic is inextricably linked with Irish immigration to Scotland. The fans of the club and the club itself should be proud of this; without Irish immigration to Scotland there would be no Celtic Football Club. The club has represented Scotland on the world stage, bringing home cups, awards, friendships and reputations. It's still very much a focal point for expressions of Irishness. The Harps Project has no working relationship with Celtic plc. Undoubtedly, Celtic is the largest sporting and cultural institution which has come as a direct result of Irish immigration and, accordingly, has a responsibility in this regard. We would be delighted if Celtic were on board with regards to the census campaign or as part of the broader Irish community to tackle anti-Irish racism.

Within football settings evidence of anti-Irish racism can be vicious. The Famine Song is an extreme example, however, there are more subtle expressions which are arguably more dangerous. The Hugh Dallas episode was particularly relevant as his position and the role of the SFA as Scottish football's administrators deemed it highly inappropriate for employees to have been communicating anti-Catholic emails. There is a perception within the Irish community that organisations such as the SFA will have an element of anti-Irish sentiment. This stems from incidents such as the SFA asking Celtic to remove the Irish tricolour from flying above the old jungle at Celtic Park, the sacking of Jim Farry over the Jorge Cadete transfer saga or, more recently, the evidence that SFA employees indulged in sending anti-Catholic emails, lying to the Celtic manager and the nonchalant attitude of the authorities towards songs such as the Famine Song.

These worries are compounded by attitudes within the media that songs such as the "Famine Song" are merely "banter" or that in response to the booing of the minute silence for the late Pope John Paul II the Celtic fans responded "with one of their sectarian anthems". In actual fact, the song the mainstream Scottish BBC and *Daily Record* journalist was referring to was the Irish national anthem, a song sung for almost 100 years by Celtic supporters. It would be unfair to focus solely on the SFA or print media in relation to anti-Irish racism as they are symptoms of an issue which is rooted within Scottish society; however, they also have a responsibility to recognise it for what it is and attempt to combat it along with other relevant organisations. Anti-Irish racism certainly existed in employment and recent research shows that although Scotland's Catholic population, which is mainly of Irish extraction, make up 17% of the population they also make up 26% of the prison population. The Church of Scotland commissioned a report in 1923 called *The Menace of the Irish Race to the Scottish Nation*. Why would sport be immune from an issue which has clearly affected other dimensions of society? Personally speaking, I'm not convinced that Scotland has a massive sectarian problem. Relations between the Church of Scotland and their Catholic counterparts are very cordial and ecumenical services are celebrated routinely, indeed the Church of Scotland recently apologised for the writing of this aforementioned report and its consequences.

What does seem to be prevalent, though, is a lazy anti-Irish racism or misunderstanding of Irish culture. Scots-born Irish international footballers vilified for choosing to represent the country they have an affinity for, for example. What we seem to have is sports journalists doubling up as sociologists and commenting on matters which, although they have a valid opinion the same as everyone else, they are utterly unqualified to have the defining say on. This is fundamentally correct when a community group feels that racism against their community is valid, it is not for people outwith this community to cry paranoid or traitor but to engage them in meaningful dialogue to resolve any problems. This spirit is enshrined in law after the murder of Stephen Lawrence. The Macpherson report recommendations state that: "A racist incident which is perceived to be racist by the victim or any other person".

We've had numerous instances of murders in Scotland of a similar vein: Mark Scott and Thomas McFadden are two names which spring to mind. I believe we would be closer to dealing with Scotland's "shame" if we recognised these crimes for what they were, attacks because these people were Celtic fans and through this association, Catholic and Irish and unfortunately for a small minority of the population, "Fenian bastards". The Famine Song, therefore, like its perceived predecessor, the Billy Boys, is no joke or banter. It's insulting, racist and perpetuates an anti-Irish culture which has existed in Scotland in varying degrees throughout the last 150 years. That's the perception of the community the joke is on so, surely, their opinions should be taken into account.

Rangers have to be warned at the start of every round, says anti-racist expert

1 March 2011

Piara Powar is the Chief Executive of Football Against Racism in Europe (FARE). Previously the CEO of the Kick It Out organisation in the UK, he is highly influential in the corridors of football power in Europe.

Speaking exclusively to this journalist about the behaviour of the Rangers fans in Europe this season and UEFA's lack of response so far to a tirade of discriminatory chanting over the past eight games in Europe, he said: "One of the challenges about anti-Irish racism and anti-Catholic sectarianism is that UEFA need to warn Rangers at the start of every round. There is no point in blaming UEFA for perceived inaction on this matter. The problem resides in Scotland and has to be dealt with by the SFA and the club. What is clear to everyone is that action needs to be taken; these levels of abuse just can't continue," he said. "We are prepared to sit down with the SFA and both Glasgow clubs to help."
I put Piara Powar's views to Kieron Brady, an equality expert with Celebrate Identity Challenge Intolerance (CICI), and put the following questions to him.

Piara Powar has revealed that Rangers Football Club requires a warning about fans' behaviour at the start of every tie whereas every other club with problematic fans have only to be reminded at the start of a European campaign. What does this, in your professional opinion, reveal about the extent of the problem at Rangers?
This reinforces the view that the issues that exist within Rangers do have unique components. Of course, other clubs throughout Europe are presented with difficulties around racism and religious intolerance. In terms of regularity within games, however, the numbers responsible,

frequency across the season and the lack of any bona fide condemnation and unprecedented action from the club, illustrate that this is a profound problem. We have not yet reached a stage where the club, or the many decent Rangers fans who love their club without this baggage, feel empowered enough to instigate change by challenging what is in their midst.

Does this mean that RFC have the worst discriminatory chanting problem in European football?
We are unaware of any other club where these matters exist to the same extent as outlined above.

Piara Powar said that, ultimately, this is a job for the SFA to tackle. What should the domestic association do?
There has to be a wholly new approach that is based around equality and what that entails, including deconstructing the belief system and removing the notion that some forms of discrimination are more unacceptable than others and that some have greater rights in having grievances around abuse.

While Scotland has facets and features that are unfathomable for many, in reality we are dealing with the hostility towards a racial and religious minority and the reactive measures that can come with such realities. To that end, Scotland is no different from other nations, but the Scottish Football Association and the Scottish Premier League have to tackle this on that basis, they have to consider whether they have been addressing these matters with any conviction, whether their present arrangements are proving productive, and crucially, that by offering immunity they are sowing the seeds of intolerance for generations to come.

Given that Scotland is seen as more problematic in this area than other countries across Europe with similar issues, including nations in central and eastern Europe, I think it is just to assume that these arrangements are proving anything but productive. An annoyance is that, with the will, I believe many of the outstanding issues within the national game could be resolved in a relatively short period of time. I do not, however, believe that the will is there presently and I fear we may sadly have to have some form of human cost which will prompt what is necessary. In this area a constant failing, not least from within the mainstream press, has been the recent phenomenon and incessant focus on characterising bigotry as being exclusively around offence as well as being unprepared to point to a correlation between verbal hate crime and it emerging physically.

To highlight that this is not an issue solely within football per se, we have the incomprehensible situation presently where the police refuse to respond to requests about the release of data around Section 74 offences. It is difficult to envisage improvements in any society around intolerance when the police force is uncooperative regarding simple requests from religious minority groups, particularly those among the most susceptible to serious abuse and hatred.

George Galloway slams Justice Secretary MacAskill for failing to condemn Famine Song at Hampden

21 March 2011

Controversial politician George Galloway has rounded on Scottish Justice Secretary Kenny MacAskill for praising the crowd at yesterday's CIS Insurance Cup final at Hampden and failing to mention the incessant discriminatory chanting of the Rangers fans.

Galloway, who is standing for election to Holyrood in Glasgow in May, said: "I suppose a man like Kenny MacAskill, who has been nicked by the police at a football match for allegedly being drunk and disorderly, finds nothing untoward about fans singing racist and sectarian songs at the game. For most of us it's a continuing and shaming embarrassment to the country. The Famine Song, just one of the hate anthems which assaulted us from the television, has been ruled as racist by an eminent judge. The police, who praised the fans and the comparatively low number of arrests, clearly stood back and allowed the sectarian and racist abuse. Is that now police policy? To ignore the law? And does Mr MacAskill endorse this or, indeed, did he give guidance to Strathclyde Police in their policy of non-interference?"

A Scottish Government spokesperson said: "We must unite as a society to combat all forms of bigotry and sectarianism – not divide – and that is exactly what we are doing in Scotland. We support the police in taking action to clamp down on all unacceptable behaviour – at the ground and outside the ground – and there have, for example, been arrests and football banning orders imposed for this particular totally unacceptable song. Such conduct will not be tolerated. Strathclyde Police, the clubs, football authorities and government all take our responsibilities very seriously – the recent summit facilitated by ministers was requested by Strathclyde Police precisely because they see at first hand many of the wider social problems in relation to Old Firm matches."

Danny Boyle, project manager of the Harps Community Project, speaking in a personal capacity, said: "Although the minister MacAskill was correct in that it was a good spectacle on the field, it has not gone unnoticed in the Irish community that, once more, anti-Irish racism has been allowed to be flaunted inside a Scottish soccer stadium with impunity. The 'Famine Song' is racist and we are sick of hearing it. No other ethnic group in Scotland is subjected to this level of racist abuse."

MacAskill responds to Irish community

8 April 2011

I have been authorised to release the following correspondence between the Irish community in Scotland and Justice Secretary Kenny MacAskill. This email was sent by the Irish Diaspora in Scotland Association (national umbrella of Irish societies) to the SNP headquarters on Friday, 25 March 2011.

Subject: Letter to the Scottish establishment on anti-Irish racism/Catholicism

Dear Sir/Madam,

May we bring to your attention the comments made by Scottish Justice Secretary Kenny MacAskill and Assistant Chief Constable of Strathclyde Police, Campbell Corrigan, following the Celtic v. Rangers cup final on 20 March 2011.

"The players, management and fans contributed to a memorable occasion and I urge that their positive example inside the ground is replicated outside it over the course of the evening and beyond," said Scottish Justice Secretary Kenny MacAskill.

"I think the atmosphere at the ground was excellent and the match was a great advert for our football. I hope that this atmosphere is replicated across the force and that we see a drop in the levels of alcohol-related violence that blights so many communities," said Assistant Chief Constable Campbell Corrigan of Strathclyde Police.

In the lead-up to the aforementioned match we had been led to believe, following the high-profile summit involving the First Minister and government representatives, Strathclyde Police, Celtic Football Club and Rangers Football Club, that a zero tolerance approach to bigotry, racism and sectarianism would be implemented. The cup final of 20 March 2011 saw tens of thousands of football supporters indulge in vicious discriminatory chants expressing anti-Catholic and anti-Irish sentiments in the form of songs outlawed by Europe's governing football body, UEFA, and recognised as both racist and sectarian in Scots law. The songs in question were the Billy Boys, the Famine Song and No Pope of Rome.

These songs call on British citizens of an ethnic Irish background to return to their country of ethnic origin, while expressing an intolerance of around 17% of the country's population who follow the Catholic faith from a multitude of ethnic backgrounds beyond the Irish, including Scots, English, Polish, Italian, Indian, Nigerian and Sri Lankan, to name a few. These communities, along with Scotland's largest ethnic minority group, the Irish diaspora, have helped build and develop the infrastructure of the country and should feel comfortable to play a part as full citizens while maintaining and celebrating their ethnic heritage.

It is noteworthy that previous Scottish governments have addressed this issue only within a distorted "sectarian" framework, while they continue to miss the fact that much of the noted behaviour and attitudes amount to discrimination against one particular ethnic and faith community. It is time that the government and relevant stakeholders started tackling the real problem within the discrimination legislative framework and moved beyond the constructed narrative, as the problem goes deeper than popular superficial understandings of so-called sectarianism.

It is with regret that in Scotland in 2011 songs which expose both anti-Catholic and anti-Irish sentiment are expressed with impunity within such a high-profile showcase event screened around the football world. Of the 51,181 attendees at Sunday's game, we are told that the zero tolerance policy towards religious prejudice and racial abuse yielded two arrests – 0.0039% of the capacity crowd. The comments attributed to our Justice Secretary and Assistant Chief Constable are incomprehensible within the context of the reported "positive" nature of the atmosphere and behaviour of supporters.

Scotland's Irish community recognise fully our responsibility to celebrate cultural diversity and promote active citizenship. We look to interact with people from all backgrounds in cultural initiatives expressing both our Irish heritage, promoting cultural diversity and submitting fully to the idea of *One Scotland Many Cultures*. Indeed, this was reflected in the positive nature of cross-party support expressed by MSPs, led by the SNP and supported by Scottish Labour and Conservative colleagues respectively at the members' debate held on 12 January 2011 in the Scottish Parliament. At this event all parties roundly praised the work of Scotland's Irish community and its importance in the dynamic of Scotland.

It is with concern that we highlight the continual inaction of government, NGOs and the Scottish football authorities to address the overwhelming issue of anti-Catholic bigotry and anti-Irish racism in the Scottish sporting arena, which has contributed to undermine the Irish community as active citizens. We recognise the need for positive dialogue to address these problems and look forward to engaging with the relevant bodies in the near future.

We call on the future government, the European Human Rights Commission, the police, the voluntary and education sectors and all relevant stakeholders to start looking into existing, as well as new, methods and initiatives which can be deployed to address these problems.

Is mise le meas (with respect)

Irish Diaspora in Scotland Association – national umbrella of Irish societies
Danny Boyle – Project Manager, Harps Community Project
Joe O'Rourke – Secretary, Celtic Supporters Association
Ciaran Kearney – Scottish Development Coach, Gaelic Athletic Association
Patrick Callaghan – Scottish Development Worker, Scottish Region, Comhaltas Ceoltóirí Éireann
Seán Ó Gallchóir – Chairman, Conradh na Gaeilge Glaschú
Pat McAleer – *An Scéal*, Irish Community Newsletter
Joe McAleer – Chairman, Glasgow St Patrick's Festival Committee
Danny Gallagher – Glasgow St Patrick's Festival Committee
Jack Trow – Chairman, Harps Community Project

*

Date: Sun, 3 Apr 2011

Subject: Re: Letter to the Scottish establishment on anti-Irish racism/Catholicism

Dear Sirs,

Thank you for your recent email regarding the issue of sectarianism.

Let me firstly agree with you that all forms of sectarian and racist abuse and chanting have no place in our national game, or indeed anywhere in our national life. It is totally unacceptable and indeed illegal – we support the strongest possible action to deal with it, which is one reason why we convened the recent summit, with the full and willing support of both Old Firm clubs, the three football authorities in Scotland, and the police.

It identified eight areas for further work – including addressing sectarianism, alcohol misuse, domestic abuse and violence, and hate crime on the internet; the practicalities of new fixture scheduling; the expansion of football banning orders; the potential role of a dedicated policing football intelligence unit; and indeed supporting the expansion of the excellent existing community and social partnerships between the Old Firm in order to take every opportunity to demonstrate cooperation and mutual respect.

The joint action group established at the summit – involving the Scottish Government and the organisations named above – has already met twice in order to develop proposals and report to ministers before the start of the new season. These issues are regrettably deep-seated and long-standing, and change will not happen overnight, but let me assure you that there is agreement on all sides to look at what more can be done, and a recognition that we all have a responsibility to ensure that football is a force for good in society – in every regard. I hope this helps to answer your query.

Kenny MacAskill

*

4 April 2011

Dear Mr MacAskill,

Thank you for your reply.

While we appreciate the sentiments and issues addressed in your reply we continue to have reservations about the current settings in which anti-Irish racism is being addressed. As outlined in our original letter, the "sectarian" framework has, in our opinion, helped mask the reality of anti-Irish racism. This is of particular concern to us within the settings of a Scottish parliamentary election campaign where the Irish community has been somewhat isolated by the silence from all relevant parties to the overwhelming issue of anti-Irish racism. This is not only an issue which afflicts the SNP but also the Labour party, Conservative party, Strathclyde Police and NGOs, whose specific remit from public funding is to tackle "sectarianism", including Show Racism the Red Card, Nil by Mouth and Sense over Sectarianism.

The abject failure of any relevant party to publicly utterly condemn anti-Irish racism outwith the sectarian framework and in the public sphere is central to our concerns. It is with frustration to again have to utilise the analogy that if "Irish" was replaced with "Jew", "Paki" or "gypsy" then the public condemnation, particularly within the context of an election, would have been widespread, expected and as vociferous as the tens of thousands of individuals who have expressed the opinion "the Famine is over, why don't you go home?" with gusto and impunity for the last three years.

This song was first sung at a soccer match in 2008. In the following three years, to our knowledge, there have been two convictions for singing the Famine Song. This is utterly contemptible. It is obvious that anti-Irish racism is being dealt with either in a completely lackadaisical attitude or the current mechanisms for recognising and tackling this problem are failing.

In order to find a solution and path which addresses the problem of anti-Irish racism, the Irish community must be included and consulted in this process with government, police, NGOs and educational programmes supplemented by the publicly funded NGOs. We are perplexed by the current failure to open any dialogue with the Irish community. Celtic Football Club nor any of the other organisations involved in the joint action group speaks on behalf of Scotland's Irish community.

These proposals are hollow as they have received no input from the community to whom the racial abuse is directed. We agree that these prejudices are deep-seated and long-standing and failure to recognise them for [what] they are will merely perpetuate the problem. We look forward to discussing this with yourself in the very near future. It is important for the Irish community to have this dialogue with the SNP before the 5th May.

Kind regards,

Danny Boyle – Project Manager, Harps Community Project
Ciaran Kearney – Scottish Development Coach, Gaelic Athletic Association
Patrick Callaghan – Scottish Development Worker, Scottish Region, Comhaltas Ceoltóirí Éireann
Seán Ó Gallchóir – Chairman, Conradh na Gaeilge Glaschú
Pat McAleer – *An Scéal*, Glasgow Irish Heritage Group
Joe McAleer – Chairman, Glasgow St Patrick's Festival Committee
Danny Gallagher – Glasgow Irish Heritage Group
Jack Trow – Chairman, Harps Community Project

SFA response to Irish Diaspora in Scotland Association

14 April 2011

This letter from Stewart Regan of the SFA to the Irish Diaspora in Scotland Association is important simply for its very existence. Here is the head of the SFA acknowledging the existence of the Irish community in Scotland.

Moreover, the final sentence of the first paragraph gets to the core of the issue. Anti-Irish racism in the sporting arena has and does undermine the Irish community as active citizens. After this correspondence I cannot see Mr Regan being able to call for round-table discussions at a future date on these issues and not invite representatives of the Irish community. From the back of the bus to the top table. That is why this letter is important. Tip of the hat to Mr Regan.

7 April 2011

Dear Sir,

IRISH DIASPORA IN SCOTLAND ASSOCIATION

Thank you for your recent letter bringing to our attention the comments made by Scottish Justice Minister Kenny MacAskill and Assistant Chief Constable Campbell Corrigan following the Celtic v. Rangers cup final on 20 March 2011. Additionally, we note your concerns that there appears to be a continual inaction by the authorities to address the overwhelming issue of anti-Catholic bigotry and anti-Irish racism in the sporting arena which has contributed to undermine the Irish community as active citizens.

Shortly after the cup final, I issued a statement making it quite clear that the Scottish FA condemns all kinds of sectarian and discriminatory behaviour, indeed this was a view endorsed by the president of UEFA, Michel Platini, at the UEFA convention in Paris on the same week. I advised that we at the Scottish FA are committed to the newly formed joint action group set up by the Scottish Government, the police and all Scottish football authorities to ensure a collective approach to addressing the ongoing problems including sectarianism. Indeed, prior to the cup final I met with representatives from the anti-sectarian charities, Nil by Mouth and Show Bigotry the Red Card, as part of the Scottish FA's plans to help formulate a new series of practical measures that can be implemented to help tackle the issues that continue to arise. I also further intend meeting with member clubs and the league organisations to seek their assistance in eradicating sectarianism and other forms of unacceptable behaviour from football.

Subsequently, and as part of our commitment to the joint action working group, I have agreed with the other members of the group that before the start of the new season we will look in depth at four key areas:

- To ensure that the existing rules and regulations of Scottish football are rigorously applied and respected
- To explore jointly and understand the practicalities of new fixture scheduling opportunities to minimise damage to communities
- To support the expansion of the excellent existing community and social partnerships between the Old Firm to take every opportunity to demonstrate mutual respect and cooperation
- To offer full support to all the work by clubs, authorities and police to work with communities to address alcohol misuse, sectarianism, racism, domestic abuse and domestic violence

I fully believe that these initiatives will further improve the already good work that has been ongoing but also realise that it will not change overnight, however, it will provide a solid foundation on which to build upon. As I'm sure that you are acutely aware, sectarianism is unfortunately a long-standing societal problem, particularly in the west of Scotland, that manifests itself at our football matches by so-called football supporters who choose to bring their own unwelcome prejudices to our national sport.

Football is for all regardless of race, religion, sexual orientation or ethnicity.

Please be assured that I and the others on the joint action working group will use every opportunity to reduce and with time eradicate this unacceptable behaviour from our game. It is vitally important to us that everyone who supports football in Scotland feels they are part of and proud to belong to the football family without prejudice.

Again, thank you for your comments which will assist in the greater debate on this whole issue.

Yours sincerely,

Stewart M Regan

Chief Executive

Trade Union equality officer
is Famine Song defender

15 April 2011

Exclusive

The National Association of Schoolmasters Union of Women Teachers (NASUWT) reacted with horror when they learned that Stephen Smith, their principal official for equality and training, had tried to defend racist chanting by Rangers fans.

When I spoke to a NASUWT press officer he had no idea that Smith is currently the public face of the Rangers Supporters Trust (RST). In 2008, at the height of the Famine Song controversy, Stephen Smith, speaking as a representative of the RST, said in an interview with the *Sun* newspaper that the reaction to fans singing the Famine Song was "completely over the top". The following year, Lord Justice Carloway ruled in the High Court of Justiciary that the Famine Song was indeed racist and aimed at people of Irish heritage in Scotland, urging them to go home to Ireland.

In 2009 the union nominated Smith as a judge on the prestigious Anne Frank Awards. When this journalist spoke to Gillian Walnes, the charity's CEO, she was horrified to find out that the NASUWT-nominated judge was defending something like the Famine Song in his spare time. Mr Smith is well known to the inhabitants of the planet Scottish football, where he is often the public face of the Rangers Supporters Trust. Only last night – 14 April 2011 – he was on *Sky Sports News* discussing Rangers' most recent bit of European bother with Jim White. In that interview, the equality officer posed the question to Jim White: "What is racism? What is sectarian? What is offensive?"

I hope Mr Smith was more confident of these issues when on Thursday, 9 July 2009 at the Holiday Inn, Bromsgrove, an internal NASUWT document stated:

Organising for equalities

Stephen Smith, principal official, equality and training, ran an interactive session looking at how to organise for equalities using the equalities calendar. Delegates were asked to identify a month and come up with ideas and identify the resources they would use and develop an action plan.

   The feedback discussion included:

- *the need to ensure the anti-violence material and events covered all sections of members*
- *young members' engagement in equality*
- *younger members' engagement with the union*
- *broadening the categories of members to 'new to teaching'*
- *anti-semitism and anti-fascism to include Islamophobia*
- *using the Stonewall* Spell it Out *DVD for tackling all forms of bullying*

Chris Keates, General Secretary of NASUWT, said: "The union has a record second to none in promoting anti-racist policies, defending members against all forms of discrimination and campaigning against racist and fascist organisations. The NASUWT condemns unequivocally any form of racist behaviour. The union's rules make clear our anti-racist stance. The union's contract of employment and codes of conduct for staff are equally clear on these matters. The NASUWT disassociates itself fully from the 'Famine Song' and recognises the judiciary's view that this song is racist. In light of these reports, the union will be conducting a thorough investigation into the allegations that have been made."

Sources inside the union informed me that NASUWT due process should be completed within two weeks. A spokesperson further added: "In response to media interest, Stephen Smith would like to make it clear that he recognises and accepts the judicial findings that what is known as the 'Famine Song' is illegal and racist. He neither condones nor encourages anyone to sing the 'Famine Song' and would like to make it clear that he is committed fully to opposing racism in all forms."

Campaigning for a Famine memorial

12 July 2011
This article first appeared in the Mayo News

With a father born and reared in Westport, the folk memory of An Gorta Mór was always around. It was part of the narrative of my childhood. One of my first memories was of listening to my grand-mother and her sister, my aunt Nora, talk about it at the fireside in the house on James Street.

Only with the passing of years can I understand what they were say-ing, but it is like a tape recording in the part of my head that is still a toddler. As a young man of 21, I spoke to my grandmother about those times. When she was born the Famine wasn't even a folk memory. The survivors were still alive.

As a native-born Glaswegian I can attest to the fact that the imprint on Irishness is everywhere. The city phone book is full of Gallaghers, Murphys, O'Donnells and O'Neils. The city gave the global Gaeltacht its own soccer team, though often at odds with an officialdom hostile to the club's heritage.

I was reared to be proud of what I was – a Glasgow-born Irishman. It's important to anyone anywhere to feel that they are respected for who they are. I cannot say that about my native city. Despite the huge amount of people in Glasgow who would proudly claim an Irish iden-tity, the city's biggest ethnic minority are invisible in the public space. Scotland's largest city is the only major reception centre for Famine refugees that does not have a permanent memorial to the tens of thou-sands of starving Irish who landed on Clydeside in those awful years.

Memorials are important. Recently in Ireland our attention was brought to two memorials in Dublin. During the royal visit at the Garden of Remembrance and Island Bridge the British head of state played an important role in the symbolism of the reconciliation between the two traditions on the island. We saw the monarch of the ex-colonial power acknowledging the legitimacy of the freedom strug-gle of Irish Republicanism. It would have been hard to envisage those acts of respect and perhaps penitence being carried out by the Queen had she not been standing in the Garden of Remembrance in front of the Children of Lir.

Public monuments are important in any society. They can acknowl-edge a past deed or misdeed. It can be a meeting point for celebra-tion, mourning or a warning from the past. The only argument against commemorating the displaced An Gorta Mór who landed in Glasgow is that it would be vandalised. Should such people control the public space of any city? Of course they shouldn't.

The *Irish Post* is the weekly publication which serves the Irish com-munity in Britain and they have launched a campaign to have a Famine memorial in Glasgow.

Glasgow is overdue its memorial to the great Irish Famine

21 July 2011
This article first appeared in Caledonian Mercury

During her recent visit to the Garden of Remembrance and Islandbridge in Dublin, the British head of state played an important role in the symbolism of the reconciliation between the two traditions on the island. We saw the monarch of the ex-colonial power acknowledging the legitimacy of the freedom struggle of Irish Republicanism.

It would have been hard to envisage those acts of respect and perhaps penitence being carried out by the Queen had she not been standing in the Garden of Remembrance in front of the Children of Lir. Public monuments are important in any society. They can acknowledge a past deed or misdeed. They can be a meeting point for celebration or mourning, or a warning from the past. All human societies throughout history have spent considerable amounts of scarce resources to erect monuments. This means they must provide some benefit, and some meaning. The Holocaust memorial in Berlin, for example, is troubling and impossible to ignore. Just like the Shoah itself, the German nation has determined that it will not ignore this troubling spectre from its past. Respect.

Glasgow is almost unique among the major receiving centres of survivors of An Gorta Mór (the Great Famine) in that there is no city centre memorial to those awful years. Great cities such as Boston, Liverpool, New York, Sydney and Toronto all memorialise the humanitarian disaster of the Famine. Why should Glasgow be different? Currently it *is* different. Certainly, the city was the reception centre for tens of thousands of Famine refugees and the only argument against a memorial I have been able to garner is that it would be vandalised by racist thugs. Can you imagine the proposed memorial to Dr Martin Luther King not being put up in Washington DC because of what the good ol' boys of the Klan might do? Of course not. Their time is gone and the reclaiming of the public space from the racists included taking down the Confederate flag from state buildings in the Deep South at the start of the new millennium. This is what mature, well-adjusted societies do about the traumatic events of the past.

The story of the arrival of the Irish in such city-altering numbers in

Glasgow cannot be told. A glance at the Glasgow phonebook will tell you that the city of my birth has as many Irish names listed as does the one for New York. Why, then, is the central act in the Glasgow Irish drama not acknowledged in the city's public space? The survivors of those cadaverous refugees propelled the city into a powerhouse of Edwardian vigour with their sweat and their blood, but the only acknowledgement that An Gorta Mór has in Glaswegian life is the refrain of the racist "Famine Song" from some football fans. Glasgow's Irish community deserves better of the city that has given the world a unique part of the Irish diaspora. All the public authorities need to do is to pledge the small footprint of ground, say on the Broomielaw or in George Square or at Glasgow Cross.

The site – as well, of course, as the design – could be put out to a competition. My own preference would be the Broomielaw by the Clyde. This is where boatloads disgorged tens of thousands of skeletal, disease-ridden Famine survivors. It would connect with the sculpture on Custom House Quay in Dublin. However, that is merely my opinion. The judging panel would have representatives from the Irish community in Glasgow, historians who have researched An Gorta Mór and input from the artistic world. It would be my earnest wish that politicians wouldn't be allowed in the room. They shouldn't be allowed in because they are not going to be asked for any taxpayers' cash. The only act of good authority that those in power should have to take is to grant planning permission for something suitably tasteful, evocative, haunting and appropriate. It would be a memorial to the tragedy of An Gorta Mór, but it would also be a strong statement that Glasgow finally acknowledges and values the city's Irish community.

A country in transition

7 November 2011

It's good to talk. That is the main message I took away from a great weekend in Ullapool.

Gerry Hassan and Jean Urquhart MSP have been running the Changin Scotland weekends for the last nine years. This was my first time at one of these events.

Gerry Hassan is *the* complete Scottish politics junkie with an encyclopaedic knowledge of the dialogues and debates around the Scottish question. His cerebral database on Scottish politics is matched by his energy and enthusiasm. You ask him a question, any question, and watch him go. He's great company. Jean Urquhart is a list MSP for the SNP in the Highlands. She has a quiet presence and doesn't miss much. It is an awful cliché in politics that people go into it to "make a difference", but it's easy to believe in Jean's case that it is actually true. The venue for the event was the Ceilidh Place hotel. A quick name check and thanks to Effie, Emmett, Fiona and the rest of the staff. Great people.

Gerry invited me to speak on the subject of being second-generation Irish in Scotland. The weekend started with a spirited debate between Elaine C Smith and Alan Cochrane of the *Daily Telegraph*, with the latter putting the case for Scotland remaining within the union. There was a wide range of opinions represented, from unionists to those in favour of full independence for Scotland. The weekend was finished off by Douglas Fraser of the BBC, journalist Joyce McMillan and the young and brilliant social media adviser to the SNP, Kirk Torrance, who all contributed to an excellent discussion on the state of the Scottish media.

My own offering was on the existential challenges of being second-generation Irish in Scotland. It was part personal testimony and part sociological analysis of the situation of Scotland's oldest ethnic minority. My settled view is that Scotland is changing. Joyce McMillan and I discussed over lunch the Famine Song controversy and the subculture that produced this racist ditty. Joyce's view was that, deep down, these chaps in the cheap seats at Ibrox know "that they are on the wrong side of history". As I was giving my talk in Ullapool there was a demonstration going on at the BBC offices at Pacific Quay in Glasgow by a group of Rangers supporters claiming that the corporation was biased against their club. Ah bless …

A modern, outward-looking, confident Scotland – multicultural and welcoming to all – cannot shelter the sentiments contained within the Famine Song. I am increasingly convinced that Scotland is a' changin'. The new Scotland has the possibility to be a very different one to the country I was born in fifty-three years ago. That gave me a good feeling as a fiery sun was setting over An Teallach as we left Ullapool yesterday.

Telling the world

9 August 2012

They say that travel broadens the mind. I am here in Philadelphia to take part in a Q&A and book signing in the *Fadó* Irish bar and I am looking forward to that hugely. This piece is being written in that very same place and there is a great, warm, friendly vibe from the staff and patrons alike.

Given the isolating nature of being an online writer, these occasions are hugely important for writer and reader alike. However, I have a more important engagement tomorrow and that will be to speak at a ceremony of remembrance at the Irish memorial in Philadelphia. Unlike the city of my birth, Philly remembers An Gorta Mór respectfully and appropriately in the public space. Glasgow remains unique in being the only major reception centre of Famine refugees that does not commemorate those world-changing events. There is much work to be done on this issue back in Glasgow.

However, this is an opportunity to tell the global Gaeltacht the state of affairs in the Scotland of many cultures. With occupational parity only achieved for the Glasgow Irish in 2001 – a century after the Irish in New York – the old discriminatory attitudes remain in place. The Irish diaspora is honoured across the world for their amazing fortitude in what they endured and how they won through. Everywhere we made landfall in the nineteenth century, escaping from genocidal conditions imposed by a brutal aristocracy at home, we have worked, served, led and enriched.

The Irish who landed in Philly were allowed to be proud Americans and to retain their Irish heritage. I hope that my sojourn in Philadelphia brings some attention to the cultural realities of modern Scotland. The people who are taking very good care of me have several media opportunities lined up and I am happily at their disposal. Hopefully I can broaden some outlooks while I am here. I am sure I will, as Philly people are open-minded and understand the vital importance of tolerance and respect for the heritage of their neighbour.

Nil aon tintean mar do thintean fein

17 August 2012

Home truly is where the heart is. After a long oul haul I was back on home turf last night. I stopped off with BTF in Dublin and had the craic with him. I also consumed a mind-altering substance called "sleep". It's good to be home. It is an atavistic exercise to try and tell someone where you think they should belong to suit your own pre-ordered agenda. You

cannot impose a cultural identity any more than you can excise an ethnicity. This is my island. That seems to irk some folks. I rather suggest
it is they who have the problem.

When I first landed in Philly, the lad standing next to me at the bar
in Fadó told me that he had first seen the light of day in Aberdeen.
His dad had worked in the oil industry. He wore a wristband in the
colours of Colombia. It is the land of his parents and it is his land too,
according to him. I wondered if this lad had been a star footballer and
decided to play football for Colombia, if he would have been booed by
the Scots. Then I considered it probably would not happen, as that racist delight is reserved for the Irish in the Scotland of many cultures. Of
course, what happened to McGeady is called "sectarianism"; the Irish
aspect doesn't even get mentioned and that's part of the racism.

Today there is a discussion in the Scottish Parliament based around
Scottish–Irish relations. The S-word will be freely mentioned, yet anti-
Irish racism is a term that remains *verboten* in the Holyrood lexicon.
While I was in the USA, it would appear that a clutch of clairvoyant
literary critics were hard at work stating that they did not like my book
on Rangers [*Downfall*]. I have been, in my time, a reviews editor for a
weekly paper here in Ireland. Unfortunately I wasn't equipped with the
same special powers that these chaps have; I actually had to read a book
before I could form an opinion of its merits as a piece of work.

Of course, these bookworms don't need to read *Downfall*. They know
that it is by me and it is about the demise of their beloved football club,
so it has to be bad. These bibliophiles were further riled to learn that
Alex Thomson of *Channel 4 News* had agreed to write the foreword.
I find it almost sweet that these keyboard hitmen thought they could
dissuade an award-winning war correspondent from a course of action
that he had freely entered into. The descent into liquidation may have
caught the extended Bear family by surprise, but it came as no shock to
me. Had they been able to read this blog and pretend it was written by
someone else, perhaps the warning signs may have been heeded. With
the publication of the book I consider my attempts to educate the Ibrox
klan over. I failed.

Now they queue in the rain to fund Sevco. So be it. They remain
an evidence-resistant subculture, easy to fool and uncomprehendingly
loyal to the nearest available male authority figure in brown brogues.
For those who have a *Schadenfreude*-based interest in the further humili-
ation of the Ibrox klan, the Sevco saga is just starting and it will not
disappoint. When I started writing about the financial problems at

Rangers in January 2009 I was disbelieved and derided. I think I am allowed a small smile.

Now that I am back home there are other projects to focus on. Having stood at the Famine memorial in Philadelphia, I am further convinced that the absence of such a commemorative sculpture in Glasgow is no longer defensible. Although I was an ocean away from my island, I was among my own. I know that there is a warm hearth in Pennsylvania; it isn't my own fireside, but the Irish welcome is genuine. People there are encouraged to have pride in their Irish ethnicity. This would not be the case had they remained a British colony. I think it had something to do with fiscal policy. The American colonists decided to Expel British Taxes (EBT). I am happy to be home, but I think I know where I'll be next St Patrick's Day.

From the land beyond the waves

25 August 2012

Irish America was hugely important in Ireland's long struggle for independence. I believe that it can now prove crucial in assisting the Irish community in Scotland in their long walk to respect.

When I was in Philly I spoke with an outstanding young man called Kevin Boyle. He is the state representative for the city. He attended the pre-match presser which delivered the announcement of a soccer academy in Philly which will involve Celtic. When I was introduced to him it took us less than 60 seconds to work out that I knew his first cousin very well and had worked with him in an Irish language project twenty years ago. Kevin's chief of staff looked on agog at the instant familiarity that Irish people are capable of wherever we meet in the world. Later that day, Kevin gave a firebrand speech at the Famine memorial ceremony. My thought was that the basic truth he had spoken would still be *verboten* in the Scotland of many cultures. We agreed to have a sit-down later that weekend.

As an Irish American, is it fair to say you didn't have too far to look back for your roots?
My father is from Glencolmcille in Donegal and my mother's parents are from Easky, County Sligo. I have many relatives still residing in Glen, Mount Charles, and Inver in my father's county.

You spoke at the memorial on Friday about your awareness of anti-Irish racism in Scotland and how that played out in soccer.

I think McGeady and McCarthy are probably pretty representative of the Irish in Scotland. They don't have the freedoms that I have as an American to celebrate my heritage. There isn't an anti-Irish bias in America where people feel marginalised. I think when FIFA and UEFA talk about "anti-racism" in soccer and you still hear the Famine Song being sung and it is not being eradicated from Scottish football, there's obviously a clear problem and there is a double standard.

As a state representative here in Pennsylvania, do you see a role for the global Irish community?

Oh yeah. I see it as my role as an Irish American. I am not restricted by any of the barriers I see in Scotland. That isn't my day-to-day reality. I can call it as I see it and I commented on this in my speech at the memorial. When you see the abuse that Neil Lennon has had throughout his career in Scotland, if that happened in the United States to a racial minority or if it happened in Britain to any other racial minority except the Irish, well, the action would have been very different. When I spoke to Neil Lennon after the event on Friday I told him of the huge respect I have for him, for all that he has had to put up with. That's coming from an American perspective and an Irish perspective.

Your father didn't go to Glasgow from Gleann Colm Cille – you caught a break there.

Obviously there is a long legacy of tension in Scotland going back to the 1800s. It is somewhat connected to the Troubles in Northern Ireland and that contributes to that mindset.

The term you used at the memorial, anti-Irish racism, in political discourse in Scotland is largely verboten. *Instead, when the Famine Song is mentioned the term sectarianism is used. Yet, the clear motivating force is a hatred of Irish people.*

Yeah, I think that takes the ethnic out of it. It diminishes the offence and the hurt caused to people. I think this issue, like the conflict in Northern Ireland, would be better understood if we stopped using the terms Catholic and Protestant instead of focusing on the ethnic, because that is what it is really about.

I have become convinced over the last few years when writing about this

*issue that we cannot have any faith in the body politic in Scotland to tackle
the issue of anti-Irish racism honestly for what it is. That is why I am so
grateful for your interest and your energy and for that I thank you. It is good
to know that the Irish community in Scotland has such a friend.*
Thank you, my pleasure.

As we sat outside the *Fadó* Irish bar on 15th and Locust, I had to do
a double-take when I considered that, had this confident young man's
father decided, like many in this country, to go to Glasgow instead of
the USA, how different and how much less enriched his life would have
been as someone of Irish ethnicity. As an American he is free to express
his Irishness. As a Glaswegian he would not have had that freedom and
he understands that. The Irish in Scotland have a real friend in this
young man and I think we will be hearing more from him in the future.

A son of Sligo

27 August 2012

A childhood lasts a whole lifetime. Andrew Kerins from County Sligo
lived through the most catastrophic years in Irish history. Born in 1840,
he was seven years of age when An Gorta Mór fell upon the Irish people.

At the height of the Famine, those fit enough to provide a decent
burial for the dead were overwhelmed and hundreds of thousands were
interred without shroud or coffin in mass unmarked graves. It was the
final indignity of a people dispossessed of decent lands centuries earlier and ethnically cleansed by Cromwell's troops into the boglands of
Connaught. My father was a Mayo man and his mother reared me on
tales of those terrible times. Family research I carried out some years ago
revealed that her father's brother had died as a four-year-old during the
Famine years in a Mayo village where no household escaped the ravages
of the great hunger. Such events can leave a psychic wound that never
fully heals.

Brother Walfrid's grave in Dumfries is suitably humble for a man
who would have been horrified by anything ostentatious or grandiose.
Yesterday, he was remembered in a ceremony organised by the Celtic
Graves Society. Although we gathered around his graveside to honour
the man who founded Celtic, it was An Gorta Mór that commanded
my attention as we travelled back to Celtic Park. I suspect that those

awful years never ever left Walfrid in peace. Childhood trauma is like no other. The wound is seared into the most vulnerable of psychological tissue. The emotional pain never really goes away. Was this the fuel that drove him to provide food for hungry children? He was certainly a driven man, possessed of great energy and focus. The Irish who escaped to Glasgow left an impoverished land and found themselves in probably the most anti-Irish city on the planet. As a fifteen-year-old immigrant to Scotland, Andrew Kerins experienced that racism first-hand. It was in that awful situation that Brother Walfrid grew to manhood and entered the church for a life of duty and service.

As the football club he founded steps out on Wednesday night to the strains of "Zadok The Priest", Handel's coronation anthem would make the Sligo man smile wryly as his life was not concerned with those of elevated status. Celtic Football Club has a unique narrative that the entire world should be aware of; An Gorta Mór created the community that gave birth to Celtic. Brother Walfrid was no dilettante missionary reared in comfort and indulging in *noblesse oblige* among the starving; he was serving his own people and doing his God's work by using any means necessary. He devoted his life to the service of others.

On Wednesday night in the Lisbon Lions stand this atheist will remember him as I gaze upon a living, breathing monument of one man's liberation theology. Last year, the Celtic charity foundation helped to feed and save over 60,000 children in Somalia. The existence of the Celtic family is the wonderful legacy that Walfrid gave to the world. My childhood was lit up by a love of Celtic and I have a Sligo man to thank for that.

Progress on a Famine memorial for Glasgow

31 August 2012

Glasgow City Council will be asked to throw its weight behind a Famine memorial for Glasgow. The motion will be moved by Councillor Feargal Dalton of the SNP. Here is the draft wording:

Council notes the significant cultural, economic and social impact of Ireland's An Gorta Mór and the Scottish Highland Potato Famine on the modern day character of our great city. Council recognises the efforts made by Glaswegians at the time to provide relief and sanctuary to those affected,

a tradition that continues now as our city and its citizens continue to pro-
vide hope and assistance to those throughout the world affected by famine
today. Council therefore agrees to create a working group to examine the
feasibility of, and to make recommendations for, a memorial to those who
perished and to those who migrated to this city, and elsewhere, to escape
starvation and forge new life for their families.

Over the last twenty-four hours a series of discussions has taken place
within the wider Irish community as how best to advance this project.
Developing story.

A good day for my city

14 September 2012

An Gorta Mór helped to create modern Glasgow. In fact, it is difficult
to think of any other event in the last 150 years that had such a lasting impact on the city's demography and culture. Therefore it became
increasingly puzzling to me that this event was not commemorated in
the public space in the city before now. Subsequently, it was heart-
warming yesterday to hear of Feargal Dalton's motion being passed in
the City Chambers.

As had been reported here, the SNP councillor for Partick decided to
put this before his colleagues in the City Chambers at the first available
opportunity. Clearly, some in Glasgow will have an issue with this –
clue: they sing the Famine Song – as it suits them fine enough that there
is no public recognition in the city of An Gorta Mór. Any country that
harbours people who would take offence to and trash a 70th-anniver-
sary memorial to Irish children killed in a tragic fire, as happened in
Kirkintilloch in 2007, has some serious issues. Now that there will be
some kind of memorial, the next move for such folks is to carry out the
sculptural equivalent of ethnic cleansing. They want historical revisionism written into stone or bronze.

However, the historical issues are not in question. What they now want
to achieve as a fall-back position is a Famine memorial that isn't really a
Famine memorial. Anyone who has a problem with a sculpture that specifically commemorates An Gorta Mór in Glasgow simply has a problem
with the Irish and Irishness. The condition is commonly referred to as
racism. Yet, such backward people should not define a great city.

I am told that Feargal Dalton was listened to in silence as he put forward the motion and was loudly applauded across the political divide in the chamber. However, some in the city will have a problem with the very idea of commemorating this seminal event in the creation of modern Glasgow. In the words of an Irishman currently living and working in Glasgow, they really should have a good look at themselves. An Gorta Mór claimed many victims; in the main they were poor rural people and the Famine did not discriminate on the grounds of religion, cultural background or political persuasion.

My grandmother's uncle was not much more than a toddler when he died during the Famine. A major beneficiary of this humanitarian disaster was the Catholic Church in Ireland. For anyone interested in following this strand of the story I can recommend the late Emmet Larkin's prolific work on the subject. Yesterday was an important first step and there is much work still to be done, but we will get there.

There were people within the Irish community who told me that I was wasting my time bringing up the Famine memorial issue. They said that it would never get any official traction and that the entire campaign was futile. I have three words for them in the language that the Famine almost extinguished: Is feidir linn. Yes, we can.

From Famine Song to Famine memorial

22 October 2012

One of the common themes in memorials to the Irish Famine across the world has been a distinct lack of politics or religiosity evoked within bronze, iron and stone. Right-thinking people look back at those awful times and they just see a humanitarian disaster and a criminal failure of government.

The latter aspect was the subject of an apology from the British Government on the 150th anniversary of the Irish Famine. The memorial that I envisaged when I started writing about the subject is something like the one at Custom House Quay in Dublin. There is nothing to suggest the ethno-religious background or politics of the figures depicted. These are just desperate starving people clinging to life.

I stated that a secular city-centre memorial to An Gorta Mór was required and that it would be a good thing to counteract the anti-Irish racism there and in the west of Scotland generally. The proposed

Famine memorial from Glasgow City Council is newsworthy because of how the Irish Famine has been viewed by some people in the city in recent times. The Famine Song is a particularly nasty little racist footnote in the social history of this part of the world.

Rangers were unique in being a senior football club in Britain which had not had a Republic of Ireland international play in their first team since the Football Association of Ireland (FAI) was officially recognised by FIFA. The emotional contract seemed be that no one in the light blue shirt would stand under the Irish tricolour on international business. The connection was clearly made; here was a group of football supporters singing a racist song who just happened to follow a team that did not have any of the targeted nationality playing for them.

There was a time in late 2008 when I seemed to be the only journalist that was interested in flagging up these issues. There were questions asked about it in Dáil Éireann and in the European Parliament. Eoin Ryan MEP visited Scotland in November 2008. It was largely ignored by the Scottish media but I travelled from Ireland to cover the fact-finding mission. On Rangers message boards the legal experts from the Govan stand guffawed that the Famine Song would never be brought before the courts, but it was and a conviction resulted. It was appealed to the High Court of Justiciary and the conviction from Kilmarnock Sheriff Court was upheld. The Famine Song, in Scots law, is racist. There is no debate. This has been in case law since 2009.

I am told that the Famine Song has not been totally excised from the Ibrox songbook and appears to have come over on the TUPE bus. Now that those awful events are in the process of being commemorated in an inclusive and respectful manner in Glasgow, I hope that we have heard the last of this racist ditty. Those who defended the Famine Song in 2008 and 2009 should reconsider their stance if they do not want to be characterised as defenders of racism.

Finally, the "one side is as bad as the other" narrative is stripped away and people outside Scotland are starting to learn the forensic truth. I believe that the general acceptability of anti-Irish racism in Scottish society back in the day and the absence of a Famine memorial in Glasgow are not unconnected; the Irish in Scotland were a barely tolerated invisible ethnic minority. Thankfully, the Zeitgeist has changed.

Of course, some will squeal at the pain that equality is causing them. The old days at the back of the bus are gone and they're not coming back. Feargal Dalton of the SNP, in proposing the motion last month, stated that the sculpture should also remember the victims of the Highland Famine and those fleeing modern famines who want to make Glasgow their home. Moreover, the proposed memorial is not to recognise the migration patterns from the island of Ireland to Glasgow over the centuries. Of course, those who now wish to row in behind this laudable project are very welcome to do so.

However, if they have a previous history in defending the Famine Song, they must address that issue and do so publicly. An apology for the offence caused to Glasgow's Irish community would also be welcome. Clearly, any organisation now wishing to support the Famine memorial project cannot defend a song that mocks the victims of An Gorta Mór or their descendants. Perhaps they should issue a statement to that effect, just to clarify matters.

A voice of authority

2 January 2013

As regular visitors here will know, one of the major irritants in my life is the debilitating condition of historical illiteracy. There is a lot of it around. When it was announced last year that Glasgow City Council was planning to erect a memorial to the Irish Famine, I was concerned that historical accuracy might be sacrificed in order to get people on board. That is why I am delighted at the news that Professor Tom Devine will now almost certainly be invited onto the City Council working party, formed to establish the nature and setting of the memorial to An Gorta Mór in Glasgow.

He is the acknowledged authority on modern Scottish history by his peers within academe. In a piece in the *Herald* by Gerry Braiden, Professor Devine warns that the memorial must be grounded in historical fact rather than the narrative that some may wish to peddle for their own twentieth-century agendas. As I have written before, my wish for the memorial is for it to be in the city centre – my preferred site is the Broomielaw – secular in nature and eschew any political message. The sculpture on Custom House Quay in Dublin is, for me, the benchmark.

What is depicted there by the Liffey is a humanitarian tragedy. However, it was an avoidable catastrophe, to say the least. The island of Ireland remained a net food exporter throughout those awful years.

Westminster looked on, perhaps approvingly, as a million died and a million left never to return. The British Government of Tony Blair apologised to the Irish people for the criminal negligence of the British state. That apology was accepted and we move on. Now it is time for Glasgow to finally acknowledge in the public space that the Famine played a crucial role in the city's narrative.

I am now more confident than ever that this job will be done properly and the city that gave the world the Famine Song will finally pay respect to those who died and those who fled An Gorta Mór. With Professor Devine on the team I am sure that whatever the working party decide on will be grounded in historical fact.

Links

http://www.philmacgiollabhain.ie/the-laughter-of-my-children/
http://www.philmacgiollabhain.ie/the-anger-that-reveals-impotence/
http://www.philmacgiollabhain.ie/
  anti-irish-racism-is-treated-as-non-issue/
http://www.philmacgiollabhain.ie/
  irish-politician-writes-to-rangers-about-famine-song/
http://www.philmacgiollabhain.ie/in-a-parallel-universe/
http://www.philmacgiollabhain.ie/show-hypocrisy-the-red-card/
http://www.philmacgiollabhain.com/wp-content/themes/original/
  ip081108.pdf
http://www.philmacgiollabhain.ie/an-important-visitor/
http://www.philmacgiollabhain.ie/forbidden-word-hidden-truth/
http://www.philmacgiollabhain.ie/groundhog-day-at-celtic-park/
http://www.philmacgiollabhain.ie/blowing-the-whistle/
http://www.philmacgiollabhain.ie/preventing-further-offence/
http://www.philmacgiollabhain.ie/
  peter-lawwell-unhappy-about-lack-of-action-on-famine-song/
http://www.philmacgiollabhain.ie/a-day-to-remember/
http://www.philmacgiollabhain.ie/the-power-of-myth/
http://www.philmacgiollabhain.ie/
  interview-with-danny-boyle-of-the-harps-community-project/
http://www.philmacgiollabhain.ie/rangers-have-to-be-warned-at-the-
  start-of-every-round-says-anti-racist-expert/
http://www.philmacgiollabhain.ie/george-galloway-slams-justice-min-
  ister-macaskill-for-failing-to-condemn-famine-song-at-hampden/

http://www.philmacgiollabhain.ie/
    macaskill-responds-to-irish-community/
http://www.philmacgiollabhain.ie/
    sfa-response-to-irish-diaspora-in-scotland-association/
http://www.philmacgiollabhain.ie/
    trade-union-equality-officer-is-famine-song-defender/
http://www.philmacgiollabhain.com/pdf/Mayo_News_1207.pdf
http://heritage.caledonianmercury.com/2011/07/21/opinion-glasgow-
    is-overdue-its-memorial-to-the-great-irish-famine/002912
http://www.philmacgiollabhain.ie/a-country-in-transition/
http://www.philmacgiollabhain.ie/telling-the-world/
http://www.philmacgiollabhain.ie/
    nil-aon-tintean-mar-do-thintean-fein/
http://www.philmacgiollabhain.ie/from-the-land-beyond-the-sea/
http://www.philmacgiollabhain.ie/a-son-of-sligo/
http://www.philmacgiollabhain.ie/
    progress-on-a-famine-memorial-for-glasgow/
http://www.philmacgiollabhain.ie/a-good-day-for-my-city/
http://www.philmacgiollabhain.ie/
    from-famine-song-to-famine-memorial/
http://www.philmacgiollabhain.ie/a-voice-of-authority/

Part II: Neil Francis Lennon

Introduction

As I stood in a bar in Glasgow's West End on a cold February evening, chatting GAA and sports psychology with an engaging, witty, polite Irishman in his early forties, my mind was cast to the representation versus the reality of the man standing beside me. I was in the company of the Neil Lennon that most people in Scotland do not know. The guid folk o' Scotland are reliant on a media that would portray him as a snarling thug, and that isn't his fault. In fact, none of the incidents documented in this chapter are the fault of Neil Francis Lennon from Lurgan in County Armagh.

When Lennon first saw the light of day in 1971, the statelet established in 1922, Northern Ireland, was facing an uprising from people who no longer wanted to be at the back of the bus. In the late eighteenth century, Ireland was convulsed with revolutionary ideas imported from regicidal France and the rebellious colonies in North America – people even adopted a hairstyle that made a political fashion statement. While the establishment "Whigs" favoured luxurious locks, the advocates of a French Republic cropped their hair close. In Ireland, those who adopted the style became known as "croppies".

There was even a Loyalist song, "Croppies Lie Down" – reportedly written by George Watson-Taylor and dating from the 1798 rebellion in Ireland – celebrating the defeat and suppression of the Republican rebels. It could have been written for the shaven-headed Lennon; his hair remains militarily cropped and, as the klan were to find out, he didn't lie down. Buzz-cut and proud, he didn't accept his place at the back of the bus.

The Orange subculture was imported into the west of Scotland in the nineteenth century as skilled shipyard workers were decanted from the Lagan to the Clyde. The explosion in the number of Orange Lodges in west central Scotland in the latter half of that century was an indicator of how the Orange tradition of Ireland had found a new home across the North Channel. These Ulster artisans, the descendants of Scots who had been moved by royal charter to the north-east of Ireland in the early seventeenth century, helped to solidify the position of the Catholic Irish in Scotland as the *Untermensch* on the Clyde. In doing so, they pandered to an ancient hatred that shames an otherwise fair-minded and tolerant nation.

Neil Lennon is a winner. He bossed the Celtic midfield for both Martin O'Neill and Gordon Strachan. He deliberately riled opponents to put them off their game and opposition fans detested him for it. However, there was more to their hatred than sporting rivalry and it is hardly ever discussed in polite company in Scotland: anti-Irish racism. Not only is it rarely discussed, the phrase is almost wholly excised from the lexicon of Scotland's socially concerned classes.

Veteran sports journalist Hugh Keevins once said, on the Clyde 1 *Superscoreboard* radio programme, that Lennon had cause to have a very low opinion of the country he lived and worked in. The treatment he endured over more than a decade could have been scripted by John White and executed by Billy Fullerton. That man of the cloth and the fascist street thug from Bridgeton intersected on a vengeance diagram of victim-blaming as Scotland's greatest city grew exponentially from Irish inward migration.

There is nothing new or remarkable about the hostility the Irish suffered when they arrived on Clydeside in great numbers in the nineteenth and early twentieth centuries. What is distinct is the extent to which the ethnic component of that hatred was studiously denied and ignored by the host community in the modern period. Subsequently, the official reportage of what happened to Neil Lennon as he tried to live his life in Scotland, first as a player and then as a manager, was lacking the appropriate emphasis on the centrality of his ethnic background. If, in a parallel universe, Lennon was an Israeli national and had signed for a Polish club, similar treatment would almost certainly be characterised as anti-semitic. I doubt that any Polish sports journalist would cite his robust playing style or even hint that Lennon the Jew "brought it on himself".

The number of Lennon's footballing crimes throughout his career would get him booted out of the ball-winning midfielders' union – his card count was minimal. Not a natural athlete, he patrolled a beat in front of the defence, often intercepting misplaced passes from opponents instead of scything them down with tackles that would inevitably be penalised. Lennon played a smart game which bested those playing against him and made many in the press box seethe with a hatred they could barely conceal in their copy.

I cite the analogy of Israel and Judaism because, like Sikhism, it encapsulates both a religion and an ethnicity. For the people who hate Neil Lennon it is similar, for he is an Irish Catholic and that, in the worldview of the Famine Song choir, marks him out. The Lurgan man did not want to become a *cause célèbre*, much less a target for racist nutters. He wanted to become a professional footballer and he achieved his goal. What was not known until the publication of his autobiography, *Neil Lennon: Man and Bhoy*, in 2006 was that he suffered from clinical depression. That he could struggle with such a debilitating condition and play football at the highest level was a glimpse of a determination constructed out of titanium and reinforced concrete.

When the klan decided to run Lennon out of Scotland they rather miscalculated. I am reliably informed that Lennon took a substantial wage cut to move to Celtic from Leicester City in 2000. Until then he had enjoyed a successful career with the provincial club. His only brush with controversy was when he had the temerity to viciously assault the boot of England captain Alan Shearer with his head in April 1998. Not for the last time, his manager, Martin O'Neill, rushed to his defence. The English media found him guilty of causing all-round good guy Shearer emotional damage. Apart from that, Lennon was a contented young man playing for the eponymous club that took its name from King Lear. It was all rather fitting because the life that awaited Lennon in Scotland was truly Shakespearean.

Someone somewhere will turn his experiences north of the border into a movie someday, beginning with how signing for Celtic effectively finished off his international career with Northern Ireland at the age of 29. On 21 August 2002, an anonymous caller phoned the BBC in Belfast. He claimed to be from the Loyalist Volunteer Force (LVF) and said that if Lennon took to the field of play that evening against Cyprus, he would get seriously hurt. That night should have been the 41st time Lennon represented his country and his first time as captain. However, the police took the threat very seriously, and Lennon didn't play. He would never again take to the field in the shirt of the Irish Football Association.

The LVF was a breakaway from the Ulster Volunteer Force (UVF), formed by Billy Wright. Known as "King Rat", he was one of the Troubles' most notorious killers. At the time of the threat on Lennon's life they were viewed as the most dangerous and most out-of-control of the Loyalist paramilitary groups. The splinter group showed it had none of the usual boundaries observed in the Troubles when a journalist was murdered in September 2001. Martin O'Hagan was gunned down by the LVF as he walked home with his wife in Lennon's hometown of Lurgan. The *Sunday World* journalist had been a real thorn in its side as he exposed criminal and racketeering activities.

His death was claimed by the Red Hand Defenders, a *nom de guerre* used by the Loyalist Volunteer Force. Therefore, when the same group made a threat in 2002 against Lennon it was taken seriously by the police. The previous year, on 28 February, he played for Northern Ireland during a friendly match with Norway. This was the first time he had played for his country since signing for Celtic. Every time he touched the ball his own fans booed him. In a post-match interview, Norway's Ole Gunnar Solskjær, who then played for Manchester United and was well known to Northern Ireland fans because of the popularity of the Old Trafford club, asked why Lennon had been booed by his own fans. The Scandinavian was baffled and the TV interviewer from Northern Ireland fell silent.

It was a shameful incident and left an indelible stain on those who follow the Northern Ireland international football team. In January 2011, during his tenure as Celtic manager, Lennon and two of his Northern Irish players, Paddy McCourt and Niall McGinn, were sent bullets in the post. A journalist colleague of mine in Northern Ireland with excellent police sources confirmed to me that the PSNI believed this threat had originated in the North Antrim Brigade of the Ulster Defence Association (UDA). Just like the LVF a decade earlier, these UDA chaps were considered by security forces to be the most renegade and most dangerous of a fairly threatening bunch of zealots.

It is only a deranged minority that wants to maintain the old supremacies. The North Armagh triangle, where Lennon was born and reared, is the crucible of the belief system that would socialise his attackers and detractors. They inhabit the same worldview as the Glasgow-based Billy Boys. As Lennon bossed matches with the arrogance and aplomb that all so-called midfield generals need, the klan on the other side of the city cried out for a great white hope.

It is an appropriate analogy, as the Irishman truly became a Jack Johnson figure in Glasgow football for those who sang about wading in Fenian blood. Johnson was the first African-American to be the world heavyweight boxing champion, and the term "great white hope" was coined. The boxing public hoped and prayed that somewhere there was a white man who could beat Johnson. It was an affront to the white male ego in the land of the free that the best in the world in the square ring was a black man. In the end, it was a match against the giant Jess Willard on 5 April 1915, in front of a huge crowd at the new Oriental Park Racetrack in Havana, Cuba, where Johnson was finally knocked out, in the 26th round. Johnson married three times, and all of his wives were white, which enraged racially segregated America. When professional sport, where masculinity is asserted by proxy, is poisoned by discrimination and hatred, the exponents of the sport can become ciphers for a wider societal conflict.

Lennon, like Johnson, enjoyed rubbing their noses in it. The man from Lurgan loved going to Ibrox, and, under the guidance of Martin O'Neill and with the peerless Henrik Larsson spearheading the attack, his Celtic were often victorious over their Glasgow rivals. I remember one piece of post-match taunting when Lennon mimicked the smoking of an imaginary cigar as he left the field to send the message that the previous ninety minutes had been rather easy. As his "cigar" came to an end, he spat out the water he had swigged from a bottle handed to him by a trainer. It was taunting *in excelsis*. He was saying not only did we beat you, but it was no big deal. Similarly in the ring, Johnson taunted his white opponents with his talent. This, for racists, was the stuff of nightmares. Adolf Hitler was to suffer the same appalling vista a generation later in Munich as Jesse Owens rather spoiled the Aryan master race sports day in 1936.

Lennon ticked all of the boxes for the klan as someone whom they should not only hate but consider inferior in every way. In the arena they held to be theirs he strutted his midfield stuff. Celtic's midfield generals have, throughout my decades of watching Glasgow derbies, gone to Ibrox and put manners on the opposition. Players like Roy Aitken would rattle the fillings in their teeth with tackles that were not approved by the Geneva Convention. However, although feared and respected, he never became the hate figure that Lennon did.

In terms of playing style, Lennon was a shrinking violet next to his buddy, Alan Thompson. On the field of play, the Geordie was a brawl waiting to happen. He was sent off several times against Rangers for violent conduct. All the while, Lennon was intercepting passes and passing the ball to teammates with aplomb, demonstrating how it should be done. Built like a typical GAA player, he was rarely pushed off the ball.

Off the field, Lennon confounded the klan just by being himself. He became a close personal friend of Rangers skipper Barry Ferguson.

Lennon could leave the conflict on the field where it belonged, but others, consumed with hatred, could not. Reared in the sporting tradition of the Gaelic Athletic Association in Ireland (GAA), for Lennon this sportsmanship was taken in with his mother's milk.

The GAA is the heartbeat of Ireland. Like America and baseball, if you don't understand "the Gah" then you probably know little of Ireland. One of the great sporting occasions on the planet is all-Ireland final day every September in Croke Park. Lennon played for his county at youth level. The first time we ever shared a non-work-related word – in the foyer of the Hyatt Hotel in Philadelphia in August 2012 – it was about how Armagh were doing in the championship. As we both went up in the lift to the pre-match press conference, our conversation was entirely about the GAA.

He told me he thought Jim McGuinness, the manager of the Donegal team, was working wonders. Not surprisingly, perhaps, the Donegal man joined Celtic to work with the Next Generation youth squad a short time later. McGuinness is a qualified sports psychologist and brought a focus and determination to his charges in Donegal, taking them from nineteen out of thirty-two to number one. Lennon was delighted to have the Glenties man as one of his backroom staff. His new role was to instill the self-belief that the Celtic manager always had in spades into the young team.

Lennon's Irishness is not in doubt and that made him a hate figure for some. They ignored the glaring fact that his life partner, Irene, the mother of his young son, was the niece of Rangers legend Peter McCloy. The real Neil Lennon wasn't anything like the man they referred to on message boards as "the Lurgan bigot". This ignorance would have been hilarious had it not been the worldview that would produce Trevor Muirhead and Neil McKenzie.

In March 2011, Lennon was targeted by a letter bomb that was intercepted at the Royal Mail sorting office in Kirkintilloch. Initially police asked for a press blackout; it was informal, with only a couple of newspaper editors aware of events. When I learned of the bombs I did not see the need for the blackout. I knew that, despite what was said publicly, one of the recipients was less than happy with this ad hoc press blackout. I discussed the situation with several senior colleagues in the NUJ. They agreed that I should publish. None of them could see how the police investigation would be hampered and, as it turned out, it wasn't.

I then started to work with the *Guardian's* Scotland correspondent,

Severin Carrell, on the story. Between us we pieced together what was happening behind the scenes. Trish Godman MSP and Paul McBride QC had also been targeted by the would-be bombers. It later emerged that the Sinn Féin support group Cairde na hÉireann was also an intended recipient of one of the devices in the post.

It is fair to say that in the immediate aftermath of this news going viral there was a feverish scramble at the higher levels of Strathclyde Police. We learned that Prime Minister David Cameron had been on the phone and wanted to know what the hell was going on. Police resources on the case rose exponentially within forty-eight hours of the story breaking. On 12 May 2011, two men were arrested in an early morning swoop in the west of Scotland. They were charged under the Explosive Substances Act 1883. This was less than four weeks after I went public with the story.

If someone had been scripting a drama based upon Lennon's experiences in Scotland up until that date, two characters resembling Trevor Muirhead and Neil McKenzie would have been rejected as crude stereotypes. Muirhead, 44, a father of six from Kilwinning, Ayrshire, and McKenzie, 42, of Saltcoats, were motivated by a vicious hatred of Celtic FC and Irish Catholics. Muirhead, a van driver known locally as big Trev, was a former member of the Orange Order and the Apprentice Boys of Londonderry. Police found that his home was full of Rangers and Loyalist material. His partner in crime, McKenzie, was a career criminal with Loyalist links. In terms of anti-Irish racism in Scotland, these two fine fellows were straight from central casting, and in Neil Lennon they had the perfect focus for their hatred.

Tragically, another of their intended victims, a close personal friend of Neil Lennon, did not get his day in court. Paul McBride QC died suddenly on 4 March 2012 while in Pakistan. On 5 March the judge suspended the trial for one day as a mark of respect. Lennon and the brilliant QC were especially close, and the Celtic manager was very affected by his sudden passing. On social media there was something akin to a party atmosphere as Paul McBride's death was celebrated by the same chaps who incessantly targeted Lennon with hatred and smears. There was nothing particularly unusual about the worldview of Muirhead and McKenzie. There was rarely a day that passed without another Facebook page being set up, dedicated to the hatred of Lennon. One of them had a Photoshopped image of the Celtic manager on the touchline with a bullet hole added to the picture.

Just before Lennon arrived at Celtic as a player in 2000, the club employed John Barnes as a manager. It is generally accepted that, although a wonderfully gifted player for Liverpool and England, the Caribbean-born English international was a complete flop in the dugout. As I left that West End bar after chatting with the klan's number one hate figure, I considered how the world would have reacted if John Barnes had been subjected to the same campaign of abuse which Neil Lennon had endured.

I wondered what the media's reaction would be if far right groups had sent him a bullet in the post and two chaps with a stated hatred of black people had constructed something that looked very much like a letter bomb and sent it to him at his employment. How would the media have styled the motivations of the perpetrators of such acts? I doubt that a journalist back in Barnes's homeland would have had to argue that what befell him in Scotland was anything other than a series of racist attacks. Had this level of hatred and ethnically focused vitriol been aimed at the ex-Liverpool player it would have been on CNN. Moreover, the great and the good in Scotland would not have been slow in coming forward in their condemnation.

The extent to which the ethnic component wasn't even considered by Scotland's culturally aware classes is probably best illustrated by how the *Scottish Review* dealt with the subject. An online arts and culture magazine run by Kenneth Roy, it was the last place you would expect to find something insensitive or obtuse, especially regarding hate crime. Yet, on 20 April 2011 (issue 392), a cartoon portrayal of Lennon was published next to a piece about the possible motivations of the as yet undetected bombers. I immediately saw the significance of the depiction and took a screen grab. I sent the image to several friends and colleagues – all Irish – and asked for their responses. One of those people was a senior civil servant with the Department of Foreign Affairs (DFA). I asked her to open the email and tell me what she thought of the image. She shrieked and simply said, "*Punch* cartoon!" – mirroring the thought that had leaped into my head when I saw the slightly apelike caricature of the Celtic manager.

In the nineteenth century the *Punch* cartoon had regaled English readers with depictions of the Fenian ape-man threatening good order in Ireland. The term "*Punch* cartoon" entered the lexicon of those studying anti-Irish racism as a particular low point in how people in Britain saw their Irish neighbours. All of the recipients of the email containing the *Scottish Review* image of Lennon agreed that it depicted the Lurgan man as apelike.

I called the *Scottish Review* and spoke to a contact there – I had until that point contributed a couple of articles. I asked my contact if the words "*Punch* cartoon" had any significance to her and she said no. I believed her. She wasn't the cartoonist and I was perfectly happy to accept that any racist depiction of Lennon was the last thing on the artist's mind. However, if a football manager in Scotland of Afro-Caribbean background was being targeted by racists, would he have been so stereotypically depicted? The extent to which anti-Irish racism is almost entirely subliminal in Scottish society allows this sort of imagery to pass largely without comment.

After the letter bomb incident, Lennon and his young family lived in a world of safe houses, close protection officers and panic buttons. No other football manager in Europe required this level of personal security and yet the very obvious basis for this hatred was largely ignored. Anything other than the ethnic was offered up as explanation, but it would easily be swatted away by pesky evidence.

Some pointed out that former Celtic manager Martin O'Neill had come from the same background, had managed Celtic in a period of dominance over Rangers and there had been no equivalent targeting of him. However, following a cup defeat by Rangers in 2002, the O'Neill family were startled when a large Union flag was planted in their garden. The Celtic manager's home had been splashed on the pages of a Scottish tabloid before the incident. "It's a bit disconcerting for my family that it happened at that time of evening," O'Neill told the media after the incident. "I suppose, when you see your house in the newspapers, people do find out where it is a lot quicker. It hasn't terrified me and it hasn't terrified my wife, but it's a bit disconcerting to look out of the window to see a flag unfurled in front of you. I'm more worried about my family than myself." Regarding the tribal realities of Glasgow, he said: "It is one of a number of incidents that have brought it home to me since I've been here – as if I needed any confirmation of that."

The flag incident was as far as the intimidation appeared to go for O'Neill. With Lennon, it was his swaggering bravado that sent the klan over the edge. When he returned to Celtic in 2010 as a manager that could turn a soccer shambles into a team that looked like it could win and keep on winning, it was a nightmare for their *Herrenvolk* sense of superiority. However, the hostility was not new to Lennon.

O'Neill said at a UEFA Cup pre-match press conference in Barcelona in 2004 that his captain, Lennon, had to endure sectarian and racist abuse on a regular basis at Scottish soccer stadia. Ever the strategist,

O'Neill picked his moment and occasion well. There was a UEFA official at the event and the mention of racist abuse was taken on board. None of the Scottish hacks at the press conference sought to challenge the Irishman and his use of words. The man from County Derry sacrificed a career in law for professional football and his precision with the English language was legendary.

In November 2004, after Lennon had suffered horrendous abuse from the home crowd during a match at Ibrox, O'Neill defiantly took him back onto the pitch. He marched over to the Celtic support with his arm around his captain. O'Neill said that the Lurgan man had endured an afternoon of "racial and sectarian abuse". At the time, the reportage in the Scottish papers seemed to grasp the enormity of a Celtic manager using such language, especially the R-word.

In Scotland, racist abuse of an Irish person was habitually considered "sectarian". It was more than semantics; in styling it as such the targeted Irish lost their nationality, which compounded the oppression and the insult. Lennon was not unique in this respect, but became a high-profile case study. It was not something he wanted. He only wished to be a footballer. Had he stayed in England, his career and personal life would have been very different. During the worst of 2011, a terrified toddler and his mother were bundled into a car and whisked to a safe house while Lennon was away on duty with Celtic.

Like the African-American quarterback on the gridiron, the klan regarded a successful Celtic manger in the shape of Neil Lennon an appalling vista. In order to prevent any discussion on what kind of society produced Neil McKenzie and Trevor Muirhead, it was preferable to focus the blame on the victim; "he brings it on himself" was the standard reply when the plight of Lennon was mentioned in Glasgow to someone outside the green half of the city.

It was an instructive analysis from a group of people whose default setting was to blame Lennon. The only word not used to describe him in this online discourse was "uppity". Being born in the north of Ireland in 1971 with a clear memory of the Hunger Strikes a decade later, he was no stranger to being part of a socially excluded, oppressed minority. In such a situation there are two broad responses: fight or surrender.

If Lennon thought that the letter bomb incident was the end of his trouble in 2011, he was wrong. At Tynecastle stadium during an SPL match against Hearts, a man ran onto the track along the pitch and launched himself at the Celtic manager. His name was John Wilson, and the picture worth a thousand words of him in mid-air, hurtling towards a Lennon instinctively stooping to avoid the collision, went around the world. Once more, as with the abuse Lennon received from Northern Ireland fans, it was a clear-thinking Scandinavian with a moral compass, this time assistant manager Johan Mjällby, who told Scotland in the immediate aftermath of the incident that this was not acceptable behaviour. The big Swede looked shaken as he said, "It's a dark day for Scottish football. It's an absolute disgrace. I've never seen anything like it."

Wilson ran onto the touchline, bypassed security and sprinted towards Lennon, who was standing on the edge of the technical area, the marked-out box in front of the dugout and the nearest point that a trainer or coach can be to the field of play. Wilson leaped clumsily into the air as he tried to grapple Lennon into a headlock. Alan Thompson, a member of Lennon's backroom staff, got between the Celtic manager and Wilson, and fended off the assailant. Off-balance, Wilson fell to the ground and was tackled by stewards and police. As the incident happened, one journalist from the Tynecastle press box reported that Lennon was involved in a brawl and could find himself in trouble. It was astounding to listen to the accepted common sense of "Lennon brings it on himself" on live radio.

At Edinburgh Sheriff Court in September 2012, Sheriff Fiona Reith QC sentenced John Wilson to eight months' imprisonment after he was found guilty of committing a breach of the peace at Tynecastle football stadium on 11 May 2011. A football banning order was also served upon the convicted. However, on the charge of religiously aggravated assault against Neil Lennon, the jury delivered a not proven verdict. Lennon was aghast, and people close to him said he was as down about the verdict as they had seen him throughout the entire period.

It didn't seem credible that someone could admit to assault, have his lawyer tell a court that he was sorry for committing it, yet the jury ruled that assault could not be proven. That Wilson was only found guilty of a breach of the peace despite being seen on live television lunging at the Celtic manager baffled people who believed that they had witnessed a criminal assault. Criminal courts in Scotland have a third option besides the usual guilty and not guilty verdicts: the not proven verdict. The writer Sir Walter Scott famously called it "that bastard verdict". I suspect that Neil Francis Lennon might well have agreed with him on that.

The assault, despite being witnessed by millions and despite being admitted to by the defendant and his lawyer, was not proven on a point of law; the religiously aggravated aspect of the charge could not be proven because the testimony of the steward who said that Wilson called Lennon a "Fenian" was not considered enough by the jury to explain the motivation behind the attack. The inability to prove that element of the case meant that the whole charge was not proven.

This also happened in the Muirhead and McKenzie case, when the religiously motivated element of the charges against the pair was dropped near the end of the trial. Experts told the *Herald* that the sectarian charges were "too difficult to define" to be able to prove. University of Edinburgh sociologist, Dr John Kelly, told the paper, in a piece written by Gerry Braiden: "The term itself is misunderstood and ill-defined and for a jury this could be hugely problematic. The Crown clearly went with what it could prove." Professor Larry Ray, of the University of Kent, said the hate aspect of a crime was often difficult to prove.

The difficulty in defining sectarian and proving religious prejudice is not altogether surprising if the crimes were motivated by an ethnic, rather than religious, hatred. Cairde na hÉireann is not a Catholic organisation, it is a Republican group which campaigns for a united thirty-two county Ireland. Trish Godman MSP was targeted because she wore a Celtic strip in the Scottish Parliament for a charity event. Celtic Football Club has a close association with Ireland because its roots come from Irish immigrants in the city. In the Wilson trial, the word "Fenian" was cited as the important factor in proving religious motivation. However, Fenian is a term associated with Irish ethnicity, not Catholicism *per se*.

Subsequently, neither of the two cases was officially recorded as a hate crime in Scottish law. The motivation behind them was not properly explored or addressed. To do that would have subjected an entire belief system to forensic scrutiny.

The Muirhead and McKenzie case raised eyebrows again when the charge of conspiracy to murder was reduced to conspiracy to assault before the end of the trial. Despite having taken the trouble to mix dangerous chemicals and put them together – albeit very badly – into the structure of a bomb, the Crown was not convinced it was enough to prove the devices were intended to kill. Instead, Lord Turnbull told the court there was not "sufficient evidence" to prove Muirhead and McKenzie sent the parcels with the intention to kill, and so the charge was dropped to conspiracy to assault. Duly convicted, the pair were sentenced to five years in prison. It is fair to say that many were baffled at the notion that a Scottish court found it more believable that bomb-like devices were sent to four targets with only the intention to assault, not to kill. The consequence was that Lennon, a victim deserving of justice, was failed by the criminal justice system in Scotland.

During Celtic's first visit to Tynecastle after John Wilson was cleared of assault, Lennon was forced to endure taunting from Hearts fans, many of whom brought John Wilson masks along for the occasion. In the midst of all of this it was remarkable that Lennon, hugely successful as a player, emerged as one of the best young managers in Europe. No other football player or manager within the aegis of UEFA had to endure a lifestyle of close protection because of a campaign of threats and attacks. Being a football manager is incredibly stressful and precarious without concerns about personal and family safety thrown into the mix.

In season 2012–2013, on a football budget that would be considered impossibly meagre by the big boys in Europe, Lennon fashioned a team capable of beating Barcelona, arguably the best club side on the planet. With players from Airdrie, Honduras, Israel and Scunthorpe, he made good his promise to the Celtic support when he took the managerial job three years ago. He said he wanted to "bring back the thunder" and, speaking from personal experience, Celtic Park on European competition nights under Lennon shakes with noise and crackles with atmosphere.

Although a fans' favourite, he hasn't tried to curry favour with anyone, even the most vociferous of the Parkhead faithful. In December 2011, a small group of fans embarrassed the club with their behaviour at an away match in the Europa League against Udinese in Italy. Someone thought it was a good idea to have a banner with "Fuck UEFA" emblazoned on it, in response to the news that UEFA had fined Celtic €15,000 (£12,700) for "illicit chants" in praise of the IRA at the home game against Rennes the previous month. When asked about the incident by a journalist at the airport, a clearly seething Lennon did not hold back.

"If I was in a room with these guys right now what I would say to them would not be for public consumption. That's how angry I am about it," Lennon told Roddy Forsyth of the *Daily Telegraph*. "I am very angry because we should be talking about the players today and their efforts. They gave everything last night – every ounce of energy and quality – but today we are talking about a group of people who are just hell bent on damaging the reputation of the club. So, to say I'm upset about it would be putting it mildly. I can't understand what they are thinking, I have no idea. Are they even Celtic fans?

"I would use that term very loosely and be very dubious about calling them that," he continued. "The club has worked very, very hard to build a reputation in Europe – so have 99% of the fans. Because of all that hard work we are welcome everywhere in Europe but now we have a few people who are trying to undermine all that and tarnish the reputation of the club. We don't want them here. We are talking about a handful of people here. It's premeditated obviously – I'm just surprised they spelled the words right."

This was a not-so-thinly veiled reference to a misspelled protest banner by Celtic ultras group the Green Brigade in November 2010. They were unhappy at the decision by the club to have Celtic players displaying the Royal British Legion poppy on their shirts for the match nearest to Remembrance Sunday. "No bloostained [sic] poppy on our hoops" was a Monty Python moment for the Green Brigade.

At the end of last season (2011–2012), Lennon purposefully marched across the turf with the Scottish Premier League trophy and placed it down at Section 111, where the Green Brigade has a club-designated singing area. Both incidents were classic Lennon: speaking his mind honestly without fear or favour but also giving credit where it was due. Through the darkest days in 2011 the Green Brigade stated and restated, often with the use of cleverly designed banners, their support for the Celtic boss as he was threatened and targeted. The Green Brigade was, and remains, the backbone of the most enthusiastic element of the Celtic support on match days. With the exuberance of youth, they keep up an incessant cacophony of partisan invective. Lennon knew how important this was in driving his players, but he was also acknowledging their unflinching support when bullets and bombs were sent in the post to him.

Lennon's time as the Celtic manager saw him in trouble with those who govern the game in Scotland. The most notable incident was between him and the Rangers assistant manager, Ally McCoist, after a Scottish Cup replay at Celtic Park in March 2011. Lennon, whose team won the game 1–0, approached McCoist and offered a handshake. As Lennon put his arm around McCoist, the Rangers assistant manager was seen to say something into Lennon's ear. Lennon recoiled in surprise at what he heard – which has never been revealed – and then pointed a finger in anger and moved towards McCoist. The image of the snarling Lennon was tabloid gold. It became the library file image for Lennon for the next few weeks. It was the depiction of him that the tabloids seemed most comfortable with.

Three Rangers players were sent off during the game, and the scenes, beamed around the world, caused the Scottish Government to host an emergency summit. Millions saw two Rangers players, El Hadji Diouf and Madjid Bougherra, manhandle the referee as he tried to send one of them off. However, the only person to be punished by the football authorities for the chaotic scenes was Lennon, who received a four-match touchline ban. Just like the court decisions, it baffled the onlooker.

The late Paul McBride QC represented the Parkhead club and Lennon in the disciplinary hearings and ran rings around the SFA people like a skilful winger. However, when the ruling was given that the Rangers players involved would not face a lengthy ban, McBride, with all of his courtroom eloquence, let rip: "The SFA are tonight officially the laughing stock of world football and they have been shown to be not merely dysfunctional and not merely dishonest but biased," he told BBC Scotland, "because McCoist, who undoubtedly said something that provoked a reaction from Neil Lennon that caused a four-match ban for him, has received no punishment at all. We know that Bougherra, who manhandled the referee not once but twice, doesn't get a ban.

"We know that El Hadji Diouf, who was involved in an altercation in the tunnel with a Celtic physiotherapist, refuses to leave the park and, given a red card, throws his top into the crowd against police advice, and isn't given a ban either. What is any sensible person to think of that set of affairs? Frankly, anybody with the tiniest brain could only regard them as being biased and prejudiced. They are not rational, they are not fair and they are not consistent in the way they have approached the matter with Neil Lennon and Celtic in general. And tonight I think people will be scratching their heads in amazement and disbelief at the way the SFA conduct their affairs and continue to conduct their affairs.

"Rangers have apparently said this is a victory for common sense," he continued. "So, if a Celtic player tonight manhandles the referee, throws his top into the crowd, abuses other players, causes reaction among management and no action is taken, Rangers presumably will tell us tomorrow that's a victory for common sense. I don't believe anybody thinks that to be correct."

Lennon was pressed to comment on McBride's opinion of the SFA and its judicial process. He would only say: "I don't want to make any more comment because I will end up in the stand or have a heavy fine, but if you think it is fair then a lot of people are burying their head in the sand on this one. I find it interesting that after all the fallout from that game I am the only one who has been banned."

Although I'd had previous professional contact with Lennon through press conferences, I wanted to get a sense of the man from people who were close to him. I managed to arrange a meeting in the foyer of the

Pond Hotel in the West End of Glasgow with a man who had known
Lennon for many years and had supported him when others hadn't.
This chapter doesn't claim to be a biography of Lennon – that is the
worthy subject of a book on its own and if anyone would be the appropriate author of the Lennon biography it would be this chap. He asked
not to be identified and I agreed to that. After the initial pleasantries
and rules of engagement about what I meant by off the record, he
relaxed into a masterclass in what it was like to be close to Neil Lennon
through all of this madness.

At one point I had a lightbulb moment and I played to him a radio
interview I did with a London radio station at the time of the letter bomb campaign in 2011. With the earphone in from my mobile
phone, the audio file played and he listened intently. Occasionally he
stated his agreement with increasing vehemence. Listening to my disembodied voice and a radio anchor seemed to be cathartic for him.
When the earphone was out he was even more forthcoming about how
Lennon had been treated.

Interestingly, his ire was directed more at my trade than at those who
had assaulted and hospitalised his friend. Not for the first time, this lay
member of the National Union of Journalists had to sit through a dia-
tribe being aimed at some of my colleagues in Scotland. Try as I might,
much of the accusations were irrefutable: "He'll stick up for Scotland,
but Scotland hasn't stuck up for him."

On the location of Lennon's house being identified in the papers, he
said, "I blame the head hunters in the Scottish press. These guys have
hounded Neil. They are obsessed with him and they want him out of
Scotland. If Neil wasn't Irish we wouldn't be having this conversation.
If he had been black and had received this treatment then it would have
been a global story from day one, in the year 2000, when he signed for
Celtic and the abuse started. There is no one else in the UK who, as a
sportsman, has gone through what he has had to endure."

On the media, he reiterated that it had questions to answer: "Scottish
journalism has been the problem here. Their obsession with him is all
because of what he is – an Irish Catholic. If he was a Catholic Scot then
this wouldn't have happened. It is because he is Irish. It's the Irish background, no question about it. That is where the ignition is: 'Catholic'
and 'Irish', that is the match and the petrol. If Neil Lennon had been
Scottish, no matter what his religion was, he would have been putting
the Christmas lights on in George Square."

About the threats to Lennon, he said: "It wasn't mindless thugs. It was people sitting and planning." As we made our way back to the city centre, I told him there was nothing new or unique about the victim-blaming that Neil Lennon was enduring and that he had witnessed. It was, of course, easy, lazy and shameful. Moreover, it happens within all discriminatory situations. It happens to ethnic minorities, gay people and women.

An acceptable view about the Lennon situation in Scotland was that "he brings it on himself". This was Scotland's get out of jail free card. If Lennon was somehow to blame then everything was okay in fair Caledonia. This was clearly the agenda of the SNP Government, led by First Minister Alex Salmond, who wanted to present a marketing slogan as social reality: "the best small country in the world" was the happy-clappy Kumbaya image he wanted to sell to the planet. As the image of John Wilson lunging at Neil Lennon on the same spot where I had discussed anti-Irish racism with Lex Gold in October 2008 went global, there had to be an acceptable narrative offered up, and it wasn't the one I knew to be true. Salmond's marketing strategy was that his Scotland was a mature, modern, multicultural country comfortable in its twenty-first century skin. The Wilson trial could have been an educational turning point about the hatred that dare not speak its name in Scotland, but the opportunity was squandered.

What was not acceptable was the truth: Scotland had a long-standing problem with anti-Irish racism. Indeed, those with the education and, one would hope, the values could not even bring themselves to analyse the proposition. They certainly couldn't bring themselves to use the term anti-Irish racism. To do that would be to start deconstructing the comforting myth for many Scottish nationalists that chaps like me don't exist.

The extent of the treatment meted out to Neil Lennon was unique. However, Aiden McGeady of Celtic and James McCarthy of Hamilton Academical both attracted the ire of the klan for declaring for the Republic of Ireland despite being born in Scotland. Veteran sports journalist Hugh Keevins called out the racists who abused McGeady when he said it was the Celtic winger's "country of choice that was the problem. If Aiden McGeady's granny had come from Cardiff and he wore the red of Wales then this would not be an issue."

At the end of the traumatic season of 2010–2011, Celtic missed winning the league title by a whisker. It was a season where the club's young manager had been assaulted on the trackside in Tynecastle, received a bullet in the post from Loyalist paramilitaries and was the intended target of a letter bomb. Speaking to the Parkhead faithful on the final day of the season, he thanked everyone for their support and said that, for him as Celtic manager, it was just the beginning. However, he thought a lot of the people in Scottish game needed "to have a good look at themselves in the mirror". He was correct about many of the great and good in the national game. His advice about self-examination had a wider significance.

When I spoke at the Changin Scotland conference in Ullapool in November 2011 on the lack of cultural space for Irishness in modern Scotland throughout my lifetime, I said that trying to establish cultural acceptance as second-generation Irish in Scotland had, for me, been an existential challenge. For Neil Francis Lennon, living and working in Scotland in the glare of a hostile media had become an existential threat.

Any attempt to offer an analysis without acknowledging the ethnic is to befriend nonsense. As I write this, Lennon is in a good place, which is rare enough in the most vulnerable of professions. His team, assembled on a shoe string, defeated Barcelona in the Champions League and made it to the last sixteen of the competition in 2012. He is respected throughout Europe as a coach who can spot a player and weld a team of youngsters and free transfers into a unit capable of beating the best club side in the world. Only in Scotland does the Fourth Estate view him differently.

The financial and organisational collapse of Rangers in early 2012 ushered in a long hot summer that appeared to emotionally exhaust the klan. The new Rangers were formed as the old club was liquidated and they started life in the bottom tier of professional football in Scotland. Neil Lennon was the first manager in Celtic's 125-year history not to have Rangers to contend with on league business. Elements within the Scottish press pack continually tried to draw him on whether or not New Rangers should be given any accelerated promotion up the league structures. Lennon questioned the intentions of the hacks on this line of questioning. He told them his team was in the lead in the SPL and in the last sixteen of the Champions League. As for Rangers, he said, "They're not on my radar."

Neil Lennon didn't ask to become a hate figure for people who only have hate to keep them warm at night. It wasn't his fault he was fashioned into an Identikit picture of everything they had been socialised to despise. However, it happened. That he didn't do the sensible thing and run away to a safe country where he would be respected means that Scotland owes Neil Francis Lennon a huge debt of gratitude. I know he doesn't see it that way, he just wants to get on with things, and that is exactly why all the fair-minded people in Scotland should wish him well.

Neil Lennon

4 March 2011

Three times in the past few months, Neil Lennon and his family have been roused from their sleep in the middle of the night and moved to a safe location. Last month, Ulster Loyalists, who a security source confirmed to me "have access to weaponry", sent Lennon bullets in the post. This UDA gang is strongly suspected by the PSNI [Police Service of Northern Ireland] of having been involved in the murder of Kevin McDaid in 2009.

In the last twenty-four hours yet another hate page on Facebook was erected and, after complaints, taken down – this one was asking for information on Neil Lennon to facilitate his murder. Just banter? Facebook did their job promptly. Sadly, my trade in Scotland has once more lost its moral compass. I cannot think of anyone in British football who has to work under these conditions. This should be a national story; indeed, it should be the only football story in Scotland. This is a subject worthy of the First Minister's time and attention. Instead, when the target of these threats and abuse loses his cool, he is admonished like a difficult toddler.

Lennon and his family are under threat because he is the *bête noire* in a belief system that should have been tackled a generation ago. He is an in-your-face-not-taking-any-of-your-crap-uppity-Fenian. He manages Celtic just like he swaggered through many midfield battles wearing the hoops. He now manages the club he played for. Given that "one side is as bad as the other", can anyone remember the twenty-four hour security that Graeme Souness had to live under when he was at the helm at Ibrox? Quite.

Live bombs sent to Lennon, McBride and MSP

19 April 2011
Exclusive

Paul McBride QC, Neil Lennon and Trish Godman, the Labour politician, were sent live bombs, one of which was only intercepted at a late stage last Friday, 15 April. These devices have been described to me as "viable improvised explosive devices". I'm told there has been a voluntary news blackout, requested by counter-terrorism officers in the UK. At least one of the recipients is not happy with this blackout and doesn't see the sense of it. Developing story.

AICSC statement on Neil Lennon

21 April 2011

The Association of Irish Celtic Supporters' Clubs wishes to reiterate its support for Celtic manager, Neil Lennon, at this time. Last summer, we warmly welcomed Neil's appointment and we are delighted with the team's current run of form under his leadership, which has led us to a Scottish Cup final and in contention for top spot in the SPL.

All of this has been done with a brand of football played the Celtic way and we have every confidence in Neil becoming one of Celtic's greatest managers in the years ahead. Since joining Celtic as a player, Neil Lennon has had to endure abuse both on and off the field, unparalleled to anything experienced by any other player in the SPL. At no stage throughout this time has Neil Lennon given less than a hundred per cent while representing Celtic, or taken the easy option of moving on, which is testament to the character of the man and the regard in which he holds our club.

During these past ten years it should also be noted that, on many occasions, Neil has travelled to Ireland and beyond to help promote and support various charity events, hosted by the AICSC and other groups. Neil has always been very generous with his time and support when it comes to charity work, although facts like these do not seem to take up too many column inches.

The latest incident of viable explosive devices being sent through the post to our manager and other high-profile Celtic supporters is further evidence of the disregard for human life which is held by certain people in today's society. Regardless of profession, nobody should have to contend with this sort of treatment as they and their families go about their day-to-day life, although Neil Lennon seems to be fair game simply because he is a Catholic Irishman who happens to manage Glasgow Celtic.

We welcome the condemnation from various bodies, including UEFA, of the threats against Neil Lennon and also the assurances of Scotland's First Minister that the police investigation will be given "every possible support" so that the perpetrators will be traced and dealt with. We await with interest any further developments on this front and trust the police will make this an absolute priority as it must stop immediately. Equally, we trust the media will be vigilant in pursuing the progress of these investigations.

We reaffirm our one hundred per cent support for Neil and his family. We are immensely proud that he is our manager and wish him well in leading the team through the latter stages of this season and beyond.

The Committee of the Association of Irish Celtic Supporters' Clubs
April 2011

The teachable moment

23 April 2011

This time last week, Paul McBride QC would have known that someone meant him significant harm. That is not a nice place to be. He is in my thoughts. His statement about not being bullied or silenced by this act of terrorism has been courageous and inspirational.

I was informed by a good source last weekend that Paul McBride QC had received a live bomb in the post. I tweeted the information with an "unconfirmed" warning attached to it. I then started to dig. By Tuesday of this week I had, as they say in the trade, stood up the story with three independent sources. The story was bigger than I had first suspected. In fact, Celtic manager Neil Lennon and Scottish MSP Trish Godman had also been sent bombs in the post. The second of the three sources told me that a couple of Scottish papers were "sitting on" the story.

It was, I was told, because of police advice. However, this wasn't a kidnap. I didn't see the sense in this news blackout. If anything, I thought publicity would make people more vigilant and allow the police to make a public request for witnesses. I consulted with a couple of trusted journalist friends, one of them an ex-editor. In the end, it was my decision. I decided to go with the story. I uploaded a short news piece on the basics on Wednesday 20 April at 8.45 p.m. local time. By 11 p.m. the mainstream media in Scotland, and then across the UK and internationally, was running the story. The story went global. By end of play on Wednesday, I was congratulated by senior members of the National Union of Journalists for breaking the censorship.

As a journalist, my starting point is always to see what my trade does. We are the creators of history's first rough draft. Here, the *Herald*'s headline on the Lennon story is a tad misleading. [The online article carries a link to the *Herald* online, which featured an article on 20 April 2011 headlined "Police in hunt for Celtic bomb fiend".] This unfortunate subbing didn't escape Roy Greenslade's attention in his *Guardian* media column. Roy has a sturdy moral compass on the ethics of the media. He is unequivocal that I took the correct journalistic decision to break the story.

As I have worked on the story since Tuesday, I have become aware that the police resources deployed on this case are much greater than a week ago. In the many years I have been covering these issues I have wondered at what point Scottish society reaches its "teachable moment". At what stage does the political class and civic leadership realise that there is a problem of a white underclass attached to Rangers FC? When will the leadership of Scotland decide that this anti-Catholic, anti-Irish bile is a societal pathogen that has to be tackled, faced down and, as a belief system, eradicated?

The UK can no longer afford the baubles of empire and modern Scotland cannot afford the trailer trash of its long gone global imperium to dominate the nation's discourse. After the riots of Manchester in 2008, Graham Spiers wrote that a "white underclass" had attached itself to the club. Spiers, himself from a Rangers background and the son of a Baptist minister, has been a constant, morally driven thorn in the side of those who wish to return to the old days in Scotland when the Irish knew their place.

On 6 October 2008 he said: "There is only one cure for the white underclass which has attached itself to Rangers. If I may quote Tony Blair (otherwise no great hero of mine): education, education, education." Again, on 9 November 2009, he said: "But the 'diehards' – those who love all the medieval chants and the faux-Protestant dressing around the club – certainly feel under some kind of cultural threat in Scotland. The white underclass of Rangers – I will put it no more offensively than that – feels put-upon and there is a direct link between their siege mentality and some of these repeated disturbances over the years. It is a galling image for the club to try to rectify."

The three targets of these bombs symbolise a collective threat to the worldview of the Rangers underclass that Spiers writes about. Lennon is an "uppity Fenian" from central casting and was a dominant warrior on the field of play for Celtic. He is now also shaping up to be a decent manager. A Catholic from Lurgan, in the worldview of the

Famine Song choir, he is the *Punch* cartoon figure of the Irish ape with the bomb. Of course, it is he who is threatened with bombs.

Paul McBride QC symbolises that the days of professional job discrimination against people on the basis of religion are, thankfully, a thing of the past. McBride's eloquent tradecraft bested the Scottish Football Association when defending Lennon and Celtic over a touch-line ban. Using its own rulebook, he made it look foolish and inept. Trish Godman's "crime" was to wear a Celtic top in the Scottish Parliament. Once more, she is a symbol that all is not well in the world from the vantage point of the Rangers underclass. The three of them, by their existence, tell the Rangers underclass, whether in Scotland or in the six counties, that their day has gone.

Now, in 2011, we see the result of that underclass remaining unchallenged by the soccer authorities and the Scottish political class. Their resolve has grown with each passing fixture; as the Billy Boys and the Famine Song are heard with impunity they feel more and more empowered and authorised. Only UEFA seems willing to act and discipline them into civilised norms. Have we reached the point in Scotland where these deviant beliefs of a post-imperial substratum are called out and tackled?

Since I broke the nail bomb story this week, the world's media has been shining a light on Scotland's shame. Journalists in the mainstream media in Scotland complained of their "embarrassment" as they fielded calls about the Lennon story from around the world. Indeed, they should be embarrassed. Once more it takes a journalist outside the country to break a story of huge relevance to Scotland. In February I asked a leading Scottish sports journalist: "Had you been in possession of the Dallas email, would you have broken the story?" He didn't answer. Although I broke the silence on the nail bomb story, the media blackout on me continues. As with the Dallas incident, despite breaking the story, my Irish name hasn't been in any Scottish newspaper.

[The "Dallas email" refers to an incident in 2010 in which the head of referee development, Hugh Dallas, sent an anti-Catholic email on the day of a Scottish visit by Pope Benedict XVI. Dallas subsequently lost his job.]

The outside world can see Scotland's problem clearly for what it is. I fear that those in charge in Scotland still do not. I fear we may not yet have reached Scotland's moment to learn, but I hope I am wrong.

Attack on Neil Lennon at Tynecastle

11 May 2011

I was watching the Celtic match against Hearts tonight in a bar in the west of Ireland. At the bar was a Scotsman travelling the island for a pharmaceutical firm. As the events unfolded, I made the point that this was showing up Scotland to the world. He shrugged and didn't respond.

As the second and third goals went in, I suspected he wasn't from the Celtic family. I gave him some advice on the best route to his next destination and some pharmacies that might not be on his list. I told him he would find a welcome across the places he was intending to travel. "There is always a warm welcome for a Scots voice in my father's county," I told him, "unlike over there, where it is a crime to be Irish." He didn't answer, but merely studied the remains of his bar meal. Had he been in a mood to converse on the subject, I would have told him that yesterday morning I was at the BBC in Pacific Quay in Glasgow being interviewed for a documentary on Scotland's "sectarian problem". An elderly man from Dublin asked me: "What's their problem over there with Lennon?" My answer was simple: "He's an Irish Catholic managing Celtic, an Irish club in Scotland. Everything else is irrelevant." The man at the bar didn't contradict or intervene. He left before the final whistle.

In the after-match analysis, the only talking point was the attack on the Celtic manager. There have, of course, been physical assaults on Neil Lennon before. However, this one was the first to happen at his place of work. The televised game would have been watched by millions. I hope the clip of the thug attacking the Lurgan man goes viral. It will produce iconic images of an ugly society that harbours and authorises a deep visceral hatred of Catholics in general and Irish Catholics in particular. It is instructive that this happened at Tynecastle, not Ibrox, as it takes this issue out of the Old Firm setting. When Aiden McGeady was subjected to racist abuse on an almost weekly basis for choosing to play for the Republic of Ireland it was not just Rangers fans who were the offenders. Neil Lennon's assailant is the product of a society that authorises the hatred of Irish Catholics.

Scotland, like a dysfunctional family, cannot see the destructive patterns. It normalises the bizarre behaviour. Scottish society needs help, outside help, to fix its anti-Irish pathology. A society with ingrained hatred of the Irish continues to shrug as the evidence piles up on an almost daily basis. Tonight's attack on Neil Lennon at Tynecastle is just another worrying symptom that Scotland is far from its teachable moment.

The other Neil Lennon

20 July 2011

This is a Neil Lennon that many in Scotland may not recognise. [The online article carries a link to an interview on Irish television's *Saturday Night with Miriam*, by Miriam O'Callaghan.] This Neil Lennon is relaxed, amiable, intelligent, and comes equipped with self-deprecating humour. This is not the scary, nasty Lennon that is portrayed in the Scottish media. Why the difference? Split personality? Alien abduction? Identical twins on a job share? No, it's much more prosaic: this time Neil was being interviewed in Dublin.

Although this is a soft seat, soft focus format, Miriam O'Callaghan is a very tough lady. She also fronts RTÉ's flagship current affairs programme, *Prime Time*. Many an Irish politician has been skewered by her. Around eleven minutes in, she cuts to the chase about the motivations behind those who have tormented, threatened and attacked Lennon during his time in Scotland. "It's because, you believe, you're an Irish Catholic?"

The interview with Miriam wouldn't happen in a Scottish studio because the real Neil Lennon, in this clip, is at odds with the snarling Fenian thug of Bonny Bigotland's racist imagination.

For the Record …

18 September 2011

About twenty years ago I was in a little Irish pub in the East End of Glasgow when the *fear a ti* – a fine fella from Dublin – said to me: "Your story in the *Irish Post* last week. I didn't like your headline."

"Neither did I," I replied. He was bemused by this response even more so when I added: "It wasn't my headline." Now totally flummoxed, he started to cross examine me. "It was your story, wasn't it? Your name was on it."

"Yes, of course it's my piece, John, but I'm not a sub-editor." At this stage, the fact that I was not the main man at *U-Boat Monthly* probably seemed neither here nor down there. My mate behind the bar just didn't know what went into producing a newspaper. The clue lay in the size of newspaper offices; big places that housed lots of people all working towards the one aim. So, for the record and just to be clear on things: journalists do not pick headlines, sub-editors do.

Major titles like the *Daily Record* also have page editors; the entire paper is overseen just before the presses start to run by a night editor, while the main guy is sleeping. It's an industrial process involving lots of people. In my time, I've been a sub-editor and a page editor. I only once questioned our layout guy and as a hack filing copy I never crossed a sub a second time. You know your place in a newspaper.

People, especially when working collectively, can get things badly wrong. The *Daily Record* yesterday was wrong. The back page headline and layout was very badly wrong. The tone was wrong; actually, everything about it was wrong.

[The article refers to a back page headline in the *Daily Record* on Saturday, 17 September 2011, which read: "Who's more hated at Ibrox? Is it Lennon or the taxman?" The *Daily Record* later apologised for the headline after Celtic Football Club released a statement of condemnation, saying: "Clearly, given the year Neil Lennon and his family have experienced – with bombs, bullets, death threats and physical assaults – this kind of reporting is inflammatory, highly irresponsible and quite simply offensive. For this newspaper to treat the matter in this insensitive and ill-judged manner is astonishing."]

As I write this, people are getting up from their slumber in Glasgow and looking forward to attending the Rangers v. Celtic match at Ibrox. Some will already have been on the road for hours. If they have time on their hands then they might want to read this piece.

[The online article carries a link to a piece published in the *Guardian* on 17 September 2011 by Kevin McKenna, titled "Why do people want to kill Neil Lennon?"]

That's how it should be done. I realise that the *Daily Record* people are in the happy-snappy tabloid world rather than the analytical world of the *Guardian*. However, they should not be, however unwittingly, writing permission slips for those at Ibrox who hate Neil Lennon. Neil Lennon is hated by many who will comprise the home crowd at Ibrox today. It isn't "banter" or a "noise-up", it is a visceral racism that generations of Irish Catholics have had to endure in Scotland since we Irish arrived in large numbers in the nineteenth century.

I largely agree with Kevin's thesis that what we are witnessing is the outworking of a racism that is in its death throes; that having achieved occupational parity in 2001, Catholics of Irish descent in Scotland will no longer tolerate the Ibrox subculture. The "Bears" don't like this new dispensation one bit, and in Neil Lennon they have, in their deranged minds, an uppity Fenian from central casting.

I have met Neil Lennon in a professional capacity at press conferences on several occasions and he is courteous, intelligent, polite, honest and thoughtful. In the dugout he is as he was on the field of play: a warrior. Neil Lennon's crime, for many of the home crowd today, isn't that he is the manager of Celtic, but that he is an Irish Catholic managing Celtic. They do not know Neil Lennon. What they hate is what he symbolises – the Croppy who won't lie down. Here is the embodiment that tells them deep in their racist hearts that the old days are over.

There are, sadly, some in the mainstream media in Scotland who also have to play catch up. They should join with the rest of us in challenging these Victorian attitudes. That element of the Ibrox crowd is a manifestation of a belief system that should never have survived the twentieth century let alone still be around in 2011. Habitat removal is the key to extinction. The pages of tabloid newspapers in Scotland must become unfailingly hostile to those who today will, undoubtedly, pour out their racist hatred for a young man from Lurgan. You don't need to know how a newspaper is put together to read something and know that it is just plain wrong.

I hope my old buddy from the Squirrel is doing well and on Hill 16 today at Croker. The all-Ireland final is one of the great sporting occasions in the world. It is a wonderful event with a genuine life-affirming atmosphere. Funnily enough, it doesn't have Rangers supporters as part of the package. Those folks need house training and the *Daily Record* can become part of the solution. Yesterday they didn't help the problem one little bit. Must do better, guys.

Safety in the workplace

2 October 2011

Today Neil Lennon will patrol the technical area at Tynecastle stadium. He will be doing his job. It is every bit his place of work as his office in the Lennoxtown training centre. Every employer has a duty of care to the people they hire. As part of their employment they are required to go places. Subsequently, their employer must ensure that those locations are safe. Heart of Midlothian FC, as the home side, will provide match-day security through their stewards and Lothian and Borders Police.

The last time the Tynecastle technical area was Lennon's place of work, HMFC and the police failed to protect Neil Lennon. The images of John Wilson lunging at the Celtic manager went around the planet before the journalists had filed their match reports. It was a lapse in security but these things happen and it was all over in an instant. What is harder to explain is the deliberation of a fifteen-person jury in the subsequent trial. When is an admission of guilt in a courtroom not an admission of guilt in a courtroom? That's easy – when the jury decides to ignore it. The bastard verdict of not proven saw Mr Wilson beat the assault charge.

In 2008, I stood in that same technical area in Edinburgh discussing, among other things, anti-Irish racism with then SPL chief Lex Gold. There was a charity match on between a Show Racism the Red Card Select versus the MSPs from Holyrood, and it was all good-natured stuff. It was a worthy event and as the match progressed Mr Gold's understanding of these issues cognate to the event was instructive. When I put the issue of Aiden McGeady to him, his response was: "Aiden's a lot more mature and he can handle it better now."

It is hard to imagine that statement about a black player in similar circumstances. Anti-Irish racism permeates Scottish culture so much that it has become normalised and not recognised for what it is. The term "sectarianism" was used to characterise the abuse Aiden McGeady and Neil Lennon had to endure as Celtic players. However, McGeady's "crime" was, of course, his country of choice – a Welsh grandparent and a choice of the red of Wales would not have produced any problems for the young Celtic player, now safely in Russia. Similarly, Lennon's Irishness as a causative factor in the decade of abuse and victimisation he has endured in Scotland has been written out of the official narrative.

When it comes to anti-Irish racism large sections of Scottish society, including many in the political elite, are in denial. If Neil Lennon was from Lagos rather than Lurgan I suspect the stance of official Scotland would be rather different. At the time of the verdict in the Wilson case, Paul McBride QC noted that "in Scotland we have juries that don't need to read, don't need to write, don't need to count and may be full of prejudices".

The decisions of juries must, of course, be respected, even if they are sometimes baffling to the ordinary person. A basic tenet of any civilised society is that all are equal before the law and all will receive the protection of the law equally. I am sure that Neil Lennon will be safe at his place of work today. The world is watching.

Neil Lennon's enemies

3 May 2011

This week Neil Lennon was back at Windsor Park. This time he was watching, not playing for Northern Ireland. The opposition last Thursday was Norway – Neil had an interest in the Scandinavians as his young centre half, Thomas Rogne, was making his senior debut. Neil was back in the stadium where he was booed by his own fans when Norway was the opposition over a decade ago.

The same night that the Lurgan man returned to Windsor Park, another Ulsterman, James McClean, took to the field of play for Ireland in Dublin. The Irish Football Association (IFA) doesn't seem to get that many young Northern nationalists don't identify with the Northern Ireland statelet and they don't see the legitimacy of the team as a FIFA entity. Darron Gibson's views are not atypical: "It was unbelievable, you know, making the debut for your country. Everyone from Derry wants to play for Ireland. I grew up supporting Ireland, so it was a natural choice for me."

Some do, like Paddy McCourt and Niall McGinn, but the next generation seems less likely to play for Sammy's Wee Ulstur. Those two Celtic players, of course, along with Neil Lennon, have received bullets in the post. Security forces sources have briefed journalists that the authors of these threats are almost certainly a faction of the Ulster Defence Association (UDA).

The entire ambience of Windsor Park during an international match is toxic to nationalists.

[The online article carries a link to a piece in the *Belfast Telegraph* by Paul McVeigh which argues that the IFA should cease using "God Save The Queen" as its national anthem before games.]

It will take more than a new anthem to cleanse Windsor Park of the pathogens that saw the supporters boo their own player. As Ireland prepare to take part in Euro 2012, Norn Iron, as usual, are nowhere. Northern Ireland's captain against Norway was Steve Davis of Rangers.

The midfielder may soon have to find himself a new club, as the one which employs him is about to go out of business. Perhaps the Windsor Park crowd should consider finding a new home; they would find the AVIVA stadium a much more modern venue, in every sense of the word. The *céad míle fáilte* would be genuine.

Some people bear grudges and harbour bitterness for past wrongs done to them. It is abundantly clear that Lennon is not that type of man. He is a better person than those who ended his international career and who would seek to chase him out of Celtic Park.

The freedom to vent is part of the game

23 March 2012

Last Sunday I stumbled down the stairs to the press conference room at Hampden. We were waiting for Neil Lennon and there was only one question that any of us wanted to ask him. Like everyone else there, I wanted his opinion on the penalty incident in the dying moments of the cup final.

The waiting press pack hoped for good copy and the expectant tension of a cracking quote from Lenny was only broken by my offer of a dongle to assist a veteran sports journalist who looked like he had just been introduced to his laptop. With my Vodafone thingy protruding from his USB port, he carried the contraption around the room like a water diviner, but the mobile signal, like the Hampden Park wi-fi, didn't penetrate into the subterranean level to where we hacks were banished after the final whistle.

The cameras were set up and the recording devices blinked their red lights on the table. All we needed was Lenny. The opinion was split on the penalty decision and I wasn't sure. Since then the video of the incident has been analysed like the line of sight from the Texas School Book Depository window on Elm Street. However, last Sunday the best any of us had was a quick look on our screens at the time Stokes hit the Hampden turf. There was a three or four-second delay on the monitors on the media desks. It gives a replay service more or less in real time. I had quickly glanced down and I simply wasn't sure about the penalty incident. So, it was within that context that Neil Lennon was ushered into the presser.

It was observable, being just a few feet from him, that he was seething about the Stokes penalty claim. In Neil's opinion, his team was the victim of an injustice at a crucial point in the game. I asked him if he would think more of Willie Collum if the referee admitted he had messed up and he said he would. Lennon used the word "criminal" to describe Collum's decision to:

(1) Refuse a penalty
(2) Book Anthony Stokes for diving

Words can have many meanings and they are usually context-specific. If a parent tells their kid that if they don't tidy their bedroom they will "kill" them, no one hearing that interaction thinks that the child's life is in any danger, just as no one in that room thought Neil Lennon was alleging that Willie Collum was a criminal, or had committed a crime. The Celtic manager said he would be asking John Fleming for his opinion of the incident. Fleming is the head of referee development at the SFA – the post once occupied by Hugh Dallas – and he is the boss of all of the SFA's match officials.

I have been in several Lenny pressers and he's an absolute dream for a journalist. A straight question elicits an equally straight answer. Even when the question is one he would rather not have been asked, you still get an unambiguous response that you can use. He speaks in clear, easy-to-understand sentences. He is as straight in his dealings with the media as he was pragmatic with the ball at his feet in his playing days. He doesn't utilise Martin O'Neill's tactic of tying the hacks up in knots with educated sophistry and that isn't because he isn't smart enough to use such a ploy; Lenny has a soldier's staccato honesty of the situation as he sees it. You are left in no doubt. He doesn't do ambiguity. I know which I prefer.

Compliance Officer Vincent Lunny has now written to Celtic for clarification about Lennon's post-match comments about Willie Collum's decision. If there is any action taken against Lennon, post-match pressers will no longer be worth going to because managers will be even more gagged than they are at present. Certainly, Inverness Caledonian Thistle manager Terry Butcher will have to be mindful of further florid rants about "kangaroo courts" at Hampden. I can't imagine that Neil Lennon would be singled out for especially punitive action by the SFA. I'm sure that won't happen to the Irishman.

Neil Lennon at Ibrox

26 March 2012

Is Ibrox stadium a safe working environment? The question seems apposite today because of the Celtic manager's reported post-match comments after the Glasgow derby match. According to Hugh Keevins in the *Daily Record*, Lennon said: "I would've sat in the stand but I was told by Rangers' security people that wasn't a good idea. That sums up this country."

A Celtic spokesman later clarified the origin of the decision: "Further to certain media reports today, for clarification, Neil was advised by Celtic's own security and operations staff not to enter the stand or directors' box area at Ibrox at yesterday's match." A club insider told me today that the decision was almost certainly taken by the club's head of security. He is an ex-policeman with vast experience and his threat assessment has to be respected. Moreover, he has a duty of care for all of the Celtic FC staff when they are at work. What did he think was unsafe about that area of the main stand at Ibrox? I am sure that it was not a concern about the occupants of the directors' box itself, but perhaps that it was surrounded by the baying punters.

Once more, a racist "send them home" message to Glasgow's Irish community was seen at Ibrox. This time it defaced the national flag the sloganeers claim to love. Of course, Neil Lennon has more reason than most to abide by any security advice when he is at work. Consider this: would Sir Alex Ferguson, if he was sent to the stand in a bad-tempered Manchester derby, be similarly advised by United's security staff at the City of Manchester Stadium? The situation wouldn't even arise.

Once more, Planet *Fitba* demonstrates the extent of its abnormality within British soccer. We have tragic evidence that the old Ibrox stadium was not safe for its customers. The new stadium was a monument that the sixty-six did not die in vain. Years before the Taylor report, it was the safest stadium in Scotland. The stairwells and the exits are now constructed to the highest standard; all that needs to be redesigned is the belief system of some of the patrons. Note to Rangers supporters: Irish Catholics are people. Neil Lennon is a person. He has rights, just like you.

The Neil Lennon problem

27 March 2012

Neil Francis Lennon is a problem. We should all acknowledge that from the start. I am writing this in the part of Ulster that has provided Glasgow with many of its Irish people over the generations. Donegal people are, in the main, a quiet species. The archetypal *Tir Conaill* fella will keep his cards close to his chest and won't say too much. This became especially true once they landed in Scotland and got the vibe: if you kept your head down, you would be fine.

Although I live in Ulster I have few kin from this province in my line. My mother's side hailed from Carlow. They were strong Land Leaguers and the patriarch of the clan was a bare-knuckle fighter well into his fifties. He was a Fenian with a capital "F" and was completely aware of what was around him. Ironically, the Carlow Murphys came into a Scotland over a hundred years ago that was unsure of the sturdiness of its own national identity. Of course, that wasn't Paddy's fault; yet this was the generation of Scots who would produce the authors of the 1923 Church and Nation Committee report that stated that there was a "southern Irish Roman Catholic race", a document which the Church of Scotland has recently apologised for. Apology accepted.

The public portrayal of Neil Lennon is from central casting within that Kirk-scripted eugenics melodrama. In the interests of full disclosure, I do not know Neil Lennon personally, I only know him professionally. I have been in several press conferences with him and I have, on those occasions, asked him questions about his job. In these media set-pieces I have found him courteous, intelligent and straightforward. To see him in another media environment is to see the entirely different person that the Scottish press perceive him to be.

Lennon's main problem in Scotland is that he doesn't tug the forelock. First of all, his hair is too short, but, more importantly, his head is at the wrong angle – it is held far too high for that. For some in Scottish society, the Celtic manager is too uppity for the public good. Now, dear reader, consider this: if Alan Thompson or Johan Mjällby had been appointed Celtic manager two seasons ago, just think what the reportage would have been like. With exactly the same results, the good and the bad, what would the back pages have been like for the Swede or the Englishman?

Explanations that ignore the ethnic are proffered. We are told that

Lennon "brings it on himself" because of his manner. Moreover, it is a hangover from his combative playing days in the hoops. Really? Alan Thompson was sent off several times while playing in matches against Rangers. The big Scandinavian Johan Mjällby was a night-club bouncer of a centre half who did not recognise the Geneva Convention on the field of play. However, you just know that officialdom would have a different stance to those two ex-Celtic players if they were in the manager's seat.

To remove the ethnic from the analysis is to be a friend of nonsense. Look at how Neil is portrayed in the *Scottish Review*. [The online article carries a link to an article in the *Scottish Review* published on 20 April 2011 by Kenneth Roy titled: "The beautiful game is now in the last minutes of extra time".]

I asked a member of staff there at the time of publication if the term "*Punch* cartoon" meant anything to her with regard to depictions of Irish people. She said it didn't and I believed her. Every Irish person I showed the cartoon to shrieked in disbelief that such a depiction of an Irishman could be published in modern Britain. In Scotland, anti-Irish racism is so interwoven into the fabric of the culture that people don't even notice.

When any case is made for Neil Lennon, the self-educated body language experts of the hack pack say that his physical posture leaves much to be desired. This photograph in the *Scottish Sun* shows fourth official Ian Brines pressing home his point to an impassive Neil Lennon at Ibrox on Sunday. [The online article carries a link to an article in the *Scottish Sun* published on 26 March 2012 by Gareth Law titled: "Prove you said SFA, Neil", which features a photograph showing Ian Brines prodding a seated Neil Lennon's chest with his finger.]

Interestingly, one of the charges aimed at Lennon is "adoption of aggressive behaviour towards match official" … As I consider all of this, I wonder why he doesn't just walk away from it all because he and his young family could live in a better situation tomorrow. I thought about this when I saw him come into the press conference at Hampden last week accompanied by a man who makes Johan Mjällby look tiny. This American gentleman genuinely deserves the term "human shield" and follows Lennon around everywhere when the Lurgan man is at work. What other manager in British football requires this type of close protection? Quite.

The only fragment of light in all of this now is that the London media has become aware that something is rotten in the state of Scotland. The Fourth Estate in the country of my birth has had plenty of opportunities to step up on the issue of anti-Irish racism. The succulent lamb tasted too good, but this is far more important than whether or not a player was offside. This is about a country finally growing up and turning its back upon its racist history. Until that happens, Neil Lennon will remain a problem.

The price of silence

30 March 2012

The jury was not out for long before its decision was made. Trevor Muirhead and Neil McKenzie were not, as their eloquent defence counsel suggested, merely hoaxers trying to scare their targets. Rather, they were full of malice and, thankfully, only lacked the technical competence to construct a viable improvised explosive device (IED).

What Muirhead and McKenzie did possess was a quality which was fully operational and much more deadly than the bombs they tried to make: both of them are Rangers-supporting zealots from central casting and, because of that, they come fully equipped with an emotional deficiency as standard. When they were arrested I undertook some background research for a UK newspaper and what I found was not pretty. Their palpable hatred for fine people, like the late Paul McBride QC, Trish Godman MSP and Neil Lennon, just because of their perceived ethnic and religious background was, for me, the real story of this trial.

Everything has a cost, and the price of being silent on anti-Irish racism in Scotland is Muirhead and McKenzie. It is many years since I wrote a social enquiry report for a Glasgow court so I won't revisit that career now. However, these two men, convicts that are now awaiting sentence for their crimes, are products of a toxic belief system that passes for normal in their homeland. This is especially baffling for media colleagues in London and Dublin, but it is the only conclusion that can be reached when sifting the sociological evidence.

At time of writing, official Scotland still cannot use the term "anti-Irish racism" and I have no clear idea why this is the case. Perhaps it is because that would finally recognise the presence of the country's large Irish community. While the political class in Edinburgh continue to operate a discreet racism towards the Irish in Scotland as a people, the jury must still be out on just what kind of country the Holyrood elite want to be in charge of after 2014.

Anger management

18 April 2012

Getting angry is part of being human. It is an evolved response to certain stressful situations. The ability to get absolutely furious saved many of our ancestors from predator and foe. It is as much a key component of a survival kit as fear. You need both. It gives the ancient part of your brain an instant chemical choice: fight or flight.

On Sunday, Neil Lennon veered towards the former. Some may want the return of the broken posture of Tony Mowbray, a Celtic manager who always seemed to be comfortable with defeat. I was brought into the Celtic family watching Jock Stein's team. The big man was contemptuous of Scotland's football hierarchy and officialdom in general. He fought his corner and often boiled with anger, and not just in Scotland. At half-time in Lisbon he laced into the referee, Kurt Tschenscher, who had given a penalty against Celtic by questioning his integrity and his role in the Third Reich – the polyglot German probably didn't speak Lanarkshire so big Jock escaped going to the cooler.

Evolutionary psychologists have discovered that our primate cousins also experience moral outrage. The ability of chimpanzees to get angry over what they perceive as an injustice is further evidence of how close they are to being human. Of course, we learn to control our anger; that is part of life. However, the reason that sport has such a central role in the lives of many people is that it is a release valve for those feelings. That is as true for the spectators as it is for the players and the coaching staff. It is all about emotions.

Seeing a manager or player go off on one post-match is part of the theatre. When I think of Jock Stein, I am reminded of a certain genteel septuagenarian currently in England who has always considered the big man to be something of a role model. Mention the legendary Celtic manager to Fergie and he will speak in reverent tones about "Mr Stein". Before the Glazers intervened you could see that Ferguson was fashioning his own Lisbon Lions with quick, inventive players sweeping forward. He was creating the type of side that he met in the 1969 cup final. The Rangers defence was destroyed that day and Ferguson was to blame. He was the centre forward but he had married a Catholic so it had to be his fault.

He would get his own back as manager of Aberdeen. His Dons side was built around pacifists like Rougvie and Strachan. Ferguson brought them and his anger to Glasgow. It was part of the Pittodrie induction course that match officials were against them. Rage was a key part of Aberdeen's success in the early 1980s. For some reason, the nickname "Sir Furious" has attached itself to this serene, zen-like knight of the realm. Utterly defamatory, and Sir Alex really should instruct counsel to seek redress for this vile calumny.

That nice young chap Beckham and his charming lady wife could perhaps be called as character witnesses to testify to Sir Alex's genial disposition. What isn't widely known is that as a young boy in Govan he would pass by an Aladdin's cave of timepieces every day on the way to his school. The shop was owned by a frail, kindly gent of foreign extraction and he would show these amazing contraptions to the young Ferguson. The ancient watchmaker showed the young Govan lad the intricacies of his trade. It was here that Sir Alex developed a lifelong passion for the precision of timekeeping. You can still see him, even in his senior years, assisting much younger men from the Football Association to accurately assess the time left in a football match involving Manchester United.

He will often make the arduous journey down from the stand to the touchline to make sure that the officials have not miscalculated the allotted playing time. A lifelong fascination, indeed! There have also been times when Sir Alex has entered into a fair and free exchange of views with match officials. To see him do so on the touchline post-match is to witness the embodiment of the Corinthian spirit.

So, Lenny marched onto the turf after a match and berated the ref – the whistler wasn't manhandled, *à la* Bougherra. The Lurgan man shouldn't have done it, but I understand why he did. Given that Euan Norris apparently can't differentiate between Joe Ledley and Victor Wanyama, I suspect that Johan Mjällby will soon find himself up on charges relating to the incident. The laptop loyal are now starting to sound like a lynch mob out to get Neil Francis Lennon but don't expect me to join in. In fact, the more I think about it the more fucking pissed off I'm getting. One, two, three, four, five …

A culture of hatred

27 April 2012

I believe what Lord Turnbull said to Muirhead and McKenzie when he sentenced them is worth exploring. He said: "I cannot fathom what was

in your minds." Now that the two Rangers supporters have been sent
to prison for five years it is, perhaps, an appropriate time to look at the
belief system that authorised their hate.

Neil Francis Lennon ticks all the boxes for the subculture that socialised McKenzie and Muirhead. Irish Catholics occupy a central place in
the worldview of the Rangers subculture that nurtured Muirhead and
McKenzie. These two men undoubtedly acted in accordance with their
culture. Indeed, people rarely act at variance with their worldview. The
Celtic manager is an Irish Catholic from the north of Ireland and he has
a streetfighter's response to those who would try and push him to the
back of the bus. The late Paul McBride QC, almost certainly destined
to be a High Court judge, held a position that Catholics with Irish
names just shouldn't have. Trish Godman's "crime" was to wear a Celtic
top to the Scottish Parliament as a joke for charity. That was enough to
make her a target.

This *Mississippi Burning* belief system of many who follow the Ibrox
club must now be seen for what it is: a serious social problem in modern Scotland. This is not "sectarianism" nor is it a case of "one side is
as bad as the other". This is anti-Catholic hatred and anti-Irish racism
that is validated by following a football club. For them, being a Rangers
supporter is a crucial part of harbouring a xenophobic fixation on a
religious and ethnic minority. Supporting Rangers was a vehicle for
this; their hatred of Lennon was not some example of sporting rivalry
taken too far, rather it was at the core of their belief system. In their
worldview, Neil Francis Lennon should know his place. The problem
for Muirhead and McKenzie was that Neil does know his place: it is to
be heard, to be acknowledged, to have his culture respected and to be
afforded the same rights in modern Scotland as anyone else.

Mr Jackson QC for Muirhead, in his mitigation speech, pointed out
that that no one was injured by his client. He did accept that there
was intent to injure but argued the devices were "non-viable" and on
the lower end of seriousness. Therefore, all that prevented a tragedy
was their lack of technical competence. By the time these two Rangers
supporters emerge from prison I hope they are rehabilitated and cured
of their hatred of Irish Catholics. I also hope that when they are freed
they are reintegrated into a society where there is zero tolerance for their
racist worldview. The Scotland of many cultures has much work to do
in a very short time.

Links

http://www.philmacgiollabhain.ie/neil-lennon/
http://www.philmacgiollabhain.ie/
   live-bombs-sent-to-lennonmcbride-and-msp/
http://www.philmacgiollabhain.ie/aicsc-statement-on-neil-lennon/
http://www.philmacgiollabhain.ie/the-teachable-moment/
http://www.philmacgiollabhain.ie/attack-on-neil-lennon-at-tynecastle/
http://www.philmacgiollabhain.ie/the-other-neil-lennon/
http://www.philmacgiollabhain.ie/for-the-record/
http://www.philmacgiollabhain.ie/safety-in-the-workplace/
http://www.philmacgiollabhain.ie/neil-lennons-enemies/
http://www.philmacgiollabhain.ie/
   the-freedom-to-vent-is-part-of-the-game/
http://www.philmacgiollabhain.ie/neil-lennon-at-ibrox/
http://www.philmacgiollabhain.ie/the-neil-lennon-problem/
http://www.philmacgiollabhain.ie/the-price-of-silence/
http://www.philmacgiollabhain.ie/anger-management/
http://www.philmacgiollabhain.ie/a-culture-of-hatred/

PART III: AN ILLICIT ETHNICITY?

Introduction

Eleanor Roosevelt famously said that "the future belongs to those who believe in the beauty of their dreams". Next year, the Scottish people will vote to determine the future of their nation.

Among those voting will undoubtedly be women who are married to each other. Last December, the Scottish Government published its proposed legislation to introduce gay marriage in Scotland and the views of the public are being sought on a draft bill to be presented to the Scottish Parliament. The announcement was met with general approval by the population. If that image does not establish that society can profoundly change then I'd urge you to reconsider.

In the historical blink of a single century, the lives of women and gay people have been transformed from legally enforced inequality to empowerment. If that vignette of two lesbians joined together in marriage and voting for Scottish independence had been proposed when I was born in 1958 it would have been considered the offensive, blasphemous output of a diseased mind. Now it is read by most people in Scotland as an uplifting reminder of social progress and the onward march of equality.

When I spoke to the Changin Scotland conference in November 2011 I asked the audience what kind of Scotland they wanted to live in. When I took my first steps into journalism thirty years ago I was warned by a veteran reporter that all analogies ultimately fail, but that should not stop us from using them. The transformation in the social standing and the perception of wider society towards women and the gay community is, I think, a reasonable reference point in what could happen for people in Scotland of Irish heritage if society was to truly grow up and embrace diversity.

If an ethnic minority is not physically distinct, a common response to oppression is to become invisible. It is a strategy that is not, of course, open to people of colour. In the 1947 film *Gentleman's Agreement*

Gregory Peck plays the role of a reporter who pretends to be Jewish in order to cover a story on anti-semitism. In doing so, he discovers the true depths of bigotry and hatred. The film was nominated for eight Oscars and won three.

In the film, Philip Schuyler Green adopted a Jewish identity to find out the level of anti-semitism in New York City and in an affluent suburb in Connecticut. As Phil Greenberg, his eyes were opened and the story developed as he embarked upon a journey of discovery in the country he thought he knew – his own. The key to his enlightenment was a simple change of name, to one that would tell the world he was a Jew.

I have used the Irish form of my family name since my mid twenties and I'm now fifty-five. At some point in the eighteenth century some English state functionary most likely wrote Mac Giolla Bháin down phonetically. That was the theory suggested to me by the Chief Herald of Ireland, Donal Begley, while I was still using the anglicised version of my name. In Ireland, using the Irish (original) form of your family name is a way of signifying that you are an Irish speaker. In Scotland I have frequently been on the receiving end of "humour" about the spelling of my family name. On several occasions I have enquired of the comedian if they would similarly abuse someone with an Italian, Pakistani or Polish name. An embarrassed look is the usual reply.

Linguistic oppression is often an important component of any ethnic hegemony. Once the entire island of Ireland was fully under the control of the English state from the mid-seventeenth century onwards, the full extirpation of Irish ways and Irish laws could begin. A key component of that policy was the destruction, by any means necessary, of the Irish language. People lost their family names and were given English versions instead, which were either a direct translation or a phonetic rendering that meant nothing in any language. This also happened to place-names, and Brian Friel's brilliant play, *Translations,* tells how the British Ordnance Survey established its linguistic control on the Donegal landscape.

I look out of my window to see the early morning sun stream in over Muckish Mountain. This is the name that was written in the first English maps of the area. However, "Muckish" doesn't mean anything. The original name is *an Mhucais*, literally meaning "the pig's back". The mountain is very distinctive with a flat top and, depending on your vantage point, it can resemble a pig's back. Friel's play, written in 1980, is set in these mountains in the nineteenth century and tells the tale of cultural imperialism and how language can be a weapon of war and a tool of conquest.

The suppression of the Irish language in Ireland, like anti-Irish racism in Scotland, has a long history. Given the experience of Gaidhlig in Scotland, one would have thought that someone reconnecting with their Celtic language would meet with general approval. However, as we have seen, when it comes to Scotland and Irishness, there seems to be a special set of rules.

It is now recognised that a secure sense of cultural identity is a fundamental human right. The right to self-define is central to anyone's wellbeing. Abraham Maslow gave the world of psychology a model by which the various needs of humans could be categorised and prioritised. His theory, the hierarchy of needs, was published in the 1950s and it is now orthodoxy in disciplines as varied as clinical psychology and advertising.

Within Maslow's hierarchy of needs, self-actualisation wasn't the first on the list, but for any democratic society that claims to embrace multiculturalism, it has to be there. Anything that creates uplift in the general wellbeing of a section of a population enhances the entire ambience of a city or, indeed, an entire country. One would think, then, in the twenty-first century in a country that had a celebration of diversity written into the government-approved marketing slogan that there would be ample cultural space for everyone. The reality is that to establish a secure sense of Irish identity in contemporary Scotland one must overcome a series of societal obstacles.

When I spoke at the Changin Scotland conference my talk was, like this section, part sociological analysis and part personal testimony. I told the audience of a chance conversation I'd had with someone on the plane on the way over from Ireland to attend the conference. The man seated beside me on the journey from Dublin to Glasgow looked the archetypal business traveller; he was a middle-aged man in a suit on a plane full of middle-aged men in suits. He was based in Glasgow and had been in Dublin for a meeting.

He looked every inch what he told me he was; a senior person in a blue chip American-owned company travelling to Dublin to visit its European headquarters. When we exchanged pleasantries he asked me about the nature of my journey. I told him I was travelling to Glasgow and on to the north-west of Scotland to speak at a conference. I told him I was travelling from the north-west of Ireland to the north-west of Scotland and that each area was my favourite place on each island.

I told him where I lived and why I thought my children were lucky to have grown up there. Half way through our conversation, quietly, politely and almost whispering, he told me that both of his parents were from the village of *Gort a' choirce*, where I live. I was astounded. It proved to me the central point of my talk; that the Irish in Scotland could be highly invisible after a generation. That can be evidence of a highly successful integration, but it can also suggest hostile assimilation based upon racism and prejudicial attitudes.

He told me that his parents, both fluent Irish speakers, had stopped using their native tongue after his older brother had spoken Irish in the Glasgow streets and was set upon by some lads. Had these parents been from the Punjab and the language in question been Urdu, this story would have been seen through the prism of racism. However, in Scotland the young Irish Gaeilgoiri being attacked for speaking Irish was categorised "sectarian".

If something adverse happens to Irish people in Scotland that is motivated by a hate of the Irish and Irishness, it cannot be called as such. There is a special category all on its own where the ethnic is excised from the analysis. Racism against Irish people in Scotland is called "sectarianism". This isn't just a sloppy use of language, but a crucial denial of identity that is contained within the current lexicon of public discourse in Scotland.

This meant that my neighbour on the plane could understand Irish but couldn't speak it. He had a younger sibling in exactly the same situation. The man on the plane and his sister will not figure in any research, meagre as it is, on the Irish in Scotland, let alone any discourse on racism or cultural oppression. He smiled a quiet smile when I told him that I had no idea how to introduce my topic but, if he didn't mind, his story was a perfect way to get people thinking in the Highlands.

It worked. As I was getting the notes for my speech printed out at the reception in the Ceilidh Place the wonderful manager there, Effie, wanted to engage me in chat as I rushed to rip the paper out of the printer to go through it with my red pen. She wanted to chat so I obliged. She said she had been reading what I had written – I'd emailed it to her so that she could print it for me. She told me the entire experience of the Glasgow Irish was redolent of what had happened to people in that stunningly beautiful part of Scotland.

Her generation was the last that had not been taught Gáidhlig at school. She told me she thought it was great that the younger generation was now embracing the old culture. However, she said that when she looked at them, culturally confident in who they were, she felt a loss that it had come too late for her. It reminded me that the making of the Irish invisible, the cultural hostility and the monoglot linguistic bigotry was well in place before the Famine Irish arrived during Black '47.

In the march towards equality, language is important and in this case doubly so. When I lived in Glasgow in the early 1990s I taught conversational Irish to adults at the Conradh na Gaeilge club on a Friday night in Govanhill. A few of my students were in their forties or fifties and had two Irish-speaking parents but, like my travelling companion on the plane, had "benefited" from their parents' decision not to pass on the language. Subsequently, some of them felt a disconnect towards their culture.

Again, if these people attending an adult education class had two parents born on the Indian subcontinent and had been reared as monoglot English speakers because of the threat of physical attacks in the street for speaking the language of their parents, there would be no question that this was the linguistic collateral damage of racism.

Tackling the Famine Song was fairly simple. I first had to raise awareness; that was achieved by writing newspaper articles and helped to get Irish politicians involved, especially in Ireland. I hoped that if the Famine Song became something Irish-elected representatives were discussing, there was a chance that official Scotland could be shamed into doing something about it. The William Walls case, when it went to appeal in June 2009, was job done and mission accomplished. Now, if this illegal song is tolerated by the forces of law and order at any stage in Scotland, the constabulary will become the focus for failing to act. The racism of the lyrics is not up for debate. It was established in Scots law in June 2009 that the Famine Song was racist and offensive to Irish people and people of Irish descent in Scotland.

The absence of a memorial in Glasgow to those who died and those who survived the great hunger in Ireland is finally being addressed. Fine people, like Councillor Feargal Dalton, stepped into the *bearna bhaoil* to make a difference.

Neil Lennon would not bow his head and give racists the amoral victory they craved. All discriminatory systems are ultimately brought down by the courage of people who inspire by example. This section deals with something that is more difficult to quantify but is just as vital as outlawing racist songs, building a memorial in Glasgow to An Gorta Mór or acknowledging the racist nature of the hatred aimed at Neil Lennon.

The Famine Song and the lack of a Famine memorial was linked, as was the fact that the former was being belted out by supporters of a club that appeared unable to find a player from the Republic of Ireland good enough for its first team. All of these issues led back to a society with no cultural space afforded to Irishness. This was what led the Donegal parents of my neighbour on the plane to realise they had unwittingly committed a huge cultural crime in rearing an Irish speaker in Glasgow. The head-down-back-of-the-bus attitude was the default setting for most of the Irish in Glasgow during my childhood.

In the absence of the appropriate amount of serious academic research all we have is a crude correlation between faith and ethnicity in the west of Scotland. Although the Catholic Church played its own self-serving role in de-Hibernising its flock in past generations, anti-Irish racism in Scotland cannot be fully disentangled from anti-Catholic hatred.

In 2010, the Scottish Football Association's head of referee development, Hugh Dallas, felt confident enough to take an email "joke" about His Holiness Pope Benedict XVI on the day of his state visit to the United Kingdom and forward it to colleagues from his SFA email account. The email had a jpeg image of a road sign; a British red triangle warning at a road side with the depiction of a child's silhouette holding the hand of an adult. The sign is used to warn drivers that there may be children crossing the road in the area and is usually placed near schools. In this picture, the sign had been Photoshopped and under the word "Caution" it read "The Pope is coming". The implication was that His Holiness the Pope was a danger to children. I became aware of the email several months after Dallas sent it and broke the story. Three weeks later, he was dismissed by the SFA.

At the time, I never editorialised about Mr Dallas's motivations or worldview, or whether or not he really believed that the Pope himself was a danger to children. However, I do think it is fair to conclude that Mr Dallas felt confident enough that there would be no serious repercussions if he forwarded the email from his work account. On reflection, what probably tipped the balance as to whether or not Mr Dallas would survive the scandal was a letter from Peter Kearney of the Scottish Catholic media office to the SFA demanding that the football body sack Mr Dallas.

Over the years, Kearney has been outspoken in challenging the official narrative that anti-Catholicism in Scotland is something that is mainly a thing of the past and is waning. Indeed, in January 2013 he stated that the situation faced by Catholics in Scotland was akin to that of African Americans in the Deep South in the 1950s and 1960s. Mr

Kearney, citing Crown Office statistics showing Catholics were more likely to be the victims of a hate crime than those of other religions in Scotland, said: "I am certain that many voices will join this debate, bringing with them a blame-the-victim mindset. In much the same way as America's black citizens in an earlier era were urged to straighten their hair and whiten their complexions in order to 'minimise' differences with the white majority, many will surely urge Scottish Catholics to stop sending their children to Catholic schools or making public or overt declarations of faith at any time.

"Scandalously, open and wide debate on the matter in modern Scotland is neither encouraged nor facilitated. Scotland has first and foremost a problem with anti-Catholicism. This must be recognised and accepted before progress can be made. To wilfully deploy blanket terminology like 'sectarianism' in the face of compelling evidence attesting to the particulars of certain animosities is to perpetuate the problem. We could reasonably start by following the lead taken by campaigners against domestic violence. Although this behaviour manifests itself in a variety of ways, for the most part it comprises male violence directed at women. Campaigners and politicians have rightly recognised this, allowing publicity material like posters and advertising to portray women as the primary victims."

Any notion of an Irish ethnicity was, in the collective consciousness of the host community, conflated with expression of Irish Republicanism. The penchant to indulge in IRA chants and rebel songs could be viewed as an expression of something akin to a ghettoised alienation. There is an oral tradition around the Irish struggle for sovereignty that is lauded around the world as a specific contribution to world music. In Scotland, much of that tradition is currently criminalised.

Whether or not, post-Good Friday Agreement, the chanting of rebel songs has any utility, is simply bad manners or is boorish behaviour is an adjacent point to the fact that many expressions of that political Irishness are currently criminalised in Scotland. In 2012, the SNP's Offensive Behaviour at Football and Threatening Communications (Scotland) Act came into force. The new law gives powers to individual police officers to arrest persons at a football match, travelling to and from a football match, or watching a football match on television in a public place. The criteria for being arrested under the act include that the police officer deems that an incident would cause offence to a reasonable person. The act has proved to be highly controversial and cases brought to Scottish courts under the new law have been thrown out.

Given the Irish Republican subculture which exists within the Celtic support, Provisional IRA endorsements can often be heard. These are undoubtedly offensive to many people; however, they are legitimate political expressions. Moreover, after the Good Friday Agreement was signed the Provisional IRA left the stage and its political manifestation, Sinn Féin, is in a power-sharing government in Northern Ireland. Perhaps precisely because of the lack of public and cultural space to create expressions of Irishness, the only place the Catholic Church did not formally control the Irish community was at Celtic matches.

IRA chanting by a minority of Celtic supporters at football games is an echo of an earlier time. As greater respect is shown to Irishness in Scotland, the utility function of these chants will be rendered redundant. The comparison between Glasgow and large North American cities could not be starker. Across the pond, Irishness is applauded and acknowledged.

I do not know what the future holds for Scotland's Irish community. With people like Councillor Feargal Dalton and Danny Boyle of the Irish Heritage Foundation around, I can be hopeful that the end of a long journey to equality and respect is within reach. The former has been a major proponent of the Famine memorial for Glasgow and the latter is a central player in advancing the plans for an Irish Centre in the city.

At present, parents who wish to pass on a positive sense of Irishness to their children in Scotland still face societal obstacles. In Scotland, Irish people learned throughout the twentieth century to be quiet and not to draw attention to themselves in order to be tolerated. However, toleration is not respect.

I examined my own country during the preparation of this book. Here in Ireland we have racists – every country has them. However, there is no public apology made for them and there are no journalists offering the banter defence as we had in Scotland with the Famine Song. This country is bending under the pressure of IMF-imposed austerity but there has been no *Daily Mail* scapegoating of the new Irish. In the world of politics there is no Hibernian equivalent of Golden Dawn, the recently formed neo-fascist movement that shames the land that gave the world that magic word "democracy". Greece and Ireland show that there can be a different response to similar stimuli.

Being second-generation Irish in Scotland is more culturally difficult in the developed world than anywhere else I have encountered. As Irish culture and Irishness have become "cool" across the globe, Scotland has abnormalised itself by the absence of any adequate recognition for the large section of her people who are of Irish heritage.

Yet, it seems to irk many people in Scotland if someone like me, or Kieron Brady, states quite calmly, with Scottish phonetics, that we are Irish. Thinking logically, given the geographic proximity and the historical closeness, it should be the opposite of what is the case today. Perhaps it is because of how Scotland carried out the ethnic cleansing of her own Gaels before the Famine Irish arrived in the middle of the late nineteenth century. When the refugees of An Gorta Mór arrived on the Broomielaw they were like ghosts of the old Alba.

I gave one of the Terence MacSwiney memorial lectures in the late 1980s as a guest of the Greater London Council under Ken Livingstone. I called my talk *The Irish in Scotland: Despised Aliens or Guardians of the true Scotland?* It remains a thesis that I have examined and tested for the last quarter of a century. The Famine Irish arrived in Victorian Scotland just at the point the Scottish elite had its imperial ducks in a row; the internal opposition in Scotland to Pax Britannica was dealt with in a fashion that would have made Niccolò di Bernardo dei Machiavelli smile at the ruthlessness employed.

The Gaelic clans of Ireland and their cousins in the north of Scotland were destroyed. Once clan society was dismantled, clan societies, often in North America, could safely be established. The tribal social formation that threatened the Hanoverian crown was over forever.

Of course, An Gorta Mór itself was an entirely man-made consequence of the massive dispossession and extirpation that had been inflicted upon the native Irish people in the mid-seventeenth century. When the Highlands came to be "cleared", North America was a reasonably convenient dumping ground for the communities that "improving landlords" no longer required.

The Irish who arrived in huge numbers in Glasgow during those decades carried with them various diseases and this alarmed the city fathers. However, the one that the British feared most was the virus of Fenianism. Many of the starving *spailpíni* had within their heads something possibly far more contagious than the insects that lived on them; unlike the other parts of the "Celtic fringe" in Ireland, a revolutionary separatist tradition had emerged from the native settler disputes of the sixteenth and seventeenth centuries.

Drawing on the ideas of revolutionary France, the secessionist colonies in America and movements like the Narodniks in Russia, the Fenian tradition in Ireland was highly unwelcome in Victorian Scotland. The Fenian Brotherhood viewed English predatory expansionism within these islands in much the same way as the great names in Scotland's heroic age. When Robert the Bruce needed allies to defeat the English he knew where to look. In this letter to the powerful Gaelic clans in the north of Ireland, he laid out why they should be on the same side against English predatory expansionism:

> Whereas we and you and our people and your people, free since ancient times, share the same national ancestry and are urged to come together more eagerly and joyfully in friendship by a common language and by common custom, we have sent you our beloved kinsman, the bearers of this letter, to negotiate with you in our name about permanently strengthening and maintaining inviolate the special friendship between us and you, so that with God's will our nation (nostra nacio) may be able to recover her ancient liberty.

Bruce's brother, Edward, was crowned High King of Ireland and died fighting the English in Ireland at Dundalk. The Scotland that the Famine Irish fled to in the mid-nineteenth century was a very different place. The Scotland that existed at the time of An Gorta Mór was British and proud of it. It was in that Scotland that the Irish were unwelcome, but needed.

As Glasgow and its Lanarkshire hinterland exploded in an eruption of enterprise and industrialisation and there was an insatiable need for labour, the Irish provided it in huge amounts. This was the Scotland that James Connolly was born into. It is another indicator of the low opinion that modern Scotland attaches to those of Irish heritage that James Connolly is hardly mentioned in polite circles, even on the left.

I regularly pass by the statue of Connolly across from the modern Liberty Hall. In the original building, he helped organise the Dublin working class during the 1913 lockout. Connolly and his Irish Citizen Army took part in the 1916 Easter Rising against British rule in Ireland. Dying from his wounds, he was strapped to a chair and executed in Kilmainham prison. Across the world, Connolly is hailed as a hero of the oppressed and the downtrodden. Only in Scotland is he ignored. At the Cowgate in Edinburgh there is a tiny plaque to mark where he was born.

Given that there seems to be a uniquely Scottish response to Irish immigration, it is logical to look at Scotland rather than the Irish. If that can be unpacked in a national conversation then I am sure in the home of David Hume the Scottish can achieve enlightenment on this issue. Confident cultures do not suppress others.

I have noted to colleagues that in the past few years of covering international football matches in Dublin, only the supporters of Scotland put so much effort into their match-day wardrobe. It is colourful and vibrant, and the Tartan Army is rightly famous for its friendly invasions. However, having recently watched Greeks and Poles arrive in Dublin, of course speaking Greek and Polish respectively, I have been struck by how understated they are in showcasing their patriotism. They have hats and scarves and a few flags, but that is largely the entire ensemble. I don't think this is a wardrobe malfunction on their part, rather it is an indication that they know who they are and they don't have to prove it to anyone else.

They did not, perhaps, feel the need to convince others and themselves of who they were. I think this is the collateral damage of being absorbed into a union with a much larger partner. Perhaps if Scotland becomes independent and is recognised as a nation in the world and not a region of the UK, the wardrobe at soccer matches can be a bit more informal. Perhaps if Scotland is at the United Nations in her own right it might help some of her sons and daughters recognise the validity of this Glaswegian's right to have an Irish passport.

It may also prevent any repetition of the racist abuse of Scottish-born players who decide to wear the green of Ireland and not the blue of Scotland. The treatment of Aiden McGeady and James McCarthy is not something that Scottish football or Scottish society can be proud of. It was a case of patriotism being the last refuge of the racist as the "he turned his back on Scotland" defence was offered. Once more, this was not the behaviour of a confident culture.

In Scotland today, particularly Glasgow, there is a new generation of young people of Irish ethnicity who have grown up in a new situation of occupational parity. Their aspirations and needs, *à la* Maslow, can be set higher. It is something that their kith and kin had in New York a century before; however, it has finally arrived in the Scotland of many cultures. It was shameful that a settled ethnic minority did not achieve this at any point in the twentieth century.

So, the frontline of this struggle for equality and respect has moved. The central focus now must be on the culture in its widest meaning. There is yet to emerge in Scottish writing a clear positive character self-defining herself or himself as second-generation Irish. Given the size and contribution of the Irish in Scotland throughout the twentieth century, this absence in Scottish literature is remarkable.

I suspect, and it is only a suspicion, that if other ethnic minorities in Scotland were similarly under-represented in contemporary writing, there would be conferences held about it. The concerned classes would no doubt opine that something must be done. However, the old paradigm of making the Irish as invisible as possible in the hope that they culturally disappear altogether still is partly extant.

Given the existence of an anti-Irish subculture, sometimes associated with football clubs such as Hearts and Rangers, it was a smart move for Irish people and those of Irish heritage to keep a low profile. Perhaps it is not surprising within such a milieu that cultural products evoking the Irish contribution to Scottish life were rare to non-existent. The lack of acknowledgment of the existence of a settled Irishness in Scottish life is such a common sense assumption it can draw strange looks from people when it is challenged.

A key player in this process has been the Catholic Church. Ironically, it was the crude correlation between attendance at faith schools and the declaration of that faith that provided hints of a buried ethnicity. When the Catholic Church reached a *rapprochement* with the local state by way of the 1918 Education Act, "Mother Church" already knew what was expected of her.

In Ireland, where many of Scotland's new Catholics hailed from, there had been a deal in place since the eighteenth century. The British exchequer funded Maynooth, the biggest Catholic seminary outside Southern Europe. This was not an act of ecumenical *largesse* from the British state, which was officially anti-Catholic as much as it was Protestant. Although the British monarchy only recently ditched the sexist law of primogeniture – whereby the first male born, not the first born, inherited the throne and all the nice big houses – it still has a ban on the monarch being Catholic or being married to a "Papist".

The French and Spanish clerics who ran Maynooth knew what the deal was; if the flock could be steered away from rebellions against British overlords then Christ and Caesar could be, as James Joyce said, hand in glove. The Catholic Church in Scotland knew that the new flock in the teeming slums of Glasgow's East End and in the grim mining villages of the Lanarkshire coalfield was viewed as a problem for the British state because of its Irishness, not its Catholicism.

The Irish revolutionary tradition that developed in the nineteenth century was notable for its strident anti-clericalism. The Fenians clearly saw themselves as part of the continental left that emerged out of the 1848 revolutions and convulsed Europe. Moreover, they saw the

Catholic Church, quite accurately, as an agent of British rule in Ireland. Subsequently, the state-funded Catholic schools in Scotland became very effective factories of de-Hibernisation. In my secondary school, the school chaplain was a Dubliner and he had a pre-revisionist worldview as an Irishman. Briefly, I had a history teacher from down the country, possibly Kilkenny. Between the pair of them they had something of a hedge school running in this British state-funded Catholic school that was expected to turn out Catholic Scots with no idea of Irishness, despite their names and family connections. This was not what the 1918 Education Act was meant to be.

Both the British state and the Catholic Church wanted docile Scottish Catholics bending to the will of Pope and Prime Minister. Perhaps because of my education in sociology, I enjoy watching groups of people, especially when they are in a foreign environment. If you look carefully you can often ascertain quite a lot about how members of the group see themselves. When I think of the impression that the Tartan Army made on me in Dublin and as I travelled back home to Donegal, I thought I had witnessed a self-consciously insecure nation.

Does the hostility to the asserting of an Irish identity in modern Scotland point to fragility in Scottish self-esteem? The same response to the Irish is, in the main, not found in England's great cities where the Irish settled in large numbers in the twentieth century. The Scots, very much the junior partners in the United Kingdom, perhaps felt uneasy about even acknowledging this ethnic minority within their midst.

There were xenophobic responses to Irish immigration in Scotland in the 1920s and 1930s and what now remains is, as Professor Tom Devine styles it, "attitudinal discrimination". In 2009 two young men in Glasgow were arrested for singing the Irish national anthem. The officer told the court he knew it was "a sectarian song" and he, along with a police colleague, arrested the men. That this even got to court was instructive. The case was thrown out. However, the fact remains that in 2009 in the Scotland of many cultures, a constable admitted using his powers of arrest on the basis that the Irish national anthem was "sectarian". This same police force turned down several offers of equality training around matters *apropos* Irishness and Irish political expression in both 2011 and 2012.

As this book was being prepared, my attention was brought to a piece on an online football magazine which stated that Irish political chants at Scottish football grounds were "an infestation" and "the plague". I doubt that had the political expressions emanated from people of, say,

Kashmiri background and related to the conflict there that the lexicon of diseases would be used.

Only the Irish in Scotland are fair game for this type of racist grand-standing. Attempts at hostile assimilation tend to produce a reaction. One strategy is simply to leave. I knew when my son was a toddler that if my wife and I remained in Glasgow we would be bringing our child up in a society that was toxic to Irishness. That bright toddler is now a twenty-year-old undergraduate at Trinity College in Dublin, Ireland's elite university which was once the citadel of the British Raj here.

When Trinity was an outpost of that mythical place "West Britain", the idea of an Irish Republic taking its place among the nations of the world was as fanciful as two Scottish women marrying and voting to remove their country from the grip of Westminster. Our son is a product of Gaelscoileanna and he represents the new Ireland. His two sisters, the youngest born here, are on a similar trajectory. Decisions that are taken for children should be considered and thought through because it is they who have to live with the consequences.

My wife and I have often discussed over the years the decision we both made in the mid-1990s. I saw last year in Bordeaux how the French welcomed people into their country. I was there to take part in work for the European Council's Media Against Racism in Sport (MARS) project. My Spanish colleague and I were given the task of seeking out the Latin American community in the city. What we witnessed was uplifting. Of course, migrant workers from Peru and political refugees from the Chilean coup did not have any colonial baggage with the French state. Large cities in France have, let's be frank, ghettoes of people of North African ethnicity, mainly Algerian, with all of that bad history between coloniser and colonised.

However, the policy of the French state was clearly to give people their cultural space, while at the same time requiring them to abide by the mores of the French Republic. Creating a positive space for Irishness in modern Scotland would enhance active citizenship. At present it is kettled by a political elite which perhaps privately shares some of the views of the Famine Song choir.

For the denizens of Holyrood, people like Kieron Brady and I shouldn't exist. We were meant to be socialised into homogenous Scots with any trace of Irish ethnicity excised by education and the relentless public narrative. If Scottish society embraced respect for the Irish in the modern Scottish nation, those in leadership positions might be sur-prised to find that many thousands of Scottish-born people feel exactly the same way as Kieron Brady did when he reached his home parish of Cloughaneely. He instinctively felt that he was home and he would be welcomed as such.

As I was writing this section, the Scottish media was tiptoeing around why Jon Daly of Dundee United might be going to play for New Rangers. I have written for several years about the apparent inability of Rangers (1872–2012) to source a player from the Republic of Ireland. The mainstream discussed it as "curious" that the Ibrox club had never had a Republic of Ireland player in modern times – indeed, not since the Football Association of Ireland (FAI) was established as the FIFA-recognised authority for the twenty-six county state at the end of World War II.

Out of the hundred and ninety-one professional football clubs on the island of Britain, one hundred and ninety have fielded a full or under-21 Republic of Ireland international player in their first teams within the last two decades. That the odd team out had fans who could conjure up the Famine Song should have been homed in on by the Scottish media. Instead, the lack of Republic of Ireland players at Rangers was not examined.

The story of Alan Smith, a young Dubliner who signed for the Ibrox club in 2010 after UEFA received a dossier from a west of Ireland MEP in 2009 about Rangers' employment policies *apropos* the Irish was not picked up. If any team in Scotland had fans singing racist songs about, say, people of colour and it was the only team in Britain to have been unable to find a black player for their first team, I suspect that the mainstream media in Scotland would have been all over it.

Moreover, if a political representative from an African country had written to the footballing authorities about it, it would have been a huge story in Scotland. Once this discriminatory system is fully dismantled it will be no more unthinkable to have a Republic of Ireland international playing for the home side at Ibrox than having a team called Rangers languishing in the bottom tier of professional football in Scotland.

The MEP who sent that dossier also noted that the club's fans sang anti-Irish songs. This was the same year a police officer in the club's home town thought that the Irish national anthem was "sectarian". As I write this, Alan Smith has just made his first team debut for New Rangers, ironically against a team from Northern Ireland, Linfield, in a friendly match at Ibrox. When the young goalkeeper is on international duty he will sing his country's anthem, a song that for some in Glasgow remains culturally unacceptable and, for at least two police officers in 2009, an arrestable offence.

There will be no adequate cultural space in Scotland for Irishness until anti-Irish racism is called out as such. The failure of wider society in Scotland to provide cultural space and respect to people of Irish ethnicity throughout the twentieth century is more remarkable when it is stated as thus. Scotland's largest city has yet to fully embrace the concept of multiculturalism.

Indeed, denial of the space to be second-generation Irish in Scotland seems to be woven into the fabric of modern Scottish society, so much so that people barely realise they are part of that system. This discriminatory system could not operate if it was only reliant on the klan at Ibrox, the subculture that grew up around Rangers Football Club in the twentieth century; it is much wider than that.

A Scotland capable of fully embracing the Irishness of some of its people is a better country. British Scotland was forged by physically and culturally suppressing the old Alba. Subsequently, the Famine Irish arrived in a Caledonia that was demoralised and Balmoralised. They were alien in Scotland the way that Bruce's men at Bannockburn would have been out of place.

British Scotland also brought in people from the north-east of Ireland, many of them the descendants of people decanted from Scotland in the early seventeenth century. As a power play in Machiavellian statecraft, the "planation of Ulster" created the basis of a native settler dispute that has still not fully healed. That garrison community developed its own subculture: that of Orangeism.

The Orange Order was formed in Loughgall in Neil Lennon's native County Armagh after the 1795 Battle of the Diamond. It was a bloody brawl along sectarian lines and it was central to the origin myth of the Orange Order. The population of County Armagh at the time was roughly evenly divided between Catholics and Protestants. There had been a history in the county of intermittent sectarian feuds between the Protestant "Peep O' Day Boys" and the Catholic "Defenders". This violence culminated on 21 September 1795, when a well-armed Protestant mob, confident of the protection of local magistrates, clashed with Catholic Defenders and four or five Defenders were slain. That same night, a body of magistrates, squires and parsons in County Armagh met together and formed the Mother Lodge of the Orange Society.

The new organisation copied the rituals from Freemasonry and another oath-bound society was born in Ireland. This date is now the toast of any gathering of the Orange Order. It happened at the same time others in Ulster from the Protestant tradition were swelling the ranks of the Republican United Irishmen. The Orangemen won out, and the secular radicalism of the early Protestant Republicans was drowned out by the noise of Lambeg drums beating out tribal anthems.

Three years later, an uprising led by a Dublin Protestant, Theobald Wolfe Tone, supported by Protestants in Antrim and Catholics in Mayo, was brutally suppressed. The Orange Order became culturally dominant among people who are today styled as "Ulster Scots", but in the eighteenth century considered themselves Irish. The partition of Ireland at the end of the War of Independence essentially gave the Protestants of Ulster their own state. It was the United Kingdom's first experiment in devolution.

From the vantage point of Ireland and living in a border county I can see how a discourse emerged in Northern Ireland about creating space for traditions that have been historically antagonistic. Fifteen years on from the Good Friday Agreement this is a process rather than an event. There is still much to do, but much has been done.

Creating cultural space for each tradition was key to moving the process forward. What is currently lacking in modern Scotland is that which is, for example, afforded to Italians without Scottish self-esteem being in any way diminished. The future in Scotland can be that of another country. If nationalism is now the dominant force in the life of the nation then it is vital that the national dress is not a straitjacket constructed in the kailyard.

The SNP long ago embraced civic nationalism and eschewed blood-and-soil rhetoric. Quite simply, you are a Scot if you live in Scotland. Part of that narrative is that people of many cultures can make up the patchwork quilt of the new nation that the SNP wants to be fully independent. Within that paradigm, then, the expression of Irishness in all of its forms should be afforded parity of esteem.

Scotland will become one nation of many cultures when people of Irish ethnicity feel empowered to declare that in the public space without fearing arrest, assault or ridicule. When that day happens, Scotland will have arrived in the future that some of us dream about.

Scotland's British problem

21 September 2008

Racists always make sense. They make sense to themselves and other racists, presuming, of course, that they are of the same perceived racial/ ethnic group.

For the last five hundred years the dominant ethnic group on the planet has been the white western European group. That much is undeniable and self-evident. At the top of that particular racial pile a hundred years ago were the British. The Germans tried to topple the British, but they failed. However, despite their failure to take out Britain, Germany drained the strength of the London state, and in the end the colonials in America had to save the old country with Lend Lease. The North European white tribe had a new leader. The old boys in London didn't realise this until Suez in 1956.

Now, of course, it is the Americans who are the top dogs and the British bulldog knows it. The Ivy League Blue Bloods who have run the American state since the creation of the USA represent an unbroken racial supremacy dating back to Henry VIII. Within western Europe the expansion of strong states to incorporate "peripheral cultures of low prestige" was brilliantly mapped out by Michael Hechter in *Internal Colonialism* (1999). He used the example of the expansion of the London state to become the dominant power in the north European archipelago.

Of all the subject peoples of these islands, the rural Irish, remaining Catholic after the Reformation and emotionally thirled to the Brehon laws, even after Cromwellian ethnic cleansing, remained outside the emotional contract with London. Like all peoples of internal colonies they provide military and industrial recruits to the power centre. The Irish who flocked to British cities were no different to Bretons and Corsicans who provided the French republic with its soldiers and factory fusiliers. The descendants of these reluctant *arrivistes* have several paths to take and these routes are often marked out for them by the powerful. They can remain distinct by being systematically excluded and ghettoised like European Jewry. They can fully integrate and become indistinguishable like the Cornish who provided greater Wessex with agricultural labour.

The Glasgow Irish over the last hundred and fifty years are probably somewhere in the middle. At no time were the Irish locked up in ghettoes, although there was a limit to their social mobility. In Scotland there was a tartan ceiling that the Irish could not pass through.

As late as the 1960s, a certain major Scottish bank had a formal ban on Catholics being employed there. Now, of course, that Scottish bank is no longer a Scottish bank, but in the 1960s it was owned and run by Scots. Catholic was a handy badge to identify and exclude members of the Irish community. However, the social division was never truly about religion. Just like Rangers Football Club, everyone, including the Catholics, knew the rules. Some Catholics did better than others.

Rangers supporters sing and chant about "Fenian bastards" not "Catholic bastards". It wasn't a crime to be an Italian Scot. They remained fiercely Catholic. Their homeland was a republic and was home to the Pope. Italy had sided with the Axis powers in World War II. Yet, a benign integration, while being allowed to remain distinctly Italian, was afforded them. If only the Irish had been able to make ice cream!

As ever, politics is in everything. Despite being Catholic from the losing side of World War II the Italians in Scotland did not represent the threat to the entire British project that the Irish did. In the late nineteenth century a Scottish Catholic cleric, Bishop Grey, was concerned about the Irish refugees and argued with an Irish colleague, Bishop Devine. Given that both bishops were probably Catholics we can probably rule out religious intolerance in this one!

The issue was that the Irish were Fenians. The Irish had, among their number, revolutionaries who wished the empire nothing but ill will. Karl Marx was alive and writing at this time and noted a definitive difference between the Irish and the British proletariat. The Famine and the Land War in Ireland had produced the Fenian Brotherhood. The first act of asymmetrical warfare in modern times in these islands – the Clerkenwell explosion – introduced dynamite to the arsenal of the Irish revolutionary. The Catholicism of the Irish was never the issue for the host community. Fenianism was the issue. The armed threat to the state was the problem, not transubstantiation.

The Fenian fuse finally reached its logical destination in Easter 1916. The Proclamation is the written statement of a cultural revolution. It mapped out the end of Greater England. Historians may yet write that it was the beginning of the end of the London state's grip on this archipelago. The Republic of Ireland is – as Alex Salmond says – "an independence success story". That long journey to being such a success story started in Easter 1916, and is justifiably celebrated by the Irish people and the Irish state. The British send a representative, and wreaths are laid by the Irish Army and the British Army. Thankfully, all of this is in the past, and the Dublin state and the London state could not be closer allies on many issues.

Anti-Irish racism was a creation of the centrifugal force of the London state at its zenith. Although there had been writings about the barbarous Irish as far back as the twelfth century. Giraldus Cambrensis (Gerald of Wales) was also very Catholic. That centrifuge is slowing down now. We may be in the end of days for the British state. It will not, in my opinion, survive full Scottish freedom. Finally, the auld sang could begin again. That new beginning for Scotland will, necessarily, be the end of Britishness. The Scots who berate the Glasgow Irish may finally stop wearing England shirts at Ibrox and realise how appallingly they behaved when they were England's docile natives. One cannot explain the Famine Song of recent controversy without understanding the different roles that the Catholic Irish and the Protestant Scots played in the British Empire when that empire was in existence. The British Empire is, of course, a thing of the past. A historical fact, but something that is done with, over, finished and never to return.

The centre of that empire – which once spanned the globe – is now in terminal decline. The UK is now struggling even to be a junior ally of the US empire, which is also starting to stumble in the imperial game as China waits its turn. The new Scotland can have no place for the league of empire Loyalists with their visceral hatred of the Irish. Scotland, like Ireland, can play a full part in the development of a European polity. The "mother country", so loved by the England shirt-wearing Rangers fans will soon be too busy dealing with the home-grown jihadist in Bradfordistan to notice that the descendants of a successful English annexation in the eighteenth century are finally being themselves again – just like the Irish. I am confident that more and more Scots will find their confidence and their voice to take their place among nations once more.

I am glad I came home to Ireland, but I wish the country of my birth well in dealing with their British problem at Ibrox. For if Scotland is to progress and take its place among the nations of the world, the Ibrox psychosis will need to be finally dealt with.

Ibrox "racist" banner criticised

14 January 2009

An ex-Republic of Ireland international and anti-racism expert has slammed the official inaction on anti-Irish racism in Scotland after the most recent stunt by supporters of Glasgow Rangers. At the recent Old Firm match in Glasgow, Rangers supporters unfurled a banner with a bus on it imploring that the city's Irish community should go back to Ireland. The banner was made by the Blue Order, the Ibrox club's official fan club.

Kieron Brady, a Glaswegian who played for Sunderland and the Republic of Ireland, is recognised as one of the leading anti-racist educationalists in the country. Until recently, he worked for the charity Show Racism the Red Card. "The banner is undoubtedly racist," Brady said on the development. "Many familiar with recent events surrounding anti-Irish racism would opine that the banner is a derivation of the Famine Song's motivations, only expressed visually as opposed to vocally. The reference to Stranraer and how the word 'offended' is constructed leaves those who view the banner under no illusion that its target group is the Irish diaspora in Scotland, and despite what many in Scotland may think, stemming from the principles of equality, the Irish community have the same rights not to be discriminated against as any other ethnic or immigrant grouping.

"My view is that this banner is indicative of a profound intolerance of the aforementioned community," he continued. "I fail to see how it can be viewed otherwise. I personally find it sad that a supporters' collective can sate their prejudice by altering the well-documented manifestation of anti-Irish racism. To substantiate the claim of its profoundness I would point to the fact that the police, as well as anti-racist groups with expertise in this field, had deemed the Famine Song racist, yet this particular group of supporters still insisted on the creation of a banner similarly themed, and on the face of it were willing to discount any subsequent implications."

Brady fired a salvo at the Ibrox club itself: "The attitude of Rangers as a club and the accompanying rhetoric is in stark contrast to how clubs deal with racism by and large in England.

"Clubs on the whole condemn the racism almost instantaneously and take steps to ensure the racists are located and consequently prohibited from stadia. The lukewarm utterances of those in the employ of Rangers only serve to illustrate that they have comprehended that this represents a unique, significant and serious problem, irrespective of whether we deal in the semantics of a 'minority'."

Brady continued: "If there were a forthright perception that this is a small minority that continuously besmirch the name and image of the club then surely it would not be beyond the realms of possibility for those in the higher echelons of Rangers FC to issue a statement asserting that those who hold anti-Irish attitudes are no longer welcome at Ibrox Park.

"All that said, I am aware that Rangers FC does engage with groups campaigning against racism and other forms of intolerance," he said.

"However, as encouraging as education in the bowels of Ibrox may be through the week, there is a futility if there is a lack of preparedness to banish those from the stadium who are incapable of attendance at fixtures without voicing their ingrained prejudice."

Brady received support from Scottish politicians in the governing SNP. Alasdair Allan, the Scottish National Party MSP for the Western Isles, said: "However generously you try to interpret this banner, I am afraid its unambiguous message is that families who have lived in Scotland for a hundred and fifty years should be 'repatriated'. I don't think Scotland can put up with intolerance on that scale and I would welcome the fact that all Scottish football clubs are now working to eradicate these embarrassing displays of ignorance."

Professor Christopher Harvie MSP, SNP member for Mid Scotland and Fife, said: "The folk who get their kicks out of the Famine Song and this provocative football banner vegetate on their own sad wee planet. No one wants to visit it, or them."

Exclusive interview with James MacMillan

12 May 2009

Ten years ago, Scottish composer and conductor James MacMillan gave a lecture at the Edinburgh Festival, entitled *Scotland's Shame: Anti-Catholicism as a Barrier to Genuine Pluralism*. The response from the Scottish media was immediate, hostile and, on one occasion, somewhat underhand. In an interview with the *Guardian* in 2006 he related a telephone interview with the *Sunday Herald*.

MacMillan was sure that the call was being recorded or monitored in some way – perhaps set up as a conference call. Perhaps the people on the other end of the line wanted him to trip himself up or say something damning. He did hear someone in the background saying to his interviewer, "Ask him if he's Opus Dei!" The classical musician couldn't help but let out a guffaw. MacMillan had clearly touched a raw nerve.

The time and place of his lecture would have added to the collective pain the Scottish establishment must have felt. The entire artistic world spends a month in Edinburgh every summer. MacMillan has been described as Scotland's most successful musical export. In the age of celebrity this internationally feted composer and conductor was telling the world how it was to be a Catholic boy growing up in Kilwinning.

Moreover, he was saying that things were still difficult for Scotland's Catholic minority.

Ten years on from his speech, I was grateful that James MacMillan took time out from a busy schedule and afforded me the time to answer my questions so fully and frankly.

Where were you born?
In Kilwinning, Ayrshire.

You are from a Catholic background. Were you aware of any social exclusion that your community endured during your childhood?
I was aware of tensions, which manifested themselves in unpleasant ways. Prejudice was rife – seemingly part of the majoritarian attitude to Catholics in the area, and outright discrimination was very much in the living memory of relatives, who remembered jobs being advertised in the 1930s and 1940s with the proviso that no Catholics need apply. Elements within the Church of Scotland had campaigned for the repatriation of the Catholic Irish right up to the 1930s. The Kirk apologised for this a few years ago. Much of the debate here now revolves round whether actual discrimination is still current or not.

Research by Williams and Walls of the MRC Social and Public Health Sciences Unit at Glasgow University has argued that there is indeed still a lingering problem relating to social deprivation among the Catholic Irish descendants. This is vehemently challenged, though, by other academics like Steve Bruce and Michael Rosie. They, and others like Graham Walker, are also campaigners for a specific understanding of Scottish working-class Protestant culture. Not for nothing are they known as the Orange Order's favourite sociologists. Others, like Professor David McCrone, are suspiciously keen to argue that there is no such thing as an Irish community in Scotland. There are good reasons to enquire as to what motivates these non-objective, self-proclaimed experts in this matter. Joe Bradley would be worth speaking to about this.

It has been said that anti-Catholic sentiment in modern Scotland is merely a misunderstanding of another phenomenon – that of anti-Irish racism. Would you agree with that?
These two prejudices are complicatedly intertwined. I have a great deal of sympathy with those who want to stress the ethnic dimension, because they are clearly correct. However, it would be a mistake to

dismiss the purely religious aspect of this issue. Scotland has been historically vehement in its anti-popery since the Reformation, centuries before Irish immigration. The Scottish cultural Protestant mindset is programmed to be aggressive about Catholicism. Secular commentators might want to play this down nowadays, but this is the dark theological hinterland to the current debate.

Since you "went public" on your views of Scotland's anti-Catholic underbelly, what has been the response to you personally?
Catholics are generally well disposed towards me, as I articulated an argument many would make in private but shy away from expressing in the public square, for obvious reasons. Anyone who does this is attacked. Many in the media tried to assassinate my character and motivations at the time of my speech in 1999. This has made me very wary and choosy about dealing with the Scottish media and other aspects of public life here. I have just swung my wider focus onto the outside world where I can be a composer, pure and simple. I have created a little cocoon for myself in Glasgow, which is populated by family and friends.

In retrospect, though, it seems that most have come round to my analysis, in that there has been a grudging acceptance that there is a problem here that needs to be addressed. That suits me just fine, as that was the intention of the speech in the first place. The embarrassment and surprise factors were crucial at the time. This was a good lesson to learn, and will well serve the new campaign to confront anti-Irish racism in Scottish football.

What is your view of the Famine Song?
It is utterly disgraceful, nakedly sectarian and racist. It has no redeeming factors whatsoever.

What has been your assessment of the official response to this controversy?
I am not surprised that the condemnation of the fans that sing this has been less than robust. Scottish life is full of the nudge-and-wink acceptance of anti-Irish/Catholic bigotry. Sports journalists are the worst, with a few honourable exceptions. However, Kieron Brady is on to a winner with this campaign. There is no way official Scotland can wriggle out of this. I am looking forward to seeing it all develop.

What needs to be done in the future if the Famine Song continues to be heard in Scottish football stadia?

The response needs to be ultra-strict expulsions, lifelong bans. It is easy to pinpoint the perpetrators. Police cameras are trained on the crowds at every game. There is no excuse.

James, we're the same age, and I recall in the 1970s that my family in the west of Scotland were worried about the prospect of Scottish self-government as an Edinburgh parliament could bring in the policies of old Stormont, further socially excluding the Catholic minority of Scotland. Can you recall a similar fear in your Ayrshire childhood?

Yes, I remember this very well. Although the anxiety lingers a little bit in some quarters, it is clear that things have changed. Catholics just need to be politically astute in the new situation. For example, we all know that New Labour is riddled with ideological atheists who want to smash Catholic education. The SNP have been trying to make inroads into the west of Scotland Catholic vote for years. They know one way to do that is to be seen publicly defending faith schools. Politically astute Catholics know this is just an opportunist ploy, but we can use that to our advantage. It is important that, instead of throwing our lot in with one party against the other, as was the case in the past, we learn to play one off against the other. It makes life more interesting, if nothing else!

It is ten years since you gave a lecture entitled Scotland's Shame: Anti-Catholicism as a Barrier to Genuine Pluralism – *do you still stand by that view or has your view changed?*

I think my earlier answer might have covered this. Basically the disgraceful, nationwide scenes around Aiden McGeady and James McCarthy point to unfinished business. The shame clearly lingers on. I'm just amazed that official Scotland isn't willing to see it. Heads in the sand again.

You mention the treatment of McCarthy and McGeady. Had they been, say, Scottish-born of Italian heritage and had opted to play for Italy, do you think that they would have endured the abuse they have as Republic of Ireland players?

No. The Scottish nativist bigot has a special hatred for Irish Catholics because of the political dimension, which colours the relationship that Scotland has had with Ireland from the seventeenth century to recent times.

Kevin McDaid RIP

27 May 2009

I watched the news footage of Ally McCoist dancing on his toes on the Tannadice turf waving a union flag. I thought at the time, I wonder how this plays in the North. For some Rangers supporters in Coleraine, the day was almost perfect as the final whistle sounded at Tannadice and their team were SPL champions. They had waited since 2005 to be able to say that their team was the best in Scotland. In any footballing culture across the planet it would have been a signal for a party.

It doesn't matter if it is Barca or Burnley, your team has emerged at the top of the pile after a tough season. You're champions and there isn't a feeling like it for any football fan. Rangers, of course, have a great following in the north of Ireland. These supporters are loyal; unfortunately, some of them are also Loyalist. While most Rangers supporters across the world were happy to party into the night, the Loyalists in Coleraine needed something else to celebrate their team's triumph – a dead Taig. Any Taig would do. They're not that fussy.

Kevin McDaid's crime was that he was Catholic. He was 49. A family man and a plasterer by trade, Kevin spent a lot of his free time doing voluntary community work. He had just returned from a fishing trip he had arranged for young lads from both traditions. Before his murder, Kevin was arranging another cross-community trip to take young people out of the area on the twelfth of July.

His widow, Evelyn, is a Protestant. She was also badly beaten by the mob as she tried to save her husband. His bruised wife told of the man she had lost and how her Kevin would have wanted no revenge. As I write, another victim of Sunday's SPL celebrations in Coleraine, Damian Fleming, is unconscious in hospital. He is in critical condition and is unlikely to survive. Had these murders happened in Mississippi in the 1950s and the attacking crowd had used a rope and a tree, we would have described the death of Kevin McDaid as a lynching.

A feature of the lynching in the Deep South was the official tolerance of the local police. As Robert Hamill had his head repeatedly jumped on by a Loyalist mob in 1997, members of the RUC looked on impassively from a Land Rover a few yards away. That the RUC behaved in this fashion has been forensically established and is not contested.

What is now being alleged by McDaid's twenty-two-year-old son, Ryan, is that the PSNI did something similar as his father was being murdered. Ryan alleged that there was a police car only a hundred yards from the scene of the murder. Mrs McDaid said that the attackers claimed they were members of the Ulster Defence Association (UDA). The PSNI was quick to wheel out Assistant Chief Constable Alistair Finlay to rebut these allegations. Finlay stated that there was "no evidence this was anything other than a maverick group of yobs".

Local people said the group could have been as large as forty strong. Assistant Chief Constable Finlay, who defended the police's handling of the incident, also denied a claim by McDaid's family that officers stood by while he was being attacked. "This is not something that we're aware of, but if anybody has any information on that we would ask them to contact us and share that information with us," Finlay said. "Police arrived very quickly after the initial phone calls and there were up to sixty people engaged in hand-to-hand fighting. Two neighbourhood police officers moved to make an initial arrest of one of the main aggressors, but such was the hostility of the crowd that they had to withdraw and move to rendering first aid."

These officers have weapons and legal authority for their use – a man was being murdered, yet they withdrew? It is hardly surprising, perhaps, that many in the nationalist community in the six counties think that the PSNI isn't that different from the RUC. The widely held belief in some nationalist areas is that the PSNI will observe a Catholic being beaten to death, as Robert Hamill was, and it's no big deal.

Mrs McDaid claimed that the men who murdered her husband said they were members of the UDA. Moreover, she claimed they said that they were "going to clean up this Fenian hole". This, of course, is the rationale of the ethnic cleansers in Bosnia. There is, in the Loyalist subculture of Northern Ireland, a wet dream that sees the creation of something akin to an Ulster *Volkstaat*, a land free of Fenians. The PSNI has now warned Ryan McDaid, Kevin's son, that there is a credible threat against his life from Loyalists. This warning came the day after I watched Frankie Gallagher of the UDA's political wing, the Ulster Political Research Group (UPRG), state that the UDA had no hand, act, or part in Kevin McDaid's murder or the attack in the Heights area on Sunday.

I realise that there might be a certain comedic value in writing UDA, political and research in the same sentence. However, there isn't any of this that is in any way amusing. I know. I've been to Coleraine and come to close quarters with these fine fellows. I was last in Coleraine over ten years ago. I was lecturing at the school of social work at the

University of Ulster, Magee College in Derry city. The university's main campus is in Coleraine and I had a student on placement there. Subsequently, I spent a fair amount of time in the town over the period of an academic year.

One day in particular I visited my student at her placement and travelled there by car. When I came out of the health centre my Donegal-registered car was surrounded by youths, many of them in Rangers shirts. About half of them were carrying some type of weapon. I saw at least two baseball bats. They were deep in discussion about what they were going to do with the owner of the car parked in their area. I walked up behind the lad who seemed to be the leader. He was holding a golf club but I rather thought he wasn't that into the ancient game.

"Get off my car!" They spun round and were startled by two factors: one, my Scottish accent and two, my appearance. I was straight out of central casting in my tweed jacket, polo neck, clutching a University of Ulster folder in front of me like a shield. "Which is the correct road to Londonderry?" It was more of an order than a polite request. I knew the road back to Doire very well indeed, but any doubters in this underclass lynch mob melted. This was a British gentleman giving them orders! The psychological climate immediately changed. The ambience changed from menace to deference. They were being talked down to by a university lecturer and one from the mother country.

Their rapid transformation from a menacing feral pack of teenage thugs to a ragtag honour guard was pathetic and unnerving in equal measure. One of them actually attempted a salute to the grandson of a member of the West Mayo Flying Column as I drove out of that red, white and blue twilight zone. All warfare is based on deception. My view of the defenders of Coleraine has not changed. They are the trailer trash of a dead empire.

A few weeks after that incident, I bumped into the sadly departed Marjorie "Mo" Mowlam. Our paths first crossed many years earlier when I was an undergrad reading politics at York and she was a newly elected MP. She had an amazing talent for remembering faces because she remembered mine. I told her of the positive impression she had on me when she visited. She had given a lecture on being an MP and being a woman in a gentleman's club. Mo winked at me and said, "I was shaggable then!"

I blushed. Her disarming vulgarity revealed a real warm heart and great courage. What I didn't know was that she was battling with a serious illness and was wearing a wig, her hair gone due to chemotherapy. We swapped vignettes over a cup of coffee before the powerpoints began about her sojourn in the sick counties. It was clear that this left-wing Englishwoman detested the tattooed Loyalists. Looking back, it must have taken a lot for her to go into the Maze prison to speak with Loyalist prisoners. She did it for peace, but she didn't like doing it.

She asked me if I knew a place called Rathcoole. I certainly did, I told her. I had a student there on placement. She said that one of her staff was organising a trip for her there earlier in the year. He had gone out to the place she was visiting – as I recall, it was some kind of family centre. The usual gable-end murals were a bit worse for wear and clearly needed touching up. People in the fiercely Loyalist estate knew that the Queen's minister was about to visit their little loyal sink estate. They did get the paintbrushes out for the murals of Derry's Walls and King William at the Boyne. That much I expected. What I heard next amazed me: the painters – young Loyalists under the direction of senior paramilitary figures who ran Rathcoole as their fiefdom – told the lads to paint out the murals. The gable-ends were painted grey. Mo Mowlam was swished past grey gable-ends. The day after her ministerial visit the mural painters were out again and brand new murals of King Billy on the Boyne were created.

Most of my teaching time at Magee was spent filling in for a colleague on sabbatical. He taught the mental health component of the social work degree so I was covering his classes. This Rathcoole community was fiercely loyal, but perhaps embarrassed to show that loyalty to the Queen's minister. "Yeah," I thought, "there is a PhD in this lot."

There is a belief among some northern nationalists that the behaviour of these Loyalist lynch mobs has the tacit approval of some unionist politicians. DUP councillor Adrian McQuillan on the BBC's *Newsline* was classic: "Tit for tat all the time. What reason can you see for there being tricolours up yesterday afternoon, a Sunday afternoon? None other than for to get a reaction from the Loyalist community and they certainly got a reaction this time, which is very sad."

"Tit for tat"? Robert Hamill, Michael McIlveen and Kevin McDaid were all Catholics killed in similar circumstances – all battered to death by Loyalist mobs. "Tit for tat" implies some degree of reciprocity. There is none. I watched McQuillan's statement about "a reaction" and I was dismayed. It sounded like a plea in mitigation. I hope I'm wrong about that but if I'm correct then Northern Ireland remains the sick counties when I thought that the new dispensation was a way through to community health. A reasonable person might well ask: "What kind of men would do such things?"

Within a crowd of forty – even self-selecting from the Coleraine Rangers gene pool – there might be one, perhaps two genuine socio-paths. The men who murdered Kevin McDaid weren't sociopaths, nor, I am sure, had they recently been released from secure psychiatric facili-ties. Like the respectable men who strung up black men from trees in the "good ol' days" in Alabama, they were psychologically normal. What was aberrant was the belief system that socialised them. Like the men of Reserve Police Battalion 101 so brilliantly analysed by Christopher R. Browning in his book *Ordinary Men*, these particular ordinary men in Coleraine are, like Hitler's killers on the eastern front, the products of a deeply sick culture. The Loyalists who murdered Kevin McDaid are, of course, responsible for their own actions and, hopefully, they will be prosecuted to the limit of the law.

Dealing with the individuals doesn't explain, however, why it is always a Loyalist mob and the victim is always a "Taig". The murder of Kevin McDaid was an act of cultural complicity. Twenty, thirty or forty men may have beaten him, but an entire subculture affirmed their hatred and their violence. If a group sings a song that has lyrics like "We're up to our knees in Fenian blood, surrender or you'll die" then don't be too surprised if they do in fact end up splashing in the blood of Fenians.

I'm sure Kevin McDaid, if given the chance, would have surrendered to save his life so that he could continue to be a husband to Evelyn and a father to his children. He couldn't be afforded that because some peo-ple's idea of a perfect day for Rangers FC means a Taig has to die. Kevin McDaid was not as fortunate as PC Mike Regan, who escaped with his life as a pack of Rangers supporters kicked him to the ground last May in Manchester as the Queen's underclass wrecked the city. No, they aren't ordinary football supporters, but they do feel affirmed at Ibrox and that is something the club has to address one day.

After the match on Sunday, Ally McCoist enthused about Kyle Lafferty as his "big Ulster gazelle". Everyone knows that it is highly unlikely that a Rangers manager would be enthusing about a player from Cork or Dublin because Rangers have been apparently unable over the past twenty-five years to find a suitable player from the Republic of Ireland. That hard truth is a key component of the emotional contract between Rangers FC and the men who murdered Kevin McDaid in Coleraine last Sunday.

Showing respect in Coleraine

4 June 2009

Kevin McDaid has been laid to rest. His funeral, like all funerals, was an occasion of sadness, but this was a complicated grief – complicated because Kevin was murdered. The cortege stopped and fell silent and still at the spot where Rangers supporters repeatedly jumped on his head last Sunday as they celebrated their team's league triumph by killing a Taig. Across the river the silence was broken as a Loyalist band played anthems of hate. Was this an utterly cruel coincidence or a calculated mark of disrespect?

Given the sickness that infects some of the population of Coleraine you would not need to be a cynic to plump for the latter explanation. Chances are, as with most things in life, it was merely cruel chance. However, one would have thought that the drum-banging classes of Coleraine society would think that they should be keeping a low profile at the moment. Not a bit of it. As they say in the criminal fraternity, the town of Coleraine has form.

Michael Clifford, in the *Sunday Tribune*, revealed: "Back in the old days, a curfew bell used to ring through Coleraine nightly at 9 p.m. The bell tolled for the town's Catholics, instructing them to return across the river Bann to their ghetto in Killowen. By the time the practice ended in 1954, the tolling had been relegated from instruction to tradition, but still held huge symbolic significance. The town council's decision to discontinue the practice was informed by budgetary considerations, rather than any attempt at conciliation."

When David Trimble accepted his Nobel Prize during his heyday at the centre of the peace process, he told an enthralled global audience that the unionist-dominated Northern Ireland was a cold house for the Catholic minority. Although he was talking about the province generally, I'm sure he could have been considering places like Coleraine specifically.

This week Coleraine was back in the local news in the North. It was the official opening of the town hall – one hundred and fifty years after it was built. This civic ceremony was, like the Loyalist band breaking the silence on the day of Kevin McDaid's funeral, either highly unfortunate or a shabby attempt at some positive PR for the town. It was a gushing piece of TV journalism: a town crier in nineteenth-century garb was shown doing his bell-ringing hear ye! hear ye! gig. Of course, when Coleraine had a chap doing that job for real it also had a curfew for Catholics. It probably wasn't the best week to be harking back to those days. Councillor David Barbour was enthusiastic about the official opening, saying: "This is who we are!"

Not a single unionist politician saw fit to pay their respects to Kevin McDaid at his funeral, not even his MP. Given the potential political importance of this murder, one would have thought Kevin's MP would be in attendance. Gregory Campbell MP is the honourable member for East Londonderry, which covers Coleraine and, now, the remains of Kevin McDaid. Gregory Campbell, of course, is a well-known Rangers supporter. He attempted to divert media attention away from the racist and anti-Irish Famine Song late last year.

Of course, the sickness that infects Coleraine isn't a matter of religion *simpliciter*. Kevin's widow, Evelyn, who was also beaten by the Rangers mob, is a Protestant, as is local Sinn Féin councillor Billy Leonard. Just as every white person in the Deep South didn't approve of the Klan, many decent Protestant people in Coleraine don't approve of what happened to Kevin McDaid. Hopefully, in time, they will be heard above the baying Rangers mob that repeatedly jumped on Kevin McDaid's head that Sunday.

There was another victim of that awful day in Coleraine. Damien Fleming, a neighbour and friend of Kevin McDaid, is fighting for his life. A registered disabled man, he was the first to be set upon by the heroic mob of Rangers supporters that spilled out of Scotts Bar after the SPL trophy had been paraded around Tannadice. Damien's family released a picture of him in his hospital bed. Kevin McDaid's widow, Evelyn, said the man who was the love of her life and a father to her boys would not have wanted any revenge for his murder. Hopefully that call is heeded.

All decent, right-thinking people are asking for is that the law be applied fairly without fear or favour. Ultimately, there will come a time in the north of Ireland when the lynching of Taigs, just like the lynching of blacks in the Deep South, will become a thing of the past. That requires the strict enforcement of the law and the deliberate dismantling of the belief system that affirmed the Rangers mob to spill out of Scotts Bar that Sunday with murder in their delinquent minds.

That is why the text message story from the *Sunday World* is, if true, so explosive. These lynch mobs, if they feel they have the tolerance of local law enforcement, will go and kill Taigs with impunity as the mood takes them, so the policing angle is central. A stern-looking Hugh Orde saying all the correct things to camera is of little benefit if his officers locally are colluding with their fellow Rangers supporters to teach the Taigs a deadly lesson now and again. If we get the policing right in the sick counties, the other strand in this strategy for public safety is to eliminate the cultural justification that the mobs of Rangers supporters who murdered Kevin McDaid felt they had when they attacked him and Damien Fleming.

To Rangers supporters in Scotland it may have passed them by that their world-famous and highly successful football team has, in the last forty years, not had a single player from the Republic of Ireland. In towns like Portadown and Coleraine the incontestable fact that their club doesn't field any player from the Republic of Ireland is a central part of an emotional contract. It is the soccer equivalent of the act of settlement.

Among the Taig-murdering classes in the sick counties, that perceived ban on players from the Republic of Ireland at Ibrox is what defines Rangers. In that Coleraine worldview, that makes Rangers unlike any other football club. While Rangers continue to be able to be without a player from the Republic of Ireland, they are part of the problem when they could be a central part of the solution.

Rangers: No Irish need apply?

5 June 2009

Does discrimination in employment against Irish people exist in Britain today? The Irish in Britain of a certain age can recall in-your-face job discrimination. The west of Scotland of my boyhood was full of anecdotes about major employers, from shipyards to banks, who didn't employ anyone from the Irish community.

However, the plural of anecdote is not evidence. My new view on encountering the question that started this article would be an emphatic no. Moreover, the answer would have been no for at least several decades. If someone claims that there is some structural discrimination going on in this day and age in a modern democracy within the EU then I need evidence. I really do. I need numbers.

I was recently challenged in my Pollyanna view of fair employment in Britain by looking at what is, perhaps, the last place where an Irish passport is a bar to employment. I was contacted through my website by a reader who stated as an assertion that Rangers Football Club had not, in his living memory, ever signed a Republic of Ireland player. I started out as a sceptic on this, which is always a healthy starting point for a journalist on any issue.

It was once said by, I think, Walter Cronkite, the veteran American news reporter, that journalists must remain sceptical so that the public doesn't become cynical. So I decided, in as much as I was able, to look at the players who had represented the world-famous Glasgow club in the last fifteen years. This is an arbitrary timescale for sure, but it seemed appropriate. It was post-Maurice Johnston (1989) and five years into the tenure of Sir David Murray, the current owner of Rangers.

What I found was that players from forty-six countries (excluding Scotland) had been in the Rangers first team squad since 1994. These forty-six flags represented countries from every populated continent on the planet. It would be a reasonable cross-section of humanity as represented at the United Nations. However, there was one surprising omission. In the last fifteen years Rangers Football Club have not had a single player, either full international or under-21, from the Republic of Ireland.

Since the year 2000 every other Scottish Premier League (SPL) club has had an ROI international in their ranks. Since the year 2000 every current English Premiership club has had a full Republic of Ireland international. Every Championship club in England has had a full Republic of Ireland international since the year 2000, apart from Bristol City and Doncaster. However, these two clubs have had Republic of Ireland under-21 internationalists since the turn of the millennium. Also, thirty-three clubs from the leagues below the top two divisions in England have had full Irish internationals since the year 2000. Therefore, over one hundred English clubs have either had a full Ireland or under-21 international player in the last ten years, not just an Irish citizen, but a Republic of Ireland international.

This doesn't constitute evidence of anti-Irish discrimination. There could be other explanations for the absence of ROI players from the Ibrox home dressing room. Perhaps the managers at Rangers over these past fifteen years just didn't fancy any ROI players. Such things are possible.

Since former Rangers manager Alex McLeish became manager of Birmingham City just over a year ago he has signed two full Irish internationals in Lee Carsley and, today, Stephen Carr. In January he signed Keith Fahey, who was playing in the League of Ireland and who has represented Ireland up to under-21 level. The delighted McLeish stated on signing Carsley that he had admired him for a long time. The current Rangers manager, Walter Smith, signed Carsley in 2002 when he was the manager of Everton. Carsley was available on a free transfer last summer when Smith returned to Rangers for a second stint.

Any structural discrimination is very hard to prove until someone is a whistleblower. I rather doubt that Scotland's whistleblowers will be of any help with this issue. Ex-Rangers manager Dick Advocaat, now in charge at Zenit St Petersburg, very frankly stated that he couldn't sign a black player because the supporters of the Russian club would not tolerate such a signing. It was a shocking revelation of the state of racism among the Zenit supporters. However, the Dutchman is, in my opinion, to be commended for his frankness.

When Advocaat was in charge of Rangers, the little general had the light blues playing an expansive, classy game, which required the deployment of two wingers. One of the best in the business at the time was Blackburn Rovers' Damien Duff. There is little doubt that Rangers could have paid the transfer fee and met Duff's personal terms. Duff went to Chelsea when Rangers paid the Stamford Bridge club £12m for Tore Andre Flo. Perhaps Advocaat just didn't think that Duff was a good enough player for his Rangers team.

However, there is also the behaviour of a section of the Rangers supporters towards Irish players. The racist abuse of Aiden McGeady and James McCarthy is explained by the fact that they are Scots-born and turned their backs on Scotland by declaring for the Republic of Ireland. In recent years several other Republic of Ireland players have played at Ibrox stadium, some of them in friendly matches. Ian Harte and Robbie Keane were continually booed by Rangers fans. Both these players are Irish-born. Perhaps the Rangers fans didn't like their playing style.

Then consider Alan Thompson, a Celtic player with a habit of scoring vital goals against Rangers. He was sent off three times against Rangers at Ibrox for violent conduct. Interestingly, the English midfielder was never booed by Rangers fans despite them having several genuine on-field reasons for disliking him.

When Ireland was partitioned there were – for a time – two teams claiming to be Ireland and at least one Rangers player, Alex Stevenson, did play for an Ireland team. Galway-born Alex Craig played for Rangers and Ireland in the first decade of the twentieth century. However, since there has been a definitive Republic of Ireland team I have not been able to discover a Rangers player who played his international football for the Republic of Ireland. Certainly, during the stewardship of Sir

David Murray and his four mangers there have been no ROI players at full or under-21 level who have taken the field of play for Rangers in a competitive match. Is this important?

Modern football players are hardly the huddled masses of the Victorian era in urgent need of the Factory Act to protect them. These talented young men are paid sums of money that to the average person seem difficult to comprehend. The concern we should have over this apparent inability from Rangers FC to find a suitable player who turns out for the Republic of Ireland is the message it sends to Rangers supporters. The old, unwritten, unstated policy that barred Catholics from playing for the club is certainly gone. The Ibrox club have had, during Sir David Murray's ownership, a Catholic captain and a Catholic manager. However, anti-Irish racism seems, perhaps, to be the core emotional contract between Rangers Football Club and their Loyalist supporters.

I contacted ex-Republic of Ireland footballer and anti-racism expert Kieron Brady and put this question to him: Rangers have fielded players from forty-five countries other than Scotland in their first team squad in the last fifteen years. Since the year 2000, Republic of Ireland internationals – either full or under-21 – have played for every SPL club and all ninety-two English league clubs from season 2008/2009. Do these facts indicate that there may be a signing bar operating at Rangers regarding players who represent the Republic of Ireland?

"It is very difficult to definitively and conclusively say that such a policy, whether official or *de facto*, exists, but given the persistent anti-Irish racism that emanates from a section of the support I think there is a validity in raising such a question as it could be argued by some that the club is operating a policy of conformity to those with such profound anti-Irish attitudes," said Brady. "The notion of conformity to racism is not a new phenomenon as Verona FC and Zenit St Petersburg have had to contend with similar problems in recent times.

"Migratory patterns within football illustrate that Britain is the natural working environment for players who play for the Republic of Ireland, or those who represent the Republic of Ireland but have been born elsewhere, and the fact that all the major clubs have had the aforementioned players over the period of a generation or more with the exception of Rangers does point to an anomaly. When this anomaly is set against a backdrop of the racism against those of Irish origin it only exacerbates the theory of a proscription on those players."

He added: "The most suitable recourse would be for the club to outline its position and offer clarity on this matter. In the twenty-first century the idea of a football player being effectively prohibited from representing a club because of his skin colour, country of origin or citizenship is preposterous, and aside from the discriminatory practice in itself impacting on players, it indirectly discriminates against supporters who do not hold such archaic and racist attitudes."

Piara Powar, director of Kick It Out, football's equality and inclusion campaign, looked at the facts regarding Rangers' lack of players from the Republic of Ireland and said: "There is no doubt that Glasgow Rangers have worked hard to distance the club from the less savoury parts of its history. The Follow with Pride campaign is a good example of this, but if the club wishes to counter any allegation of a bias against signing Republic of Ireland players, it should clarify that its policy is to sign players of any background, and better still, actively seek out young players from across Britain and Ireland in the future."

Perhaps post-Maurice Johnston Rangers are, indeed, "bigger than bigotry". However, will Rangers finally be able to rise above anti-Irish racism? The somewhat ambivalent attitude of the club to the Famine Song indicates, perhaps, an empathy with those who sing the anti-Irish song. Until a player can proudly announce that his club and country are both Rangers and the Republic of Ireland, it is justified in remaining sceptical that the old Rangers hasn't totally gone away. Consider this when you look at the countries that Rangers Football Club have found players from over the past fifteen years:

Algeria
Madjid Bougherra
Brahim Hemdani

Argentina
Claudio Caniggia

Australia
Dave Mitchell
Craig Moore
Kevin Muscat
Tony Vidmar

Belgium
Thomas Buffel

Bosnia and Herzegovina
Saša Papac

Brazil
Emerson Moisés Costa

Canada
Colin Miller
Roberto Giacomi

Chile
Sebastián Rozental

Croatia
Dado Pršo

Cyprus
Georgios Efrem

Czech Republic
Libor Sionko

Denmark
Jan Bartram
Erik Bo Andersen
Brian Laudrup
Peter Løvenkrands
Jesper Christiansen

England
Terry Butcher
Paul Gascoigne
Mark Hateley
Trevor Steven
Gary Stevens
Mark Walters
Chris Woods
Michael Ball

Finland
Jonatan Johansson
Antti Niemi

France
Jean-Alain Boumsong
Stéphane Guivarc'h
Lionel Charbonnier
Lionel Letizi

Gabon
Daniel Cousin

Georgia
Shota Arveladze
Zurab Khizanishvili

Germany
Jörg Albertz
Christian Nerlinger

Greece
Sotirios Kyrgiakos

Iceland
Arnar Grétarsson

Israel
Avi Cohen
Bonni Ginzburg

Italy
Gennaro Gatusso
Sergio Porrini
Lorenzo Amoruso
Paolo Vanoli

Jamaica
Marcus Gayle

Latvia
Artūrs Vaičulis

Lithuania
Andrius Velička

Martinique
José-Karl Pierre-Fanfan

The Netherlands
Frank de Boer
Ronald de Boer
Pieter Huistra
Bert Konterman
Michael Mols
Arthur Numan
Fernando Ricksen

Giovanni van Bronckhorst

Peter van Vossen

Nigeria

Moses Ashikodi

Northern Ireland

Steven Davis

John McClelland

Jimmy Nicholl

Billy Simpson

Kyle Lafferty

Norway

Henning Berg

Tore André Flo

Ståle Stensaas

Poland

Dariusz Adamczuk

Portugal

Nuno Capucho

Pedro Mendes

Romania

Daniel Prodan

Russia

Andrei Kanchelskis

Oleg Salenko

Serbia

Dragan Mladenovic

Slovakia

Filip Šebo

South Africa

Johnny Hubbard

Don Kitchenbrand

Dean Furman

Spain

Nacho Novo

Aarón Ñíguez

Sweden

Joachim Björklund

Örjan Persson

Robert Prytz

Karl Svensson

Jonas Thern

Trinidad and Tobago

Marvin Andrews

Russell Latapy

Tunisia

Hamed Namouchi

Turkey

Tugay Kerimoğlu

Ukraine

Oleg Kuznetsov

Alexei Mikhailichenko

The United States

DaMarcus Beasley

Maurice Edu

Claudio Reyna

Wales

Andy Dibble

Yugoslavia

Gordan Petrić

An Irish player for Rangers?

16 June 2009

The Republic of Ireland under-19 squad recently played against Sweden. Ireland won 2–1. This, hopefully, is another good crop of young Irish players that can break into the top level within a few years. Last year the same squad, in the main, comprised the Republic of Ireland under-17 squad. In March 2008 the under-17 lads played against Finland at Kilkenny. What was different about this fixture was that there was a scout from Rangers present.

My sources in the Football Association of Ireland (FAI) thought that the Ibrox scout was watching Republic of Ireland players, but he may also have been checking out a Finnish lad. That was more than a year ago. Since then Rangers have made no enquiries about any of those players who wore the green of the Republic that night in Kilkenny. The Rangers scout hasn't been seen since.

I contacted FIFA-registered agents based in Ireland who represented these lads and I was told that not a single one had been contacted by the Ibrox club. One of the Dublin-based agents, a chirpy talkative northerner who studied law at Trinity and who is from the Rangers side of the street, was quite unequivocal: "There is still a huge barrier there," he said. I asked him to clarify what he meant. "Well, would you want to be an Irish lad going to Rangers?" he replied. It was a powerful question.

A source in the FAI stated to me that, in his opinion, the Irish lads who had yet to win a move over to Britain would rather stay playing League of Ireland than go to Ibrox. Clearly, Rangers have an image problem among Irish players. That image problem is largely, of course, of their own making. The Famine Song hasn't helped, or the fact that there are Rangers supporters in Dublin who have a banner saying that they are behind enemy lines.

It isn't that difficult to see why young Irish lads might be put off signing for Rangers. Those Rangers fans who sing the Famine Song and see nothing wrong with that racist ditty and believe that the behind-enemy-lines banner is acceptable banter are probably beyond any non-clinical help. This is the classic chicken-and-egg situation for those who own and run Rangers. If any objective third party, someone at UEFA headquarters in Switzerland, for example, looked at the situation, what would they find? Well, we have a club that has a section of fans that are openly racist to citizens of a neighbouring nation. This racism has seen some of those supporters before the courts. Moreover, the club has not signed a player from that country for fifty years. Coincidence?

I have been informed that in the 1980s, Rangers had at least one Catholic player in the youth team. It was a start. Perhaps this is a clever way to break a previous discriminatory barrier. No one saw the Maurice Johnston signing coming. Rangers supporters' buses were cancelled and some outraged fans burned their Rangers scarves outside Ibrox, but it didn't last. Ten years later Rangers had a Catholic captain. In the 1950s and 1960s there may have been hesitancy from some players who were Catholics to play for Rangers – had they been asked. An apologist for the club could have said, "Well, what Catholic would want to come and play for Rangers?"

However, that doesn't exclude the fact that there was a signing ban on Catholics. People like Sandy Jardine and Walter Smith have openly and unequivocally stated the existence of the ban on Catholic players at Ibrox. Sandy Jardine even stated that when he joined the club in the early 1960s, there were no members of staff, never mind players, who were Catholics. It was just one of those things. Unstated, but implicitly understood by everyone. So, there was a ban on Catholics playing for Rangers. The ban is no more.

How did we know there was a ban? There wasn't a single Catholic in the team. Slowly, Rangers were shamed into signing a Catholic. Most sports journalists working in Scotland at that time managed to get through their working day without mentioning Rangers were operating a ban on Catholic players. There were, of course, honourable exceptions, like the late Ian Archer. The current generation of sports journalists in Scotland report on the anti-Irish Famine Song *en passant* and fail to mention that Rangers have not signed a player from the Republic of Ireland in fifty years. As in the 1970s, the exception in the sporting hack pack in Scotland is Graham Spiers, formerly of the *Herald*, now with *The Times*.

That Rangers have an image deficit with Irish lads is actually beside the point. It is a section of the Rangers support that the club needs to lose if it is to finally lose its problematic baggage and delinquent supporters. Rangers will not be rid of – as Graham Spiers styled it – the white underclass from their support until the club loses its *de facto* signing ban on Republic of Ireland players. It is classic cognitive therapy for people with phobias to take the person with the irrational fear – say of flying – and then gently introduce them to the source of their phobia.

It is called systematic desensitisation. I have used this professionally many times and it works well with most people. In my training I saw a video of a very successful, if expensive, programme working in the USA to cure people of their fear of flying through this cognitive behavioural approach. On the first treatment session the person would be taken to the airport, the second day through check-in, and so on. Penultimately, onto the plane, strapped in and with the engines roaring on the apron, the treatment session would end and the person would leave the plane before the pilot launched the aircraft down the runway. In the final session the plane would take off with the person on the plane and the phobia was conquered.

By taking it a tiny step at a time, a person who had been completely unable to countenance flying was gently manoeuvred into a position where they took off. Once through that barrier the phobia usually disappeared. Like all major journeys, it started with a single step. Groups of people, just like individuals, can suffer from phobias and this approach can work with groups of people. How would this approach help Rangers to break their phobia of things Irish? Clearly, were the management of Rangers to persuade a full Irish international to sign for the club and that player ticked all the boxes as a Fenian, it would be a step too soon for the hordes that wrecked Manchester.

Perhaps I can suggest a tentative baby step for the fearful at Ibrox reared in a dysfunctional subculture to fear all things Irish: it would probably be good if that player was not born in Ireland but qualified via parentage. The irony of Rangers signing what they would deride as a plastic paddy is not lost on this writer. However, signing an Irish-born player without impeccable west Brit credentials is probably too much for the white underclass section of the Rangers support.

I may have the first step for Rangers to break their anti-Irish signing policy. One of the stars of the current Republic of Ireland under-19 squad is Lanre Oyebanjo. A man mountain of a young Londoner, his mother is from Ballyfermot and his dad is from London. He doesn't fit the identikit picture of the Fenian in the muddled heads of the Famine Song choir. We in Ireland just see one of our own and, hopefully, another Paul McGrath.

Lanre qualifies by birth to play for England, through his mother to play for the Republic and, via the grandparent rule on his father's side, he could play for Nigeria. He chose Ireland, it is his choice and should he turn out to be a star then I'm sure England fans will be mature enough not to boo him for being a traitor to England. At the last match against Sweden he was a complete stand-out. He currently plays for lowly Histon in the Conference. This is not the lad's true level as a footballer, that much is self-evident. They know they have a valuable asset on their books and he has another year to run on his contract.

A figure around £500,000 is the probable asking price, which is a lot for a largely untried eighteen-year-old. That valuation may be an indication of the kid's potential and why Alex McLeish is having him watched very closely. A promising lad at this level is where Rangers and, indeed, Celtic will be dealing in the future as the financial belt tightens at both clubs.

Should an offer come in from Rangers for the lad he would, quite reasonably, ask his international teammate James McCarthy about Rangers. I have met James and he is a lovely lad, as straight as an arrow. What would James tell his international buddy about the Ibrox club? What would be fair and truthful? What would be an accurate description of the behaviour of Rangers fans at New Douglas Park towards this teenager last October? Is the Rangers management anti-Irish? Well, clearly not if an offer was made for an under-19 international – something which, as far as I can find out, has not happened. Is a section of the Rangers support anti-Irish? Exactly. Is the Rangers management hesitant about signing a Republic of Ireland player to start in the first team? Possibly. Is the lad a player? Perhaps.

What is undeniable is that he is attracting interest from bottom-rung Premiership sides and Championship clubs with aspirations. One wonders if the current Birmingham manager would have bothered having the lad assessed if he was still the manager at Ibrox. One thing is for sure: Alex McLeish doesn't have to concern himself with the reaction of the Birmingham City fans to Lanre Oyebanjo's international team. Can anyone say with real belief that he could be as sanguine if he was still the manager at Ibrox?

Rangers have a problem of anti-Irish racism to address within a section of their support and, like the Billy Boys saga, they will probably need outside help to deal with it to the satisfaction of society. The house-training project at Ibrox is a work in progress.

There is no team like the Glasgow Rangers

25 June 2009

This piece is a response to those who said "show us the evidence" when I stated earlier that Rangers were unique in British football because they were, for some reason, unable or unwilling to sign a player from the Republic of Ireland.

This reality of a Republic of Ireland-free team at Ibrox could be seen over many years. In comparison, the ubiquity of Republic of Ireland players in all other clubs in Britain is striking. Here, I look at professional soccer clubs on the island of Britain and whether or not they have had a Republic of Ireland player in their first team since the start of this decade. The criteria for inclusion: full Ireland internationals and clubs they have played for since 2000 in competitive fixtures.

There are more Republic of Ireland players, either full or under-21 internationals, who have played for many of these clubs. However, only one Republic of Ireland player, at either full or under-21 level is required to make sure that Rangers are in a category of one. On the island of Britain there truly is no team like the Glasgow Rangers.

All ninety-two English clubs from the top four leagues in 2008/2009 are represented.

PREMIER LEAGUE 2008/2009

Arsenal – Anthony Stokes
Aston Villa – Mark Kinsella
Blackburn Rovers – Steven Reid
Bolton Wanderers – Joey O'Brien
Chelsea – Damien Duff
Everton – Lee Carsley
Fulham – Steve Finnan
Hull City – Caleb Folan
Liverpool – Robbie Keane
Man City – Richard Dunne
Man Utd – Roy Keane

Middlesbrough – Keith O'Neill
Newcastle – Shay Given
Portsmouth – Andy O'Brien
Stoke City – Glenn Whelan
Sunderland – Phil Babb
Spurs – Stephen Carr
West Bromwich Albion – Dean Kiely
West Ham – Gary Breen
Wigan – Kevin Kilbane

COCA-COLA CHAMPIONSHIP 2008/2009

Barnsley – Stephen McPhail
Birmingham City – Kenny Cunningham
Blackpool – Alan Mahon
Burnley – Alan Moore
Cardiff City – Alan Lee
Charlton Athletic – Andy Reid
Coventry City – Clinton Morrison
Crystal Palace – Mark Kennedy

Derby County – Rory Delap
Ipswich Town – Matt Holland
Norwich City – Gary Doherty
Nottingham Forest – Andy Reid
Plymouth Argyle – Mickey Evans
Preston North End – Wayne Henderson
Queens Park Rangers – Liam Miller
Reading – Kevin Doyle

Sheffield United – Paddy Kenny
Sheffield Wednesday – Graham
  Kavanagh
Southampton – Darren Potter

Swansea City – Stephen
  O'Halloran
Watford – Stephen Kelly
Wolves – Andy Keogh

COCA-COLA LEAGUE 1 2008/2009

Brighton – Paul McShane
Bristol Rovers – Dave Savage
Carlisle – Ian Harte
Colchester United – Graham
  Barrett
Crewe Alexandra – Graham
  Barrett
Hartlepool United – Thomas
  Butler
Hereford United – Stephen
  Gleeson
Huddersfield – Damien Delaney
Leeds United – Gary Kelly
Leicester City – David Connolly
Millwall – Colin Doyle

MK Dons – Keith Andrews
Northampton Town – Dave
  Savage
Oldham Athletic – Alex Bruce
Peterborough United – Sean St
  Ledger
Scunthorpe United – Joe Murphy
Southend United – Dominic
  Foley
Stockport County – Nick Colgan
Swindon Town – Dominic Foley
Tranmere Rovers – Jason McAteer
Walsall – Steve Staunton
Yeovil Town – Leon Best

COCA-COLA LEAGUE 2

AFC Bournemouth – John
  O'Shea
Barnet – Gary Breen
Bradford City – Colin Healy
Brentford – Stephen Hunt
Bury – Andy Keogh
Chester City – Paul Butler
Chesterfield – Jonathan Douglas
Darlington – Curtis Fleming

Gillingham – Jonathan Douglas
Grimsby Town – Wayne
  Henderson
Luton – Dean Kiely
Notts County – Wayne
  Henderson
Rochdale – Alan McLoughlin
Rotherham United – Alan Lee

Some of the English non-league clubs which have had full Ireland internationals since 2000:

Ebbsfleet
Havant and Waterlooville
Kidderminster Harriers
Lewes
Mansfield Town

Oxford United
Rushden & Diamonds
Scarborough

Under-21 Ireland internationals and clubs they played for since 2000 in competitive fixtures:
COCA-COLA CHAMPIONSHIP
Bristol City – Stephen Henderson
Doncaster Rovers – Sean Thornton

COCA-COLA LEAGUE 1
Cheltenham Town – JJ Melligan
Leyton Orient – Sean Thornton

COCA-COLA LEAGUE 2
Accrington Stanley – Jimmy Ryan
Aldershot Town – Owen Coll
Exeter City – Glenn Cronin
Dagenham and Redbridge – Peter Gain
Lincoln City – Colin Cryan
Macclesfield – Dean Delaney
Morecambe – Henry McStay
Port Vale – Dean Delany
Shrewsbury Town – Sean Thornton
Wycombe Wanderers – Paul McCarthy

SCOTLAND
SPL clubs in 2008/2009 which have had Republic of Ireland internationals since 2000:
Aberdeen – Richie Byrne (under-21)

Since 2000, every Scottish Football League (SFL) club has had a Republic of Ireland player, either full or under-21 international, except Rangers. Other Scottish clubs with full Ireland internationals since 2000: Airdrie United, Albion Rovers, Clydebank, Dundee, Dunfermline Athletic, Livingston, Ross County, St Johnstone. Most Scottish lower league clubs have an almost exclusive compliment of Scottish players. Many are part-time and Irish players would not, for the most part, relocate for part-time football.

Continental Europe
Since 1985, Republic of Ireland internationals played for, amongst others:
Ajax – Frank Stapleton   Sporting Lisbon – Phil Babb

Feyenoord – David Connolly   Red Star (France) – Tony
Marseille – Tony Cascarino   Cascarino
Inter Milan – Robbie Keane   Lyon – Mick McCarthy
Levante – Ian Harte   Le Havre – John Byrne
Real Sociedad – John Aldridge

This list of Republic of Ireland players has been drawn up to high-light the glaring omission from the list. All SPL clubs since 2000 have had a Republic of Ireland player – all except one. All ninety-two clubs in England have been able to source a Republic of Ireland player considered good enough for their first team. In fact, signing Republic of Ireland players would seem to be quintessentially British. It is a bit puzzling that Rangers seem to be out of step with all the other British clubs.

The connection between the anti-Irish racism of some Rangers fans and the club's inability to source a suitable player who wears the green of the Republic must now be taken on board by the appropriate public agencies. It has been established at the High Court in Edinburgh that the Famine Song is a manifestation of anti-Irish racism. Rangers have, within their support, an anti-Irish racism problem. That much has been forensically established.

Much was made of the change in Rangers' anti-Catholic signing policy twenty years ago. The club's first Catholic captain in modern times – and possibly the first ever – Lorenzo Amoruso, was taken into the hearts of the Rangers supporters. Like clubs in England who had an anti-black racism problem in the 1970s, signing black players throughout the 1980s did, in time, silence the racists on the terraces. If the Famine Song and other manifestations of anti-Irish racism are to become a thing of the past at Ibrox along with the sign-ing ban on Catholics, Rangers must learn to love players from the Irish Republic.

The Famine Song is merely a symptom of a problem. Those who sing this racist song perhaps feel they have some official permission from the club itself because they never have to cheer on a player from the Irish Republic in the light blue of Rangers. That reality, like the Catholic ban pre-1989, must come to an end. One day the Rangers supporters might not want the Irish in their team to go home. When that happens, Rangers, finally, will become a normal football club.

Maurice Edu

23 October 2009

The tricky thing about racism is that when you allow and approve one type of racist thought, you tend to get more than you originally authorised.

The alleged racist abuse suffered by Rangers player Maurice Edu should not come as a surprise to anyone with any knowledge of the Ibrox subculture. The possibility that some Rangers supporters had been involved in racist activity towards someone from an ethnic minority didn't exactly challenge my worldview. This is what Rangers is about for many of the Ibrox faithful. It is what defines them as a human community.

A specific type of racism lies at the heart of the bedrock support of Scotland's establishment club. The Irish community in Scotland and the Irish in general have a central place in the Ibrox belief system as the *bêtes noire*. The Irish who settled in Scotland are the enemy within *par excellence* for the followers of the Ibrox club.

Several things in this story are worth considering. The method of transmission – it was straight from the player himself via Twitter. The traditional media galloped to stay up with the story as it was disseminated via supporters' message boards long before the print editions of the dailies had been dispatched in delivery vans. Those in the old media who sneer at the digital age are increasingly sounding like defensive craft guilds rapidly being pushed into a form of cultural Luddism.

Twitter was one of the main conduits for information during the Iranian election crisis. This technology can't be referred to as the future. It is here now. With the Edu story, people reading the back pages the next day already knew the basics of the story. This makes it harder for a craven group of onside hacks to deliver for a vested interest. Edu himself said that a couple of Rangers fans had racially abused him. In the club statement it was one fan. The tabloids faithfully followed the lone racist story. Of course, what can't happen in the Scottish tabloids is for there to be an analysis of why this incident should happen and whether it could be connected to the overall identity and belief system of many thousands of Rangers supporters.

Throughout the Famine Song controversy, members of the press in Scotland effectively wrote permission slips for those thousands of Rangers fans who were singing it throughout last season. The Famine

Song has continued to be heard from Rangers supporters this season. This is after it has been established in case law that it is racist and, *ipso facto*, illegal. The response in Scotland from the governing party and the soccer authorities *apropos* this ongoing anti-Irish racism is highly instructive.

Compare this to the swift and appropriate response to the racist abuse of Maurice Edu. I have little doubt that the Ibrox club is embarrassed by this behaviour towards one of their own players. Moreover, I am sure that those who have authority at Rangers FC would pursue any of their own who behaved like this to a player from the opposing team with equal vigour.

The Rangers Supporters Trust, whose spokesperson, David Edgar, referred to the Famine Song as a "rather tasteless chant", was swift to issue a statement condemning the abuse of the young American. There are no different types of racism, or different grades of racism. Racism is racism. Once xenophobia is at large as part of an approved culture, it often finds new victims.

It is not up for debate that asylum seekers and economic migrants into Northern Ireland have, in the main, received the most hostile response from the Loyalist community. Although the central tenet of the Ulster Loyalist subculture is a hatred and fear of the native Irish, the Afrikaners of Coleraine are adaptable in the targets of their hatred.

Failure to condemn the Famine Song as a manifestation of anti-Irish racism and the disgraceful abuse of Maurice Edu is not unconnected. If the Rangers supporters involved in this incident are to be rightly taken to task for abusing one of their own players because of his skin colour then the Ibrox support at large should also be challenged about their appalling attitudes towards the Irish.

An act of remembrance?

4 November 2009

This weekend across the island of Ireland there will be commemorations of those Irishmen who died in the service of the British Crown in many conflicts. Most of those remembered died in the "Great War", but Irishmen continue to serve in the British armed forces and they continue to die for Britain.

In the Republic, people have developed a sophisticated analysis and are able to differentiate between the individual heroism of our own and the cause for which they were led to their death. I am writing these words in my father's town of Westport, County Mayo. I have yet to see anyone wearing a poppy but if I did I suspect it wouldn't be such a big deal. Earlier this year, Westport came to a halt for a British military funeral. One of our own, Robbie McKibben, died fighting for Britain in Afghanistan. Uniformed Brits carried his coffin through Westport. Every shop and business closed as a mark of respect. It was respect to the lad and his family, not the military force that had slaughtered Irish people in this county ninety years ago.

A British military funeral in Westport would have been impossible in the time of my grandmother. She told me when I was a boy in the 1970s that one of the happiest days of her life was when she heard the news that the Carrowkennedy ambush had been successful. A few miles out the Leenane Road our lads, including her young husband and two brothers, had given the Tans what they deserved. Nine of these British mercenaries lay dead by the roadside. Incredibly, two surrendered and the West Mayo Flying Column of the IRA gave them quarter and safe passage. It was mercy they scarcely deserved. The generation of people who remember the Black and Tans on the streets of Westport are now dead and gone and their children are in their eighties, so some in Ireland have been able to move on somewhat regarding this issue. However, it would be inaccurate to characterise this society as utterly transformed on the issue. Although the wearing of the Royal British Legion poppy is a symbol of the "West Brit" to many here, it is hardly a hanging offence in the modern Republic of Ireland. In the north, commemorating Britain's Irish war dead long ago became a sectarian wedge issue. Despite this, there have been moves towards reconciliation. In recent years Sinn Féin representatives have attended wreath-laying ceremonies in Belfast and worn the poppy as an act of outreach, however, for many in the nationalist half – and it is half now – of the six counties' population the poppy remains as foreign to them as an orange sash. The first of these Sinn Féin representatives to do so was Tom Hartley.

The senior Republican has done much to research the experience of nationalist Belfast marching away in 1914 to die for the British Empire. Of course, many of those Irishmen believed John Redmond's view that they were going to die "for the rights of small nations" and Irish Home Rule. His work has been thoughtful and human. Not for a second does he have any affection for Greater England's imperial designs, but he has time to see the tragedy of Irishmen dying for their enemy. I agree with him. For too long, the memory of those Irishmen who misguidedly died for England was airbrushed out of the Irish collective memory. Even the British military experiences of Irish revolutionaries like James Connolly and Tom Barry were rarely mentioned, yet it was these life experiences that made them effective on the field of battle against the British. This was especially true of Barry in West Cork.

It is from this perspective that I view the recent engagement in Scotland's Old Firm culture war. Last year's minute's applause highlighted the problematic issue Remembrance Day is for Celtic with such a large Irish following in the support. To the average British person it is simply a commemoration of poor British squaddies in the trenches of the Western Front or the RAF pilots who defeated the Luftwaffe in 1940.

Imagine, then, someone from Derry visiting Celtic Park and being asked to observe a minute's silence for members of the Parachute Regiment – shooters at Bloody Sunday – who may have stepped on an IRA booby trap in South Armagh some years later. I have no idea if, say, the murderer in Glenfada Park met such a fate, but it is possible. Imagine that scenario and you have an idea why the minute's silence for Britain's war dead isn't universally viewed as appropriate within Celtic's support.

"Poppygate" came at a good time for those with Rangers PR as part of their day job. The over-identification with squaddies and poppies at Ibrox these days smacks of a post-Famine Song PR counter-attack. If I were running their PR I would probably do the same. The man who handles Rangers' PR account at Media House is a friend of a friend. He is a solid PR professional and ex-tabloid editor in Scotland, an Aberdonian with no Old Firm axe to grind. Moreover, he doesn't even like soccer. He has certainly had a serious job of work to do handling the RFC account. His main problem wasn't Irish politicians or the few journalists not in David Murray's pocket, but the Rangers support itself. The recently added veneration of the wartime RAF to the Rangers song sheet is all the more strange when you consider the rich vein of neo-fascism that runs through the hardcore Ibrox support. Any mind that considers it consistent to give Nazi salutes in Israel and then sing back home about the RAF shooting down German bombers is in need of professional help. Add to that the virulent anti-Irish racism at the heart of the Ibrox belief system and the stream of bad stories to keep out of the media must have seemed never-ending. A counter-attack was needed.

This time last year the Ibrox club had been subjected to several months of adverse publicity due to the Famine Song. There had been consular involvement and several questions had been asked of Foreign Minister

Micheál Martin by opposition TDs about the Famine Song controversy in Scotland. At the beginning of November 2008, Dublin MEP Eoin Ryan visited Scotland for the day as a guest of the Scottish Executive after he raised the issue on the floor of the European Parliament. The Scottish Government was keen to present a squeaky-clean image to the visiting MEP. I was the only print journalist to cover the event. Members of the Scottish political class were highly embarrassed at the attention from Irish politicians. It pushed all the wrong buttons. For a start, Ryan stepped off the plane with a belief that Glasgow had a large Irish community. He was, of course, entirely correct. He called the Famine Song "racist"; the Scots spoke of "sectarianism".

At a meeting in Glasgow City Chambers, one of the primary working documents was the October statement from Rangers issued by the club and signed by Martin Bain. It was clear that some of those who follow Rangers were the problem and that was the reason that the Irish MEP was there. Rangers' reputation was under assault. They had to fight back and they did. At the end of a month which had included Ryan's visit and the first conviction of a Rangers fan for singing the Famine Song at a Scottish soccer stadium, we had "Poppygate".

Perhaps recalling the senseless slaughter of the Somme will, momentarily, distract the Ibrox support from the fact that their club is on the financial equivalent of a ventilator. The poppy issue gives them a British stick to beat Celtic with; their Fenian rivals being "unpatriotic" and disrespectful to the war dead etc. In the end, this is just about PR. That, of course, devalues the entire commemoration of those who went to war and didn't come back. Perhaps the PR people who work for RFC could come up with something more appropriate for the bankrupt club than hijacking the Royal British Legion's sombre and respectful symbol of remembrance. Rangers need their own special event. Pauper Day for the club with no poppy.

James McCarthy

3 March 2010

It has been a difficult few months for any of us who follow the boys in green. If the punch in the gut equaliser from Italy in Croke Park was the injury then the Henry handball in Paris was the insult. For those of you who follow the Republic of Ireland, you'll know about that sense of injustice. It's still there. It just is.

So it was, that last night we started to move on; time to begin again. The national team took to the field of play to take on Brazil in the Emirates stadium in a friendly match. The noise from the crowd was decidedly high-pitched. Thousands of Brazilian girls screamed in adoration at their heart throb Kaka every time he touched the ball.

A largely male crowd will growl in anticipation as the play approaches a critical juncture or bark in collective anger if one of their guys is fouled. The oestrogen-fuelled crowd at the Emirates had a different take on things. For these very fetching soccer fans, their Joga Bonito was all about Real Madrid's playmaker with the matinee idol looks. All Kaka needed to do was to be on the ball for a second anywhere on the field of play for his female following to be convulsed in screams of adoration. As for the rest of his colleagues, it was business as usual. The boys in the canary yellow shirts romanced the ball across the turf at every opportunity. This was soccer with a smile on its face.

For the first half the Irish were, well, Irish. We were dogged and determined. Only a cruel own goal a few minutes before the interval saw the Brazilians leave the field at half time 1–0 up. The second half saw the South Americans ease up the gears. Their second goal was pure samba. It is why we love the game and why most of us love Brazil – even when they're scoring against us.

Before that happened, something took place that caused me a smile of satisfaction. With sixty-nine minutes played, young James McCarthy received one of the louder Irish cheers on the night when he was summoned for an international debut in place of the tiring Liam Lawrence. Slotting in on the right side of midfield, he didn't look out of place.

After the game was over I sent a text to a senior club official at James' first professional club, Hamilton Academical. The small west of Scotland club is where the lad was developed as a player. It was only right and fair to acknowledge what they had done for James and, now, for Irish soccer. It didn't surprise me to learn from the club official that he had spoken to James twice in the last couple of days. That is the kind of lad James is.

I met this club official and James on the same day in October 2008 at new Douglas Park after he had endured a solid forty-five minutes of racist abuse as he played towards the St Mirren goal. I sat among the St Mirren crowd that day. The abuse was undeniable in its character and clearly audible. Despite that, it didn't make it into any match report the following day. Only the local paper – the *Hamilton Advertiser* – had a reporter there, Andy McGilvray, who didn't have hearing problems.

Almost exactly a year later I interviewed James McCarthy after he played in the green of Ireland at under-21 level against Georgia. That night in Shamrock Rovers' stadium in Tallaght it was clear he had grown a bit in the year since I had first seen him. I also met with his mother and sister that night. James' mother was incensed about the abuse that her teenage son had taken from soccer crowds in Scotland. She was happy he had made the move to play in England where he was not a target for racists. It was self-evident that this young man wanted to play for Ireland and he had strong Irish heritage on both sides of his family. The genealogy was strongest on his mother's side, with James having a Donegal-born grandparent.

I asked him that night in Tallaght what it was like to stand for "Amhrán na bhFiann" facing the tricolour. The west of Scotland lad was straight as an arrow: "Brilliant, really brilliant," he said. As we say here in Ireland, the lad is one of our own. Back in January this year there was some speculation – and that is all it was – that James was about to reconsider his soccer nationality. At the time this story broke I spoke with people inside the FAI. They were mystified. A source inside the FAI told me that Trapattoni had been alerted to this story and would phone James immediately.

The same day, I called the McCarthy household in Scotland and spoke with James' father, Willie. I haven't met Willie but I know if I did I would like him. After that conversation I was convinced that James was fully committed to the cause of Ireland. However, until James played a game for the full international, then the Scots could have some hope.

Not any more. Last night the issue was finally put to bed. As far as FIFA is concerned James McCarthy is Irish. Sadly, in the land of his birth that emotional attachment to Ireland is still considered something of a social crime. I'm glad that he now plays in England where his soccer nationality isn't an issue for anyone. Had he remained in Scotland the abuse would have continued. It isn't the fact that he isn't playing for Scotland; it's that his country of choice is Ireland.

That tells me that young James made the correct decision. Just as I know I made the correct choice for my own midfield trio as they grow in a country where having an Irish name isn't a no-no. James made the same choice as, among others, Ray Houghton, Tommy Coyne and Aiden McGeady. Across the soccer world it doesn't raise an eyebrow for a player to declare for his country of ethnic origin rather than his country of birth.

Diomansy Kamara is French-born, but the Parisian plays for Senegal. Madjid Bougherra is French-born, but plays for Algeria. This is their right and I'm sure that in civilised France there is no issue that they declared for their country of ethnic origin rather than the country of their birth. Bougherra qualifies to play for Algeria by dint of one Algerian-born grandparent. These are the same qualification rules that allow Aiden McGeady and James McCarthy to play for Ireland.

In England, many young men have declared to play for their emotional home rather than the country of their birth. Here are a few:

Emmerson Boyce – London – Barbados (Wigan Athletic)
Jason Roberts (MBE) – London – Grenada (Blackburn Rovers)
Jamal Campbell-Ryce – London – Jamaica (Bristol City)

English crowds did not berate any of these players for being "traitors" to England. I have yet to hear of any English-born Afro-Caribbean player being subjected to racist abuse because he turned his back on England.

As I write this I am learning that Jamie O'Hara of Spurs (currently on loan at Portsmouth) has intimated that he wishes to declare for the Republic of Ireland. The young midfielder is English-born and once togged out for England under-21 but did not take the field of play. Now the Football Association of Ireland is merely waiting for paperwork to clear. I am sure if he does play for Ireland crowds in England will not subject him to the treatment that Aiden McGeady and James McCarthy have had to endure in Scotland. Grown-up societies do not behave in such a fashion. Sadly, only in the Scotland of many cultures does it remain a problem to be proud of an Irish heritage.

The unwanted

23 March 2010

At time of writing it would appear that the interest of Mr Andrew Ellis in buying Rangers is no more. There are many reasons why anyone with the necessary millions would not want to buy the Scottish champions or, indeed, any SPL club at the moment. Most of these reasons have been explored comprehensively in the Scottish media. The league is very poor both in monetary and footballing terms.

The gene pool that produced Jim Baxter, Denis Law and Jimmy Johnstone now cannot produce players that would be of interest to major clubs in Europe's top tier. Darren Fletcher is in exalted company at Old Trafford for his work ethic rather than his flair. Scottish clubs can't rear players of real quality and certainly cannot afford to import the best from abroad. Subsequently, there is no sustainable model for any club in Scotland that can put a team on the pitch capable of even a modicum of European respectability. The people in charge at Celtic have been trying to think round that problem for several years by seeking out youth players in other parts of the world. So far, that strategy has yielded very limited returns. The problems of little home-grown talent and poor revenue streams remain for all SPL clubs. Anyone buying a Scottish club, even the champions, would have to face up to these limited possibilities for success on and off the field.

There are, however, specific issues for Rangers. One reason, perhaps, for the lack of serious bidders for the club – apart from the level of debt – is the people who follow it. The new owner of Rangers will not only buy a football club, that person or company will also adopt some seriously delinquent people. After the defeat by Kaunas in August 2008, the Rangers owner and then chairman, Sir David Murray, admitted in several TV interviews that the scenes from the Manchester riots a few months earlier had made the job of finding a new owner for the club very difficult.

The scenes from Manchester were beamed around the world. Councillor Pat Karney from Manchester City Council said it was the "worst twenty-four hours in Manchester's history". Millions saw the CCTV footage of PC John Goodwin being pounced on by the thugs wearing Rangers tops. Even the initial spinning in Scotland that "these weren't real Rangers supporters, most of them were English" seemed strange coming from the "quintessentially British football club".

Yesterday, cab driver Scott McSeveney (21) denied assaulting PC John Goodwin and violent disorder on 14 May 2008. He was found guilty of both charges after a trial at Manchester Crown Court and will be sentenced later this year. Prosecuting barrister Ricky Holland said McSeveney was among a "seething mass" of Rangers fans who kicked and punched the police officer unconscious amid "appalling scenes". The court was told that McSeveney, from Shotts, Lanarkshire, was part of a large group who "marauded their way down Newton Street in pursuit of retreating police officers". PC John Goodwin probably owes his survival to the inability of the pack of feral Rangers fans to pull off his helmet. The policeman, who continues to suffer from post-traumatic stress disorder, is convinced that had the mob been able to get his helmet off he could have been killed. PC John Goodwin was rescued by his police colleagues. He was lucky.

A year later Kevin McDaid in Coleraine, County Derry, had neither PC Goodwin's protective clothing nor the assistance of police officers as he was kicked to death by Rangers fans celebrating their League championship win. Graham Spiers wrote at the time of the Manchester riot that a "white underclass" had attached itself to the Ibrox club. His Pollyanna view was that Rangers were essentially a decent outfit that had recently attracted some unfortunate followers.

When the withdrawal of the Ellis bid was reported in the Scottish media, Graham Spiers conjectured on a Radio Clyde phone-in that it was amazing that no one of substance had put in a bid for Rangers. The one-time chief sports writer with the *Herald*, now with *The Times*, could not understand why a Fergus McCann equivalent had not emerged from the North American business community and rescued Rangers. The conviction of McSeveney yesterday in Manchester and the inability of Rangers Football Club to find a suitable buyer are not, perhaps, unconnected.

Wanted as long as you're not Irish

23 April 2010

"Gers want Jim … he wants Scotland", *The Sun*, 22 April 2010

Upon reading this piece from Roger Hannah in the *Scottish Sun* I can't help but think that the former may depend on the latter. Perhaps the sub-editor would have been closer to the mark had the headline read "Jim wants Scotland now Gers want Jim".

Jim O'Brien has apparently declared for Scotland and now he is also, we are told, a Rangers target. Would Rangers seek him if he were planning to turn out in the green of the Republic? There is, potentially, a huge story that is not being addressed by the Scottish sports desks: why is it that Rangers can have scores of nationalities in their first team over, say, a twenty-year period, but not one from a neighbouring country? At the same time, players from the Republic of Ireland have played for every team in the SPL and almost all of the teams in England. A strange set of coincidences.

In criminal cases the law works on beyond all reasonable doubt. In civil cases, like libel, the balance of probabilities is the threshold for credibility. On the balance of probabilities, what are the chances that Rangers in modern times have not been able to find a suitable player for their first team who just happened to play for the Republic of Ireland? In the last two years, of course, Rangers' lack of signing any player has been down to the bank moving in to stabilise the Ibrox club. One thing that Rangers could not have endured over the past few years of financial crisis was to have been boycotted by their hardcore support.

What could have triggered such a protest? Perhaps signing a player from the Republic of Ireland would be too much to take for the supporters that sing the Famine Song. Hatred of Irishness goes to the core of the Ibrox belief system. The people who run the club know that the days when such prejudice was acceptable are coming to an end. However, the same people that belt out the Famine Song are the first in line to renew their season tickets. Unlike in the English Premiership, season ticket sales make up a significant chunk of the revenue of any SPL club. Rangers are no different. The emotional contract between club and supporter at Rangers is particularly well understood.

Rangers, as a vehicle for anti-Irish racism, needs to be decommissioned. I am sure that if the people who run Rangers could do so and maintain their revenue streams they would do so. Now it appears that they will be able to purchase players once more, they should not exclude those who play for the Republic of Ireland. In the meantime, the day still seems far off when a player can be described as Rangers and Republic of Ireland.

The least desirable

10 May 2010

Some cities connect with you. They leave a lasting impression on you like a lover. For a time when I was much younger, Boston was a regular haunt, south Boston to be precise. I loved the place and its people and I clicked. I love Boston. Subsequently, I was horrified to learn earlier that this wonderful vibrant city with a huge Irish community might be visited by the Famine Song road show.

This piece of performance art wrecked Manchester in 2008. If the quintessentially British football club can do that to an English city, what chance does Irish Boston have? Thankfully, the friendly against Celtic will not now go ahead. Celtic are, of course, welcome in Boston. In fact, it is difficult to think of cities that would not welcome the people that Sepp Blatter was wowed by in Seville.

Just before this madness was announced, the story leaked from Manchester that the Gary Neville testimonial committee had considered inviting Rangers to Old Trafford to honour the Reds veteran captain. No, me neither. A leaked memo from Greater Manchester Police stated that Rangers as opposition in the Gary Neville testimonial would be the "least desirable". Least desirable: a prefect strap line for this club's supporters.

Those who support Rangers have little idea what people think of them. The good people of Barcelona, Pamplona and Manchester don't want them back. They think this is the result of green propaganda from people in the media out to tarnish the reputation of this dignified, quintessentially British club. No, chaps, it is because the denizens of these cities don't want the trailer trash antics of Underclass FC turning their city into something between the world's biggest urinal and a battlefield.

Rangers' very decent chief executive, Martin Bain, has correctly pulled out of the Boston match. He knows only too well what would have unfolded. Drunken Rangers fans surrounded by symbols of confident Irishness; well, they would not be able to help themselves. The poor dears. Instead, Rangers will travel down under to play in Sydney, so Boston will be spared these awful, awful people who bring trouble, crime and the stale smell of super lager and urine wherever they stumble. My condolences to the people of Sydney. They deserve better.

Plastic Paraguayans

4 July 2010

One of the features of this current World Cup competition – now in its semi-finals stage – has been the performance of the minor footballing powers. I am not referring to England, but to countries like the USA, Algeria and Paraguay.

Although the United States is the pre-eminent power on the planet it is, in soccer terms, a minnow. I had thought since USA '94 that grassroots investment and the continuing influx into the USA from

Central America would give Team USA a Hispanic foundation of flair and inventiveness. However, the team that topped England's group tended to be all-American boys welded together by patriotism. It was engaging to watch.

I noticed with a wry smile that of the team that took to the field against England, seven were not born in Algeria. Quite a few of them qualified on the FIFA grandparent rule. It could not be argued that they lacked commitment to their ancestral homeland. Truly they tackled and fought for Algeria.

These "artificial Algerians" were French-born. Some of them play in France, the land of their birth. France and Algeria have a difficult history. Colonialism almost always creates a problematic narrative. The freedom struggle by the Algerian people in the 1950s brought the French armed forces to the brink of mutiny. The French state itself was in peril. Despite all of this, there remains a substantial Algerian community in France. French-born lads consider themselves, in some ways, to be Algerian. Some French footballers have declared for Algeria. They feel Algerian. It is an emotional connection. I wonder if they attract the opprobrium of French football crowds.

I suspect that the relaxed, culturally confident French do not concern themselves with such nonsense. In the land of rational discourse, a player such as Madjid Bougherra is allowed to express his love for the land of one of his grandparents. Bougherra regularly wears a wristband in the colours of his nation as he takes to the field of play for his club. He is routinely referred to by the Scottish media as Algerian. He has one Algerian-born grandparent. This qualifies him, under FIFA guidelines, to declare for Algeria.

Compare and contrast the treatment of Aiden McGeady by the Scottish media; has Aiden ever been given his nationality in Scottish sports reportage? Aiden McGeady is as Irish as Madjid Bougherra is Algerian. Both should be respected for their decisions.

Last night I watched a totally outclassed Paraguay team battle against the guile and inventiveness of the current European champions. Finally, they were breached, but only after they had given Spain a major examination of their determination and mental fortitude. These players were not Plastic Paraguayans. They rallied to their flag. They gave and gave.

Like Algeria, several of the Paraguayan team were not born in the country they were playing for. Several of the Paraguayans were born in Argentina. There is a strong tradition of Paraguayans being economic migrants in Argentina. Argentina is the big affluent neighbour next door. If a lad shows well as a soccer player in Paraguay, Argentina is the nearest major league, similar to the Bundesliga for Austrians and La Liga for Portuguese.

Paraguay and Argentina have history. In the nineteenth century in the War of the Triple Alliance ninety per cent – yes, ninety per cent – of the male population of Paraguay was killed by the combined armies of Brazil, Uruguay and Argentina. The country was largely repopulated by Italian immigrants. The Paraguayan national team certainly seems to have a penchant for *catenaccio*.

I am not aware of any of these – let's call them "heritage players" – being abused in the country of their birth. New Celtic player Cha Du Ri is German by birth. Born to parents from South Korea, he declared for his father's country. I understand his choice. Had I been a footballer I would have made the same choice and I would have declared for Ireland. It would not have been a second choice or a fall-back position. Ireland would be my only choice. Had the Ireland manger not wanted me I would not have turned out for Scotland. I have one heart and it is Irish. True Scottish patriots will get that.

I think of one friend in particular who first saw the light of day in Cape Breton. In his heart he is Scottish. That's good enough for me. Probably by the time the new football season starts in Scotland, Aiden McGeady will have left Celtic and the land of his birth. I wish him well. He is a talented young man and his choice of international soccer allegiance was based on a rich Irish heritage. Like the writer, he had no choice in his birthplace, but he could make a choice about his nationality, just like Madjid Bougherra.

Aiden will play somewhere outside Scotland. In whatever country he is in, the fact that he is a Republic of Ireland international will not be an issue. Only in the land of his birth is an Irish heritage a social crime. That is why his life is about to become more tolerable, as he moves to a city that doesn't harbour so many that hate the Irish and Irishness. Ádh mór ort Aiden.

The sash cloud

14 July 2010

Last weekend Northern Ireland was treated to a spectacle some people believe should be viewed as being comparable to the Rio Carnival. They

argue we should treat the Battle of the Boyne celebrations as manifestations of street theatre, cultural pageant and a general good day out.

In recent years the annual Twelfth of July Orange parades have been
rebranded as Orange Fest. To this untrained eye it looks like fife-and-
drum bands being followed by historical illiterates in strange outfits. Part
Ministry of Silly Walks, part Eugene Terre'Blanche. When in their company, it would be impolite to mention the League of Augsburg in 1686.

It certainly would not be on to point out the fact that the Papacy, as a
key member of that anti-French alliance, was one of the main paymasters
of William's army on the Boyne. Many Orangemen are Presbyterians.
Their unshakeable belief that King William's victory on the Boyne won
their religious rights is as historically illiterate as one can get about the
late seventeenth and early eighteenth century in these islands.

Orangemen believe in the legend that they are no different to any
other tribe. Because it is a legend it is unshakeable, precisely because it
is a legend. It pushes an emotional button. It is not amenable to reason.

The weekend before, there was a full fancy-dress rehearsal in Glasgow.
In Scotland the social decline of the Orange Order has been marked in
recent decades. In Northern Ireland the Orange Order is still a power in
the land. Only recently decoupled from the Ulster Unionist Party, it is
still socially acceptable for men of education and social standing in the
Protestant community to walk on the Twalfth.

There is one part of Ulster where the Orange parade has a different
social context. In Donegal there is an annual parade at Rossnowlough.
In Raphoe in recent years there have been parades by the Royal Black
Preceptory. What is lacking in Donegal is the Stormont experience. In
Donegal, it has to be said, the Orangemen don't have political power,
quite the opposite. Hence triumphalist coat-trailing by Orangemen in
Donegal would be ridiculously out of place. In Scotland the Orange
Order has clearly been on the wane for over a generation. However, in
Northern Ireland the bang of the Lambeg drum still has real meaning.

Political unionism and the wider unionist community have moved on
post the 1998 Belfast Agreement. They realise the days of their Northern
Ireland is over. If the polity is to have any stable future, for it has not had
a stable past, then it will have to be a shared space. The political future is
a form of local self-governance that enshrines power sharing. The growing nationalist demographic means that the internal conversation in a
polity set up on a sectarian headcount has changed utterly.

As I write this, north Belfast has just had its third night of rioting
in the nationalist Ardoyne. Worryingly, there are reports of shots being

fired at police. The spark for this rioting seems to have been the passing through the nationalist area of drum-banging Orangemen. The Great Northern Route comes from Ligoniel into Belfast. There is an alternative route that they could take through the Shankill but that wouldn't be as much fun as going through a nationalist residential area.

Lord Trimble, when he was First Minister, stated that he hoped that the Twelfth parade in Northern Ireland would, one day, rival the Rio Carnival. The people of Ardoyne know the reality. The sash cloud has passed through Ard Eoin; sadly it will be back again next year. So expect another eruption. All very sad, all very predictable.

A first step

25 July 2010

Yesterday I spoke with a couple of very helpful men from Crumlin United in Dublin. They weren't surprised that a journalist was on the phone to them. Their young goalkeeper had just made a little bit of history. Alan Smith, originally from Cork, had signed for the Rangers under-19 team.

Celtic had the lad over two weeks before he signed for the Light Blues. Crumlin could have claimed up to €450,000 in compensation for him, but that, of course, would have killed the deal. I have a sense that isn't what the folks who run Crumlin United are about. The club official told me that, as far as he was concerned, Alan is the first Republic of Ireland player to sign for Rangers. Certainly in modern times this is correct.

Alan Kernaghan is a youth coach and the club did attempt to sign Alan Maybury some years ago. Now they have signed a young Republic of Ireland player from a Catholic background. This is progress. I'm sure that Rangers have signed Alan because he is a fine young footballer and not as an act of tokenism.

Rangers never had a written policy that no player from a Roman Catholic background would wear their colours and play for the first team. Discrimination is rarely written down. When it is it writes its own death warrant. Think apartheid. It was indefensible. However, it was out there and it could be tackled head on. There was no pretence that the regime valued or respected South Africans of all racial backgrounds. Nods, winks and glass ceilings are much harder to tackle.

A key to extinction of any species is habitat removal. It is no different with racists. For generations, being a Rangers supporter has been a vehicle for anti-Irish racism. It is hard to think of any other club in Britain whose supporters could think up something like the Famine Song. Moreover, it is hard to conceive of another club issuing a statement warning their fans not to sing a racist song for fear they will be arrested, but failing in the statement to condemn the song or the sentiments contained within it. It is then that the club's putative employment policies come into stark relief.

Of the one hundred and four clubs that made up the four English leagues in 2009/2010 and the SPL in the same season, one hundred and three have had either a Republic of Ireland full international or under-21 international since the year 2000 and many of those clubs have had several Republic of Ireland players.

In the summer of 2009 a dossier on the racism of Rangers supporters was compiled for Marian Harkin MEP. Ms Harkin is the MEP for the Ireland North-West European constituency. This huge electoral area includes counties like Donegal, with a large connection to Glasgow and Mayo, which, in many ways, is the Famine county. This dossier included a statement from the anti-racist organisation Kick It Out and an Irish community organisation based in Glasgow. Ms Harkin MEP sent this dossier with a covering letter to Michel Platini. The import of this dossier, which I have seen, was to ask UEFA to make sure their match delegates were informed about the issues around anti-Irish racism from Rangers supporters. The dossier also included reference to the apparent failure of Rangers FC to find any player from the Republic of Ireland to play in their first team.

I got sight of the reply from UEFA to Ms Harkin and it was the intention of the football authorities based in Nyon to seek clarification from Rangers on these matters. This correspondence took place in June and July 2009. In August 2009 I received a tip from a well-placed source inside the Football Association of Ireland (FAI) that Rangers had registered a scout with the FAI. It was an exclusive scoop. This was, I was told, the first time Rangers FC had ever registered a scout with the FAI. The natural tabloid thing to do was to go to Clontarf and doorstep the Rangers man in Dublin with a snapper at my side. I decided, instead, to do nothing and let him get on with his job.

Although the Dublin-based Scotsman has since become Everton's scout, he passed on more than a few names to Rangers. A cynic could say that signing a lad for the under-19 team, perhaps fifth or sixth choice goalkeeper, is an exercise in tokenism that will get UEFA off Rangers' back on this issue. Football fans will always tell you that it is only a minority of the club's fans that will know or really care about what happens in the youth team. Everyone knows what is happening in the first team.

It could be argued that Rangers are moving, however slowly, from a no-Irish policy to simply an anti-Irish policy. The clear analogy would be a workplace that had been male-only back in the day. If today that same workplace has a healthy gender balance then the history of that change would find that one day there was one woman.

The culture of that workplace may still have been hostile to female co-workers, but it was a start. At some point critical mass was achieved and the workplace started to become tolerable for women. That will happen, in time, for Republic of Ireland players at Rangers. One day it will be no big deal if another Republic of Ireland player is signed for the Rangers first team squad. We aren't there yet, but it's a start.

What we can now say with certainty is that in the coming season a young Rangers player from the rebel county will stand to attention and face his flag, the Irish tricolour, and sing "Amhrán na bhFiann". When that can also be said of one or two regulars in the Rangers first team in years to come, then the habitable space for anti-Irish racism among the Ibrox faithful will be less and less. The racist in the Rangers shirt will be an endangered species. These things take time. Perhaps we should set an aspirational date for Rangers finally dealing with their Irish question. Six years from now. 2016.

Perhaps it would be fitting if, in the 1916 centenary celebrations when we on this island and freedom-loving people all over the world pay homage to the insurgents of Easter week, that a couple of members of the Rangers first team would feel the same grá for Pearse and Connolly; that they could be fully Irish and it would be no bother, no big deal, that the new project manager at the factory is called Paula, not Paul. No big deal.

Perhaps the last word should go to the fine men of Crumlin United who have reared and nurtured this lad to the young man he is. A club spokesperson said this to me: "On behalf of Crumlin United we would like to wish Alan Smith every success in his future. We hope that the media will leave him alone now. It is of no relevance which club Alan has signed for. He just wants to be a professional footballer."

Racism still raises its head in Scotland

28 August 2010

This article first appeared in the Irish Post

Last week, Aiden McGeady became Scottish football's most expensive export at €12m. The Russian club Spartak Moscow paid this huge sum to acquire his match-winning talent. His ability as a footballer is not in doubt. However, his time in the limelight thus far will be characterised by the sustained racist abuse that the young Ireland midfielder received during his time in the Scottish Premier League (SPL).

McGeady made his Celtic debut in April 2004 when he scored in the 1–1 draw against Hearts at Tynecastle and went on to make two hundred and fifty-two appearances, scoring thirty-seven goals. He won three league titles, as well as two Scottish Cups and two League Cups. McGeady's decision to choose the tricolour over the saltire was greeted with fury by fans at many Scottish Premier League grounds.

Neil Lennon, now Celtic manager and a former captain of Northern Ireland, stated when he was club captain in 2005: "Aiden had a choice to make and I am sure he has made a wise one. It was his right to pick Ireland, despite whatever a handful of media and a few people in Glasgow might think about it."

Aiden's "crime" was his country of choice. This was acknowledged by veteran sportswriter Hugh Keevins of the *Daily Record*, who opined on a radio phone-in last season that had Aiden McGeady's grandmother come from Cardiff it would not have been a problem had her grandson donned the red of Wales. The harassment and verbal abuse aimed at McGeady for the final years of the last decade as he played for Celtic was racially motivated. It was not "banter" or some misplaced Scottish patriotism by soccer fans. It was motivated by the anti-Irish invective that, sadly, makes Glasgow a uniquely hostile city in Britain for the outwardly Irish. It is hard to think of a highly-paid young footballer being the victim of workplace harassment. The pantomime booing is all part of an agreed emotional contract that the paying public sign up for.

However, there is a limit to this, and all soccer clubs and governing bodies accept that racist abuse of a player is over the line. Ex-Republic of Ireland international and now anti-racism trainer Kieron Brady, when asked to describe the response of the Scottish soccer authorities to this racist abuse of the Irish winger, said: "The response was non-existent. The *blasé* attitude of the footballing authorities to anti-Irish racism in Scotland is reminiscent of what befell many black players in England in the 1970s and 1980s. There is a cultural acceptance of anti-Irish racism."

Brady is clear that it was McGeady's country of choice rather than "turning his back on Scotland" that was the issue for many Scottish soccer fans. "When the abuse takes the form of 'Aiden McGeady, why don't you go home?' by supporters or he is verbally abused as a 'Mick' – as he was by a St Mirren fan – it does point to his national identity as the motivation behind such invective," he continued. "Aiden played in Scotland for six years and to my knowledge there were no songs and chants that took the form of labelling him as a traitor or quisling."

Aiden McGeady is the embodiment of something that remains a social crime in modern Scotland: an Irish identity. Speaking to Hugh McDonald of the *Herald*, McGeady said: "I was getting fed up with Glasgow. I wanted to leave. Nothing against Celtic – it's Glasgow." Of anti-Irish racism, he said: "There are a lot of horrible places in Scotland for that type of thing: Tynecastle, Ibrox obviously is always going to be bad with the Celtic–Rangers rivalry, Motherwell, Falkirk. Some fans there hate everything Celtic stand for and everything I stand for as an Irish Catholic playing for Celtic."

Piara Powar, the executive director of the Football Against Racism in Europe (FARE) network, stated: "Discrimination and abuse based on national origin may not be as obvious as that based on skin colour but it can be just as damaging."

In October 2008, I interviewed SPL chief Lex Gold about the Famine Song. During that interview I referred to the constant racist abuse that McGeady got at most grounds in Scotland. His reply was: "Yeah, but he's a lot more mature now and can handle it a lot better." It is hard to think that had the target of the abuse been black rather than an Irish international he would have said the same.

Returning to the scene of the shame

31 August 2010

If the UEFA Champions League draw is fixed then I think it is fair to say that the Greater Manchester Police (GMP) aren't in on it. That night in May 2008, some of their number thought that their number was up as packs of feral Rangers supporters kicked and clawed at them on the ground. Asbo FC was in town.

If any social policy analyst or politician was in doubt that Glasgow had spawned a dangerous underclass then viewing the CCTV images from central Manchester put those questions to bed. This pageant to British dignity and the Dunkirk spirit ended up with PC Mike Regan on the ground being battered and stamped on. Thankfully, he escaped.

Now for the rematch. The opening match of Group C games on 14 September 2010 will see Rangers travel to Old Trafford to take on Manchester United. Only the most deluded Rangers supporters can think that the people of Manchester and those entrusted with maintaining the Queen's peace there will be pleased to see them. The five thousand ticketed fans will, no doubt, be closely trailed, surveyed and herded to and from Old Trafford. The operation to render thousands of Rangers fans harmless will resemble a military operation. I'm sure if the GMP had their way there would be more draconian measures employed. However, some responses are not available in a democracy.

No matter what transpires on 14 September in Manchester, the reportage will be markedly different in Scotland than in the rest of Britain. On the night of the riots in 2008 one news journalist sent there by a major Scottish title was on the spot. He called in copy as the riot was in full flow. He was disbelieved by the news desk in Glasgow. The voice at the end of the phone challenged him that he was exaggerating. He told them he was witnessing a riot between Rangers fans and the police. He filed thousands of words of copy over the phone to a copytaker. None of it was published.

Only when the CCTV footage became available the next day was it undeniable. Some of the Rangers fans in the city of Manchester had rioted. Several police officers had been beaten and at least two were lucky to escape serious injury.

The London-based titles reported the riot for what it was: a riot. Rangers fans rioted. They destroyed property, attacked police officers and shamed their club. The British prime minister called the scenes a disgrace. The Scottish titles went into the defence attorney mode. The spinning the next day was relentless and ridiculous: it was Chelsea fans; only a few fans were involved; it was because the big screens failed; the police were heavy-handed.

The subsequent arrests following the CCTV footage on *Crimewatch* have all been seen in Scotland. The official report on the riots said that public disorder broke out before the match. Anyone viewing the scenes of disorder would not have been surprised if the GMP had used baton rounds.

Manchester 2008 was yet another nasty chapter of crowd violence associated with the Ibrox club. Now they are to return to the scene of the shame, this time, hopefully, it will be different. Perhaps this time they can all behave. They do, after all, profess a love for Britain.

If only five thousand (those with tickets) travel, then the numbers will be more manageable for the police. However, the five thousand will still be Rangers supporters and as the denizens of Pamplona, Barcelona, Vila Real and Manchester can testify, that often means trouble. These people who think they are the chosen people are, as the GMP stated earlier this year, the least desirable. They really, really are. On 14 September they return to the scene of the shame. I'm supporting the police.

Göring's Eleven

4 September 2010

Passing sentence at Manchester Crown Court, Judge Andrew Blake condemned what he described as "the worst night of violence and destruction suffered by Manchester city centre since the Blitz". Twelve Rangers fans were convicted of various offences. All but one of them received custodial sentences. Did the judge mention the Blitz? Yes, he did. Did he compare the Rangers supporters to the hated Hun? Yes, he did. Oh dear, another accolade. Luftwaffe FC, anyone? Göring's Eleven?

I am, of course, not referring to the team, but to the eleven heroes in the dock who were taken down for their part in the mayhem that Rangers fans visited upon a British city two years ago. The judge has been criticised for using the reference to the Blitz. However, but for the intervention of an ex-member of HM forces, this awful night of Rangers violence could have cost a policeman his life. Tom Bardsley saw PC Mike Regan being battered on the ground. Ignoring the obvious danger to himself, he intervened. He pushed a Rangers thug away before grabbing PC Regan and pulling him down the street. The father-of-one, from Openshaw, Greater Manchester, had just left an internet café in Newton Street when the violence broke out. He said he saw a man running towards PC Regan "aiming a kick" and jumped into action. Bardsley, who served in the 26 Engineer Regiment at Bulworth Garrison, said he had served in a number of war zones but had witnessed nothing like the scenes in Manchester.

"I would describe it as wolves who had not been fed for days. I did not think of any danger to me, just the safety of others and making sure everyone was getting out okay," he said. "I knew that if no one was going to get him [the officer] he wasn't going to make it. I thought 'sod it', I did not care that bottles and bricks were being thrown at me. The adrenaline just kicked in. The next day the city centre looked like a scene from Basra – like a bomb had hit it. I was angry that the Rangers fans had done this."

Now, here is an ex-squaddie who should be given the VIP treatment at Ibrox. I'm sure Simon Weston would agree. Just consider Sapper Bardsley's choice of words: "like a bomb had hit it" ... oh dear. "A pack of wolves" ... oh dear. Obviously some decent Rangers fans will be upset that a member of their armed forces is comparing their fellow Light Blues fans to pack animals. There, there.

In less than two weeks the dignified ones will be back. As in 2008, they will be drunk and wading up to their knees in Fenian blood. Hopefully, the hate crime unit of GMP will be out with their video cameras. The police have insisted that there is a dignified convoy by way of Wigan straight to Old Trafford then back out again. Now the destroyers of Manchester are whimpering about their human rights being trampled upon by a police force that they were quite prepared to literally trample upon in Piccadilly in May 2008. Are these the least self-aware people in western Europe? This is, quite possibly, the only way to transport large numbers of Rangers supporters anywhere and guarantee that there will be no major civil disorder.

As the fine fellows were led down to start their sentences, Scottish voices could be heard from the public gallery: "Fuck Manchester! Fuck PC Regan and Goodwin as well." This is the sort of media coverage that even PR companies can't stop. A multiple court appearance after rioting in a major city following a European final is going to find its way into even the most craven and venal print media. Even the Laptop Loyal are embarrassed to ignore the following statement by a judge in a British court: "The riot police were deployed in full riot gear and struggled to contain the trouble and restore order. What followed was the worst night of violence and destruction suffered by Manchester city centre since the Blitz."

Like Rangers' imminent day in court for their "tax strategy", this one is very difficult to spin and stay on message. One thing that has emerged from the spin is the official Laptop Loyal numerical value on this chaos of two hundred; only two hundred rioted out of the millions that were peacefully there. Just look at the CCTV footage on the BBC website. Two hundred? Hardly. A GMP spokesperson said the police had battled with eighteen hundred Rangers fans. Can you think of any major European city that would welcome Rangers supporters in large numbers? No, me neither. Best we move swiftly along until the next incident of "heavy-handed policing" involving Rangers.

Opinion: Scotland, the Irish, "sectarianism" and racism

13 December 2010

This article first appeared in Caledonian Mercury

The editor of the *Caledonian Mercury* asked me for a piece on an "expat's view of Scottish sectarianism". Although I was happy to contribute, my first issue was with the description of the piece and, indeed, with the lexicon around these issues in the country of my birth.

I was reminded of a conversation I had with Billy Singh, campaign director in Scotland for Show Racism the Red Card (SRTRC), as he was leaving the field of play at Tynecastle stadium in October 2008, the venue for a charity match between a "red card" select and MSPs. I had asked him about SRTRC's attitude to the Famine Song. He stated quite clearly that SRTRC considered the song racist. When he came off the Tynecastle turf he expanded: "It is wrong; it brought nationality into it."

I instantly replied: "Billy, nationality, my nationality, was always in it." I looked at the comments on my first piece for *Caledonian Mercury*, where my nationality was an issue for some of the people leaving comments. One wanted to impose British nationality; another wanted to claim me for Scotland. Writing in Ireland I am acutely aware of the folly of attempting to impose a national or ethnic identity on someone if it doesn't "fit" for him or her. These words blink to life in the west Mayo townland that reared my father and, on his mother's side, reared every generation of my clan back to before anyone was counting or caring.

When researching my grandmother's side here in Mayo, the genealogist was "fairly certain" that she had an uncle who had died in childhood during the Famine. As Ian Bell once wrote in a piece about his relative James Connolly: "History forgotten is a betrayal."

My mother's side were late nineteenth-century economic refugees from Ireland to Scotland. All the branches in my family tree lead back very rapidly to this island. I've only ever held an Irish passport. Take those basic details and substitute Italy for Ireland and what you have is an entirely different vista in modern Scotland. Therefore when I was discussing this piece, I didn't want to "discuss Scottish sectarianism from the point of view of an ex-pat", rather I wanted to explore why holding an Irish identity in Glasgow was such a problem.

To consider the point rationally, it is rather ridiculous. The Irish are Scotland's nearest neighbours and closest relatives. Go back to Scotland's heroic age and it is very difficult to disentangle the two provinces of Gaeldom. Why, then, have the Irish been seen as so alien in modern Scotland?

More than twenty years ago I was asked this question by the fine folk at the Greater London Council's Irish department. They wanted me to give one of the Terence MacSwiney memorial lectures that year on the theme of the Irish in Britain. They asked me, as an Irishman from Glasgow, to give the lecture on the Irish in Scotland. The title of my lecture was, if memory serves: *The Irish in Scotland: Despised Aliens or Guardians of the True Scotland?*

Basically, I looked at the ancient alliances back in the heroic age and charted them as Scotland became more and more absorbed into the southern polity, and as the Irish became more and more alien in Scotland. When the Irish started to arrive in large numbers in the modern historical period it was when being a "North Briton" was in vogue. The Irish, riddled with disease and desperately poor, were a social problem. Infected with Fenianism, they were also a stark political problem for the British political project.

I am glad that I decided to relocate my young family – one a toddler, another an infant and number three on the way – to Ireland out of Glasgow in the mid-1990s. They dander along in Donegal, confident Irish teenagers, where being called Cathal, Róisín or Aislinn and being gaeilgeoirí is seriously cool. This is an upbringing not available to them in the Scotland of many cultures.

So, to start with the original commissioning brief, I'm no longer an ex-pat, I was born an ex-pat but I've fixed that. The issue in Scotland isn't sectarianism *simpliciter*, it is anti-Irish racism. The Irish in Glasgow achieved occupational parity in 2001. In New York it was 1901.

Imagine three brothers leaving their rural Irish homestead in, say, 1847. The descendants of the brother that went to New York today are patriotic Americans (I have a large clan in Ohio). They love their country of birth and on Paddy's day they tell all their neighbours that they're Irish.

The second brother went to Liverpool or a large English conurbation, say, Birmingham. Today his ancestors are completely assimilated: English Brummies save only for their Irish surname, indistinguishable from the large swathe of *Crossroads* motel folk. Only in Glasgow and the west of Scotland do the Irish cling to a sense of separateness. All three places have faith schools and it isn't the effect of violent Irish Republicanism – the Provos bombed England (did I mention Birmingham?), but not Scotland. No, the only variable is the attitude of the host community.

Had my nationality been allowed the same cultural space and esteem as Italians born in Scotland, I might still be there. Rangers supporters aren't singing for the Italians of Largs to "go home". For all sorts of reasons I'm glad I relocated my little brood to where they now grow into fine young Irish people. If Scotland is truly to be a modern, culturally confident country ready to take its place in the community of nations – after centuries of being an absorbed province of the London state – it should allow the Irish in Glasgow to self-define. When this *blatt* was established, the view of its staff was to fill the gap in the market of reasoned analysis. Starting to call Scotland's secret shame what it really is – anti-Irish racism – not the sloppy tag of "sectarianism", is valuable for the country of my birth and for my people who still choose, for whatever reason, to live there.

The hate that dare not speak its name

2 April 2011

I have become increasingly convinced that anti-Irish racism in Scotland is the hate that dare not speak its name. Even when a victim of it mentions their Irish nationality as the reason for verbal abuse, it doesn't make it into the headline of a quality newspaper.

This piece in the *Scotsman* is a good example. [The online article carries a link to a piece in the *Scotsman* published on 1 April 2011 about nineteen-year-old footballer Richie Towell's experiences of playing professional football in Scotland.]

Asked if he believed the Hearts supporters would subject him in particular to more abuse, Towell continued: "Yeah, especially as I'm an Irish boy, and a Catholic as well …" Yet the headline is: "'I'll get abuse because I'm a Catholic,' says Towell."

There is not a mention in the headline of his Irish nationality, to which the lad himself had alluded. In modern Scotland Irishness has been sectarianised to hide within "Catholic". Racism directed at Irish people is then described as "sectarianism". In this way the problem is deliberately hidden. It can then be conveniently avoided and, therefore, it will not be tackled any time soon. I had hoped that the *Scotsman* newspaper would be able to give an editorial lead on these matters within Scotland. Someone needs to have a word with that sub-editor …

Why am I not represented in the culture of Scotland?

5 April 2011
This article first appeared in the Scottish Review

All human communities benefit from seeing a positive portrayal of themselves in the culture within which they live. It is affirming. It tells you, implicitly, that you belong, that you are valued. It doesn't need to be gushing or hagiographic, just a well-rounded view that says that a particular nationality or subculture has something to commend it.

I was born in the 1950s in the west of Scotland. My family was working-class Irish Catholic. My father was from Mayo and from a traditional rural Irish nationalist background. My mother's grandparents were all Irish born. Again, they were from rural stock. The counties of Carlow, Donegal and Antrim provided my mother with her grandparents. I grew up inside an Irish subculture in the west of Scotland of the 1960s. My story is utterly unremarkable in that it is so commonplace in the west of Scotland. What is remarkable, in being worthy of remark, is that I have yet to see any character in Scottish literature, film or TV with that ethnic background that could in any way be considered a positive role model. Now, if I was writing this and my father was from, say, Jamaica, all of my mother's grandparents had hailed from the Caribbean and I could, with justification, say that I had never in my childhood and adolescence in Britain seen a positive portrayal of my lived experience, you probably wouldn't be surprised that I relocated back to my father's country with my young family and that I was proud to travel the world on a Jamaican passport. Moreover, most literary types, culturally sensitive and historically literate, would readily describe the lack of positive characters in a culture as the product of institutional racism. Quite. The lack of positive role models in a culture is a form of oppression. There are great human stories to be told of the Glasgow Irish experience, yet how many great literary characters can we point to that are part of that narrative?

I can think of one or two of my classmates who were of Italian ethnicity. Becoming aware of their identity as Scottish-born Italians, they would have seen various characters that positively portrayed their contribution to Scottish society – and they weren't all played by Tom Conti. Consider the following incontrovertible facts: in my fifty-three years I have yet to be aware of a fictional character in Scottish drama that positively portrays my lived experience as an Irish citizen from the west of Scotland; Rangers Football Club has not had a Republic of Ireland player in its first team squad since I first saw the light of day and many of its supporters have an ethnic cleansing ditty called the Famine Song. It was ruled racist and criminal by Lord Carloway in 2009.

Isn't it time for the poets and playwrights, novelists and scriptwriters, to do their bit in recording Scotland's debt to their oldest ethnic minority? There are great characters to be created from a compelling narrative that has been shamefully ignored. The story of the Irish in Scotland, if told in literature and drama, would enhance the world's already positive view of the country of my birth. Scotland's story will not be fully told until the world knows why some of us always belonged to Éirinn sean.

It's still not easy being Irish in Scotland

13 April 2011
This article first appeared in the Guardian

A recent piece by Kevin McKenna painted a somewhat Pollyanna-ish picture of our community, the Irish in Scotland. McKenna and I are of the same ethnicity and the same generation. Born in the 1950s, we would both be in our thirties before occupational parity was achieved in

Glasgow for Irish Catholics in 2001. The Irish who went to New York instead of Glasgow achieved that economic benchmark status in 1901.

I know from my time in Glasgow as a youth worker in the 1980s and as a social worker in the 1990s that men of Irish Catholic ethnicity were disproportionately represented in the prison population. That continues to be the case. The Irish in Scotland also have a much worse health profile than the rest of the country.

Of the notorious Famine Song football chant, Kevin says: "It's simply not that abusive; a little off-colour, perhaps, and a tad wounding, yes. Abusive and racist? Behave yourself." Thankfully, Lord Justice Carloway disagreed in June 2009 when he ruled the lyrics of the Famine Song "racist in calling upon people native to Scotland to leave the country because of their racial origins. This is a sentiment which … many persons will find offensive."

In what other context would it be acceptable to taunt an ethnic group about a famine that extinguished a million lives and forced another million into permanent exile? What other community is told to "go home" by tens of thousands of football supporters week in, week out in soccer stadiums across the country? It can't be a coincidence that the city that gave the world the Famine Song is unique in that, despite receiving thousands of Famine refugees, it has no city centre memorial to that time and to those people. Recently a St Patrick's Day concert by a folk band from Donegal was stopped due to protests from locals in a small town near Glasgow. The city itself has no city centre St Patrick's Day parade.

McKenna may feel completely assimilated and comfortable in his Scottish skin, but he will not find any positive portrayal of his Irish forebears in the stories Scotland tells about itself. I finally left Glasgow in the mid-1990s. I wanted better for my young family. Since then my native city's intolerance of all things Irish has, if anything, got worse. The Scotland that schooled both McKenna and I was built on generations of Irish sweat and often Irish blood. I don't owe the place a thing.

If McKenna is happy to be Scottish in Scotland then I'm happy for him. It is a basic human right to be able to self-define. However, many others of Irish extraction find that their seat is still at the back of the bus in Scotland.

Last weekend, like McKenna, I also filled out a census, the Irish one. These words blink to life on Ireland's Atlantic coast in the parish that reared generations of my clan, including my father. Philip Joseph Gerard Mac Giolla Bháin has only ever had an Irish passport. This is my island. I'm glad I'm home in Ireland with my young Irish family and although we have many problems here, having become a virtual protectorate of the IMF, it still isn't a social crime to assert an Irish identity. I can't say that is the case for Scotland yet. Pretending that a cultural oppression doesn't exist merely compounds the disempowerment.

Helping Rangers

3 May 2011

Martin Bain has complained that Football Against Racism in Europe (FARE) did not "work with the club". The manager elect, Ally McCoist, said anything that will "solve the problem" is good enough for him.

Essentially what has happened is that two sets of rules have been in play for Rangers and the club's supporters, one domestic and the other European. In Scotland Rangers are the biggest, most powerful club in the country. They do not have, any more, the biggest stadium or the most season ticket holders, but they have a cultural power in the land that is peerless. Even as they stumble on the precipice of insolvency they remain "in the brick" of the Scottish soccer establishment. In Europe Rangers do not have that sway over UEFA. In Scotland they have a convivial relationship with organisations that are tasked to eradicate discriminatory attitudes from Scottish soccer.

In Europe, of course, Rangers come within the remit of FARE. The comparison is stark. In Scotland their fans behave with relative impunity. The club itself is interwoven with the establishment that runs the game in Scotland. There is no conspiracy, it is merely culture. It is unspoken and unacknowledged, it just is, hence the knee-jerk reaction in sections of the media that someone else must be to blame, a point not lost on the *Scotsman*'s Tom English.

In Europe their fans have to behave just like all other fans and in Nyon there is no special dispensation. However, Martin Bain has a point; for this problem to be fixed there will need to be outside help. Like the Northern Ireland Peace Process, there needs to be the intervention of people not reared in the local culture. If Rangers were serious about working with FARE they could be challenged on the absence of Irish citizens and Republic of Ireland internationals in their first team squad and the impact of that on the ongoing anti-Irish racism among a section of the Ibrox faithful.

Martin Bain lamented that FARE did not work with the club. Here, from 2009, is a piece of mine with a quote from Piara Powar, then head of the Kick It Out organisation, which is part of the FARE network.

[The online article carries a link to the piece *Rangers. No Irish Need Apply?*, reproduced in this section.]

Two years ago, Powar thought it really important that the Ibrox club should clarify its employment policy *apropos* Republic of Ireland players. The causal connection between a group of football fans who manifest a specific racism supporting a team that doesn't have any players from the target group is not difficult to make. As black players came to be ubiquitous in the English professional game so did the incidence of racist chanting in soccer stadia decline in that country.

As with most football teams, a club's supporters are only really concerned with their first team. Last year, the Ibrox club signed youngster Alan Smith from Crumlin United in Dublin. How long before there is a Republic of Ireland full international in the first team? Maybe if FARE had a chance of working with Rangers it is something they might want to address. Hatred of Irish Catholics is at the core of the Rangers sickness and while that is apparently tolerated in Scotland by soccer officialdom, in Europe the hatred is seen for what it is.

Ally McCoist will undoubtedly be in the transfer market for players this summer. I wonder if there will be any suitable targets for the McCoist Rangers squad that are Republic of Ireland internationalists. If there are then not only would they be good footballers, but their nationality in the first team squad would start to eat away at the anti-Irish pathogens in the Ibrox psyche. The anti-Irish chants from the Rangers support would make no sense if some of their heroes on the pitch turned out for the Republic.

A UEFA contact has assured me that from now on all match delegates attending European matches involving Rangers will be "specifically briefed", so for the next three years in Europe their recidivist fans have to behave. The poor dears.

The best small country in the world?

13 May 2011

I have recently been stating the following sociological data on several radio stations about the structural inequalities faced by Irish Catholics in Scotland. A few people have emailed me and asked for some clarification. I am happy to provide that.

Firstly, what is "occupational parity"? The term is generally understood among equality professionals as the representation of women, minorities and persons with disabilities in particular occupational categories in the recruiting area. This has generally been accepted as a primary basis for defining affirmative action goals and under-utilisation. It is a clear benchmark of whether or not there is job discrimination extant.

Occupational parity was achieved for Catholics in Glasgow in the under fifty-five years of age cohort in 1991. However, for the whole occupational cohort to sixty-five – that's the entire working population – that benchmark wasn't reached until 2001. Yes, 2001. The twenty-first century. The best small country in the world? Really? Certainly not if you're a Catholic of Irish heritage. The structural inequalities have gone, a century after they were banished from New York. These socioeconomic barriers are now down mainly because a Catholic education sector inculcated a strong ethos of self-improvement and a belief in higher education.

Now, we have attitudinal discrimination fed steroids by a media fearful of a drop in circulation. The reportage of the treatment of Neil Lennon shone a light on the darker corners of the Scottish psyche. Newspapers are giving the paying public what they want. Of course, the Fourth Estate should be leading the charge for decency. Just like the Famine Song controversy in 2008 my trade in Scotland has, with a few honourable exceptions, signally failed. Several leading sports journalists defended the Famine Song as "banter" in 2008, before the High Court of Justiciary found in 2009 that it was, indeed, racist, inflammatory and illegal.

Once more, the Fourth Estate's moral compass appears to be knocked out when the victim is Neil Lennon. The coverage of the campaign against the Celtic manager is proof that the attitudinal discrimination against Irish Catholics is alive and well in modern Scotland. Neil Lennon is a symbol, a cipher, for the old racist Scotland to hate and attack. Although the days at the back of the economic bus in Scotland are over for the Irish community, there remains much to be done before Scotland's boast about being the best among the small nations of the world has any validity.

Laethanta scoile

2 June 2011

If you are childless then I don't expect you to "get" any of this or, indeed, be remotely interested so, please, move along. The decisions taken on behalf of children have to be of the highest quality. Unlike the choices an adult makes for his or her own life it is someone else, someone powerless that has to live with the consequences.

This was a basic fact I tried to get through to people when I was a social worker. Subsequently, where you decide to raise your kids and what school they go to are pretty big decisions. My eldest has just finished with his school days. He has several weeks of exams looming, but he has had his last classroom lesson. Moving to Donegal when he was a toddler meant that his education was completely different to that which he would have experienced in Glasgow.

His secondary education was in a non-denominational Gaeilscoil and at the end of almost fifteen years of Irish medium education he has the language within him forever. There are many cognitive benefits to growing up bilingual. One advantage is that, as an adult, picking up a new language is much less of a chore than it is to a monoglot. Unlike the mainstream English-language sector where the teaching of Irish has been a dismal failure, the gaeilscoillana in Ireland have been a huge success story in both jurisdictions.

Tonight was the school prize giving. If his exam results go okay he'll be off down the rocky road to university in Dublin. The school my brood attend is consistently in the top four in the Republic when it comes to the percentage of pupils that go on to third-level education. It consistently trounces every private boarding school in the land. At the end of the night there is a highly embarrassing slide show of the young people who are leaving. The parents are asked to provide several pictures of when their children were pre-school.

It was a further reminder of the little fellow he was in Glasgow and that, had we not taken the decision we did, he would still be there. His mother and I decided back when he was the inquisitive toddler in those photographs that Glasgow was a culturally toxic place for a kid with a clear Irish identity. Our moment of epiphany arrived one day when I was picking himself and his baby sister up from a private crèche. "I got a new name today," was the proud boast of my three-year-old son in the back of the car. "My new name is Calum. My teacher said my name at school is Calum."

I still remember the feeling sinking in. I knew immediately what had happened. He was forever telling people his name and he had a "tottage" in "Dunny Doll" and that his name was Irish. In a well-adjusted society it would have been endearing, but he wasn't in a well-adjusted society. I have a flashbulb memory of those few minutes; I can still see the dash-board of the car and the clock next to the speedometer telling me when his mother's train would arrive. I had time, but should I do anything? Should I just let it go? I swung the Polo around and headed back.

"He left something behind," I told the owner of the crèche.

"Was it his coat?"

"No, his name."

She went pale; she was completely aware of what I was on about.

"His name is Cathal, not Calum. For future reference. Okay?" (Note to Calums everywhere: very fine name.) There have been men called Cathal in my father's line in West Mayo for as long as I can go back. In many ways it is *the* male name in Connaught.

So, we believed that we could give our brood a better chance of things here in Donegal. It was a seventy per cent positive, thirty per cent negative assessment – seventy per cent that Donegal had advan-tages for rearing our brood and thirty per cent that the society that we had been reared in wasn't culturally healthy for a lad called Cathal or a girl called Róisín. Here in Donegal they don't have to sit at the back of the respect bus.

Everything that has happened in Scotland over the last three years, from the Famine Song to the treatment of Neil Lennon, further con-vinces me that we made the right call. Tonight, as he and his two sisters went up on stage at the oíche bhronnta duaiseanna, I knew his mother and I had made the correct decision. Whether or not Alex Salmond can ever utter the term anti-Irish racism, there is plenty of it in the land he wants to lead to nationhood. His government uses terms like "sectarian-ism" and "bigotry". The official fiction that there isn't an ethnic compo-nent in this malaise ensures that the problem will continue.

Middle child just told us the good news that she has got one of the limited places for idirbhliain (transition year). Transition year (TY) is a year out from the academic grind with the focus on ski trips, hiking expeditions and cultural activities. Her big brother bloomed in TY. He learned to ski, got taller than his old dad and completed his Gaisce award. TY can be ruinously expensive for the bank of mum and dad but it is utterly wonderful and worthwhile for the young person that grows and develops temporarily freed from the daily school routine.

As he took his place on the stage with his buddies to collect GAA medals, I noted that today is the ninetieth anniversary of the Carrowkennedy ambush. My lad is, as they say in the Wesht, off good people. I just know that my kin, at rest near Croagh Phadraig, would be as proud as I am of the man that my big Donegal fella has become. He knows who he is and he knows where he belongs. The profession he wishes to join means that he will travel the world. Wherever he goes, he'll be welcomed as an Irishman. Meanwhile, as Scotland's First Minister thinks about how to convince the world that there isn't an anti-Irish sewer running through much of Scottish life, I'm doubly glad I brought my brood home to Ireland.

The Obdurate Order

4 June 2011

The funeral of PC Ronan Kerr back in April saw some iconic images. The photographs of PSNI officers and GAA players shouldering his coffin are hard to underestimate in terms of their significance. This was a moment of unity.

The murder of the young police officer by dissident Republicans was universally condemned. This was a society saying that the violence of the past should remain in the past. The old RUC is gone and the GAA has changed its stance on membership of the GAA for Crown forces. It is ten years since the GAA abolished rule 21. Since then, the British national anthem has been played at Croke Park, when the English rugby team took on Ireland.

If that wasn't change enough, the British monarch herself visited Croke Park, where her grandfather's forces murdered innocent civilians in 1920. The GAA has acted with maturity and magnanimity throughout the Peace Process. The "Gah" is in my blood. In my grandfather's wee town in Westmeath the idea of the team turning out without one of my clan in it was almost ridiculous. One of my treasured possessions is a photo of my nineteen-year-old father with his hurling team somewhere in West Mayo. They had won the county championship. For the non-Irish reader it is hard to convey the cultural importance of Cumann Lúthchleas Gael to this country's journey into nationhood. Huge concessions have been made by nationalist Ireland in the cause of peace. However, it has to be a two-way process.

It is sad, then, to see the behaviour of the Orange Order over the attendance of Ulster Unionist Party (UUP) leader Tom Elliott at the funeral of Ronan Kerr. The very fact that it is being discussed at a meeting of senior Orangemen, about whether or not to discipline their "brother", is very sad. The rules of the Orange Order prohibit members from attending Catholic masses. Rules can be changed. Ask the GAA.

People in leadership positions within both communities in the north have shown great courage and vision over the last fifteen years. Political unionism has moved on greatly. Loyalism, particularly the Progressive Unionist Party (PUP), has started to develop a sophisticated class-based analysis. The one organisation that hasn't moved on is the Orange Order. It remains handcuffed to the past. It is a given that the Orange Order would not pass muster of any equality audit. Its rules are an anachronism and should be an embarrassment to anyone who admits to being a member of "the Orange".

Like the Klan in the USA, their day has passed. The people they used to look down on are no longer at the back of the bus. They are still camped on the hill of Drumcree, waiting to coat-trail down the Garvaghy Road. They still don't get it. Their day is gone. They have lost their "wee country". The old Orange state is dead. They should acknowledge the new dispensation or slowly die. If they don't change, the cause of death will be their irrelevancy.

Attacks on the Short Strand

22 June 2011

The last two nights have seen the Short Strand, a small Catholic enclave in east Belfast, attacked by Loyalists. The PSNI has alleged that the attacks were organised and directed by the local Ulster Volunteer Force (UVF) unit. Hundreds of masked men were armed with pipe bombs and petrol bombs.

Like a rerun of 1970, St Matthew's Church was among the buildings targeted. Thankfully, unlike forty-one years ago, there were no armed men in the church grounds waiting for the attacking mob. Reasonable people have asked the question: "Why have these attacks taken place?" Jim Wilson of the Progressive Unionist Party (the UVF's political voice) said: "Loyalism at the minute feels unrepresented, they need representation. They need people to listen to them and if they don't listen, and I'm not saying that I know everything and that I'm Mr Smart, but if they don't listen to the concern from within those communities things like what happened there last night are going to continue to happen.

"Loyalism feels outside the process and do you know why? Because we've been pushed outside the process," he continued. "Nobody is trying to bring us in out of the cold. We were part and parcel of what's happening up at Stormont. But you know something? It's like, still a cold house for Loyalism. No one seems to want to help the communities that I come from and this to me is a result of it."

Outside the process? Really? Loyalists were given pride of place at the recent Islandbridge commemorations attended by President McAleese and the British Queen. This was much to the annoyance of some politicians from Northern Ireland. Loyalists, despite their minuscule electoral support, get asked to the top table in this Republic at any function that remotely concerns them. That said, they are held in utter contempt by middle-class unionists. So what do they do? They attack a small nationalist area like the Short Strand. *Plus ça change* …

PUP candidates stand at elections. However, very few of their own community trust them with a vote. In what way, then, is Loyalism "disenfranchised"? Because people won't vote for them? That isn't being disenfranchised, that is just being a political failure. Is Fianna Fail currently "disenfranchised" in the Republic because it got hammered at the last election, the worst election result in its history? The old Norn Iron is gone. The new dispensation symbolised by the enforced partnership at Stormont means that the "Protestant parliament for a Protestant people" is never, ever coming back.

With the shipyards almost entirely gone, they have to compete in a fair jobs market with well-educated Kierons and Siobhans. This isn't how it was meant to be in Sammy's Wee Ulstur. Equality is a terrifying thing for bigots everywhere. The major sociological indicators for working-class Protestant communities in the six counties are grim, especially for young Protestant men.

The late David Ervine attempted to develop a class-consciousness among his UVF comrades. He tried to stop them obsessing about working-class Catholics and instead fix their steely eyes on the unionist business class that so rapaciously exploited them while banging the tribal drum. Sadly, he failed. The Loyalists remain locked in a good ol' boy mindset that sees the terrifying of Taigs as an answer to all of their community's ills. The resignation of his successor, Dawn Purvis, from the party last year was a clear sign that the UVF was not going to leave the stage in the way that the Provisional IRA had. While that subculture exists, the only response from the state must be the iron fist. Failure to do so would see the authorisation of a twenty-first century Billy McKee and no one should want that.

The Irish Government's failure to acknowledge anti-Irish racism in Scotland

24 June 2011

In the week that saw the shambles of the Scottish Government trying to rush through legislation to deal with a problem it had ignored, the sectarian framework remained in place. There wasn't a single politician or expert at Holyrood that uttered the words "anti-Irish racism" during the parsing of the hastily assembled bill.

It is little wonder that the core issue is still under the radar when the Irish Government itself remains wedded to this official fiction. The letter reproduced here from Tánaiste Eamon Gilmore to Donegal South-West TD Thomas Pringle indicates the task ahead for those who wish to be part of the solution to anti-Irish racism in Scotland. The original missive from Thomas Pringle TD to Eamon Gilmore wasn't "concerning sectarianism in Scotland" it was clearly *apropos* anti-Irish racism in Scotland. "Sectarianism" was not mentioned in the original letter.

The Irish Government's failure to recognise the existence of the Irish community in Scotland remains a real obstacle to progress. The Irish Government has a consulate in Edinburgh. Did the Department of Foreign Affairs seek to make a submission to Roseanna Cunningham and her civil servants? At this stage, one must ask if it is a matter of policy at the Department of Foreign Affairs to excise the term anti-Irish racism from the Irish diplomatic lexicon. No doubt the Tánaiste will be asked exactly that question in the weeks to come.

James MacMillan calls on Lamont to apologise or resign after rant on Catholic schools

27 June 2011

The following is an exclusive interview with James MacMillan.

What did you think of John Lamont's contribution in the Holyrood debate on the "sectarianism bill"?

Lamont's contribution to this debate was inept and drew attention away from what some might say was Ms Cunningham's mishandling of the bill, and focused public attention on how divided the Tories were and how incompetent their justice spokesman is. The SNP must be delighted at his shenanigans. The fact some are talking about him as a possible Scottish Tory leader points to how dire the party's prospects in Scotland have become.

Were you surprised by Mr Lamont's views?

Disappointed, but not entirely surprised. It is odd that at the very time the Tories are trying to widen their support in Scotland, one of their front bench spokesmen comes across as being as out of touch as ever. He should have known that all evidence pointed to the startling success story of Catholic schools in Scotland, their deep integration in the state system and their positive impact on bigotry at all levels. I'm afraid that there are too many John Lamonts still in the Tory party in Scotland – petty provincial "golf club snobs", with nothing to be snobbish about – the type that still bridle indignantly when the local Catholic businessman applies to join.

Is his position now, in your opinion, untenable?

He is completely out of step with his party and openly contradicting party policy, which is to support faith schools and the principle of educational choice. He is clearly not competent of political responsibility at this level. He should apologise and publicly give his support to his own party's policy on this matter. Failing that, he should enunciate his opposition to his party. If he does this, he can no longer be the party spokesman and should resign.

If he does not resign, what should David Cameron do?
The Tories down south must be shaking their heads at all this. No wonder the Lamonts of this world have become such a political liability for the party. He should be sacked. But it would be better for the party in Scotland to be seen to be dealing with its own problems rather than big brother down south having to step in again to sort it out.

If he remains in post what message does this send to Scotland's Catholic community?
The Scottish Tories would dearly love to attract more Catholics to vote for them. In many ways this is the best time to do that, when the Labour party seems to be abandoning the values that social conservatives, like Catholics and others, hold dear. Labour has been taken over by a middle-class metropolitan elite, hostile to traditional values and at odds with many in the country on a whole range of issues, from social and international justice, the family and marriage to abortion, embryo experimentation and choice of schooling. Thanks to this clown Lamont, bang goes any opportunity of *rapprochement*, or even dialogue, between Scottish Catholics and the Scottish Tories. Some of us feel that is a pity.

The colour orange

12 July 2011
Today is historical illiteracy day in Ireland. In the north-east of this country an entire subculture dedicated to a false interpretation of events in the late seventeenth century parade their allergy to learning.

First, the victory they celebrate wasn't a victory at all. It was an inconclusive draw. The real victory of the Williamite forces came a year later at Aughrim in County Galway. The Williamite war in Ireland was part of a wider conflict to stop France becoming the dominant power in Europe. Opposing the French were the states that became part of the League of Augsburg in July 1686. They all feared the might of the French army.

Pope Innocent XI, who had wanted the French under Louis IV to mount a crusade against the Turks, secretly supported and funded the League. Therefore, the Papacy was main financier of the Augsburg military effort. William of Orange was selected to head up the army on the basis of his abilities as a general. So, let me get this straight: in 1690, two kings fought a battle in Ireland; one was British and the other one was Dutch, and the battle ended in a draw. So, today people in Ireland who want to remain British will carry banners of the Dutch king and wear orange sashes, because it is the national colour of Holland, to celebrate the victory he never won at the Boyne. Today is historical illiteracy day in Ireland.

Sing a rebel song

19 November 2011

Today there was an anti-British rebel song played over the PA at Ibrox. The song celebrates those who opposed the Crown in arms to break away from London rule. These rebels in a British colony wanted an independent republic with separation of church and state. Unable to face down the might of the British military, they used guerrilla tactics where they could, utilising their local knowledge and support of the people. Sound familiar? Today was a celebration of Americana at Ibrox.

How many of the home crowd at Ibrox know the origins of the United States of America? The thirteen colonies treasonably rebelled against the British Crown. The Americans engaged the Brits on their own terms. There was no essential difference between the Minutemen and the IRA flying columns. They used the same tactics against the same enemy – the British. They established a republic that was modelled to be the antithesis of Britishness; elected head of state with a written constitution and checks and balances written into the DNA of the new state. The constitution of the United States of America screams with every line: "We are not British and we aren't like them in any way."

It isn't just the Americans, of course. There are fifty modern states from Kenya to Cyprus, Ireland to Iraq and India and from Swaziland and South Africa to the Solomon Islands. Many are small nations or island communities, and I don't doubt many of them would have suffered from oppression from the British, but would not have had the population to resist a global superpower. That fifty includes Israel and the British mandate over Palestine, and Cameroon, which got its independence from both Britain and France. There is also Pakistan, which got its own nation after partition with India.

Some of those states were granted their freedom very graciously from the London imperium. Others, like the Americans and the Irish, seized it violently. It is nice to see the quintessentially British football club having no issues with this concept, just like the British monarch honouring the IRA in the Garden of Remembrance in Dublin earlier this year.

As if secession from the empire wasn't bad enough, the newly constituted upstart republic declared war on the "mother country" in 1812. The empire struck back, but was ultimately defeated. A key target for the British was to blockade Chesapeake Bay and seize Baltimore. The defence of Baltimore's Fort McHenry in the battle inspired Francis Scott Key to compose the poem "The Star-Spangled Banner", which later became the lyrics of the national anthem of the United States of America. It was this anthem that was heard over the PA at Ibrox today.

There are many national anthems around that are "rebel songs". It would appear that some treasonable secessionists who establish a republic by force of irregular arms are more acceptable at Ibrox than others. I have some questions after today:

(1) Are the people running the showbiz side of things at RFC historically illiterate?
(2) Do they have a complete irony bypass?
(3) Or do they believe that the only bad guys in the RFC worldview are Irish rebels?

So, to all my Fenian cousins in America, have a great Thanksgiving this Thursday. You got the better of the deal in growing up in a country where public expressions of Irishness aren't *verboten*.

A clear and present danger?

24 November 2011

I often travel through Glasgow Airport and the huge steel bollards there remind me of that awful day in June 2007. It could, of course, have been so much worse. In the post-9/11 world all is changed, changed utterly.

I think how the security people there must be run off their feet given that Glasgow is a busy international airport getting direct flights from places like Egypt, Dubai and Turkey. Those planes disgorge so many people who are, of course, entirely innocent of any ill-intent. That said, there could be one among the crowd, and it only takes one. The suicide bomber intent on reaching paradise is a security game-changer.

At the top of a pile of people trying to keep the airport a safe place are the police officers tasked with sifting through the thousands of innocent travellers. It goes without saying that the value to society of these highly trained and specialised police officers must be on a par with heart surgeons. Wasting police time is a criminal offence. Wasting the time of a Special Branch officer must be something worse. At the end of the day they follow orders and someone higher up the food chain prioritises their tasks.

With that in mind, I was fascinated when I was recently contacted by a forty-two-year-old man, a native of Antrim, who lives in Scotland where he works as a civil servant. This is his story:

> "I was over for a family wedding and flew over on Monday afternoon with no problems at all. I spent the week with my family in Larne and then flew back on Friday 5.35 Belfast International to Glasgow Airport. I noticed two Branch men in the departure lounge in Belfast International but never paid it much attention. There was a group of Rangers fans heading to Glasgow on the same flight so I thought they might have been watching them. The flight passed without incident.

> "I then came up through the arrivals bit at the airport and passed the departure lounges. When I had got past the two guys on the security desk one of them shouted, 'Excuse me, sir'. I blanked it and walked on, and he shouted, 'Mr (he called me by name), could you come this way please?'

> "At the security desk he asked for my passport and started flicking through it, asking where I'd been, where I was going etc. Then he was asking why I'd been to Lithuania, Israel, the States and Russia. That went on for five minutes and he said they'd need to ask me further questions. Not to be alarmed, it was just routine. They took me downstairs to an empty departure lounge (it's the one Aer Lingus use for flights to New York via Dublin).

> "There was already an Asian-looking man sitting in the lounge. He never spoke throughout my time there and was

taking notes. He handed the first guy two brown folders. The first guy then sat on the benches opposite him and motioned to me to sit beside him. I was expecting to be questioned about dissident Republican support in Scotland or something like that so I was taken aback when he looked at me and said, 'Are you a member of the Green Brigade?' I was looking at him like it was a trick question, so I said, 'No!'

"The next questions were: 'Do you know any members of the Green Brigade?', 'Are you aware of the politics of the Green Brigade?', 'Do you have any involvement in the planning of the Green Brigade?'

"All of the answers to which were 'no'. So, he goes into one of the folders and produces two photos: one of me outside Celtic Park at the poppy protest and one in George Square at the Fans Against Criminalisation (FAC) protest and asked me to explain them. So, the first one I told him was a legitimate protest by disparate groups of Celtic fans against the poppy on the shirts, and the second I was in George Square feeding the pigeons.

"He then went on about me going to these protests and drinking on the Gallowgate, yet I don't know anything about the Green Brigade. How could that be? Then he started on why I sit in section 414 at Celtic Park. Was I a lookout for the Green Brigade? Then he asked what my employers would think about my involvement with the Green Brigade and how did I get clearance for the job I have. I was one of the founder members of the Green Brigade back when we split from the Jungle Bhoys but have had nothing to do with them for years. Certainly nothing since 2007.

"He then started on the Green Brigade's opinion on Irish politics. Did they support the shooting of policemen? How did I feel about the shooting of policemen? Why at a time when everybody is working towards peace are they trying to be divisive? Couldn't help him with any of that and told him I wasn't interested in politics. He then gave me the PTA form (Prevention of Terrorism Act) to fill in. He wrapped it up then by saying he had a feeling I was being deliberately uncooperative and would be looking for me to be more helpful next time we met.

"I phoned my mate in the Green Brigade when I got out the airport to let him know about it and logged it with my solicitor yesterday in case there is any more contact from them."

He concluded: "Almost twenty years after the cease-fires, the Irish community in Scotland are still enduring political policing. I refuse to be criminalised because of the football team I support. One Scotland, many cultures should be more than a catchphrase." I said to him that it is good to know that the Al Qaeda threat has lessened to such an extent that Special Branch officers at Glasgow International Airport, a very scarce resource, now had time to assess the threat to the realm from the singing section at Celtic Park. We both laughed.

Anthony Stokes

29 November 2011

"Being Irish probably doesn't help either. It's just the way it is up here." In those final eight words, Anthony Stokes of Celtic states a truth that many in the country of my birth would rather went uncommented upon: "It's just the way it is up here."

Football is not the cause of anti-Irish racism in Scotland but it does provide it with a powerful arena. Stokes ticks all the boxes in the anti-Irish Edwardian mindset that still exists in Scotland. Within that worldview Stokes, his partner and their unborn child are fair game. To a racist it all makes perfect sense.

These racist views were common sense in British cities a century ago. They have vanished from England's cultural landscape yet they remain stubbornly in place in many areas of Scotland. The political class in Holyrood remain locked into the sectarian framework and seem keen to "even things up" with the new legislation. Until they recognise that they have a problem of anti-Irish racism, being Irish in Scotland will remain a cultural sin in the eyes of a shamefully large minority.

An illicit ethnicity?

13 December 2011

Last month I posed some questions to a room full of Scottish politicians, journalists and policy wonks at the Changin Scotland conference
in Ullapool. The title of my lecture was: *Being Second-generation Irish in
Scotland. An Existential Challenge.*

One of the questions I put to them was: "What kind of Scotland do
you want?" The Scotland I was born into in the 1950s was a cold house
for anyone with an Irish identity. Would the new Scotland, fully independent and sovereign, that many of them wanted be any different? In
the Scotland of many cultures, is my Irish culture okay? If Americana
can be celebrated at Ibrox for Thanksgiving, can Irishness be expressed
at Celtic Park? If it is okay to laud eighteenth-century American insurgents against the British Crown, can I celebrate Theobald Wolfe Tone?

Recently, I suggested an old Irish folk song for the PA at Celtic Park
to a club employee. The song was "Óró Sé do Bheatha 'Bhaile'. Primary-
school children are taught this old song here in Ireland. It's hardly controversial. There is a sixteenth-century version and a twentieth-century
version by Padraig Pearse. I offered the latter, which is the one that is
taught to the kids here. He got back to me and said, "We can't touch
this. It's about Irish history." Indeed it is about Irish history – the history that gave birth to Celtic. The same club employee had earlier taken
on board my suggestion to include a Proclaimers song into the Celtic
match-day experience.

The SNP's Offensive Behaviour at Football and Threatening
Communications Bill, likely to be passed tomorrow, will give, in effect,
carte blanche to any zealous law enforcer who doesn't take too kindly
to any manifestation of Irishness in his country. Under the new law, a
St Patrick's Day banner at Celtic Park next March could be illegal. As
I reported earlier, it would appear that in these days of Al Qaeda the
most pressing matter in the mind of a Special Branch officer at Glasgow
Airport was whether or not an Irishman was a member of the Green
Brigade. I will have more to report on this individual's case soon.

Meanwhile, the reality is that hard evidence exists – when it isn't
accidentally shredded, of course – of the targeting of an ethnic minority
in Scotland. Even when some raw data reaches the tabloids the truth is
hidden. Within the sectarian statistics hides the reality of anti-Irish racism, a term that seems to be *verboten* by the SNP Government. Speak to

them about it and they talk about sectarianism. This is more important than semantics.

The representatives of the Irish community in Scotland have consistently petitioned for the political class in Holyrood to think outside the sectarian framework. So far, they have been met with zero success. There was not a single Irish community organisation invited to speak to the Justice Committee about this new law. The Harps Community Project, funded by the Irish Government, did send in a written submission. The Catholic Church was invited, Celtic fans, the Tartan Army and people who run unofficial Rangers websites. All of these groups and individuals were afforded the opportunity to speak to the lawmakers, but not the Irish community, not the people who are the targets of the abuse and the aggression for being who they are.

Can you imagine this happening if the new law was brought forward after prominent members of the Nigerian community in Scotland had been sent letter bombs and one of the recipients had been attacked at a televised sports event in Edinburgh? Moreover, an Edinburgh jury then does not find his assailant, despite being seen by millions in the act, to be guilty of assault. Can you conceive of that actually happening? It is an irony, to say the least, that when manifestations of anti-Irish racism in Scotland and an attack on an Irishman at his work went viral, the Scottish Government, embarrassed by the fact that they had sat on their hands over this issue, created a law whose main target would be people expressing their Irishness.

If I was still in that room in Ullapool with the same people I would ask them this: "Given the reality of anti-Irish racism in your country, do you consider a law that effectively criminalises entirely legitimate expressions of Irishness to be the sign of a mature political class worthy of greater powers?"

A bad law

20 December 2011

Hard cases make bad law. The Scottish Government, for the first time, has used its overall majority to pass legislation against a largely united opposition of Labour, Liberal Democrat, Tories and Greens.

I believe that the SNP's new law will fail on two accounts. First, it criminalises that which should be legal. The freedom of speech argument has been repeatedly made in the run-up to the bill being passed so there is no need for me to rehearse that once more. Suffice to say it is fairly rudimentary for any criminal justice system to be able to discern the difference between an opinion which offends and an outburst which incites hatred and violence. The second fatal flaw within the bill's DNA has largely gone unreported in the mainstream media. This "anti-bigotry bill" does not acknowledge the ethnic component in Scotland's so-called "secret shame".

The SNP policy wonks can't claim the excuse of ignorance as there were enough of them at the Changin Scotland conference last month in Ullapool. I told them that, born in the west of Scotland in the 1950s, the derogatory terms I grew up with for Catholics all had a distinct Hibernian edge to them. Despite the presence of kids of Highland, Italian and Polish extraction at Lanarkshire schools, it was a specifically Irish badge of disdain that was attached to all Catholics. Wherever our ancestors had originated we were all, in the eyes of the host community, "Fenians".

There is a paradox in that Catholic Scots had this Irish otherness imposed on them while at the same time anyone wishing to embrace an Irish heritage was told that they could make no such claim. I know that when Irish politicians raised the issue of anti-Irish racism with Scottish officials they were answered with policy *apropos* "sectarianism". It was as if the denizens of Holyrood feared mentioning the I-word and that the mere acknowledgement of Scotland's largest ethnic minority group would somehow fatally undermine their nationalist project.

When Eoin Ryan MEP visited Scotland in November 2008 as a guest of Alan Smith MEP, I was the only journalist to cover his visit and working lunch at Glasgow City Chambers. He had raised the Famine Song issue on the floor of the European Parliament and had been invited over to see that everything was in fact hunky dory. When he spoke to the assembled group about "racism" they spoke of "sectarianism". I discussed this Derry/Londonderry issue with Eoin Ryan's savvy press officer. It was clear to us that these functionaries of the Scottish Government were incapable of discussing the Famine Song controversy as a manifestation of anti-Irish racism.

Three years on, the Scottish political elite are no further forward to being able to utter the words anti-Irish racism. During the dying months of 2008, as the Famine Song controversy raged, I saw correspondence between several opposition TDs and the Scottish authorities. All of the TDs stated that they were writing about the racism contained in the

newest addition to the Rangers songbook and they would get a standard letter back about "anti-sectarianism". This is what Danny Boyle of
the Harps Community Project refers to as the "sectarian framework"
and refusal by official Scotland to recognise the Irish as an ethnic group
and ditties like the Famine Song as a manifestation of anti-Irish racism.

[The online article carries a link to an interview with Danny Boyle,
reproduced in this book.]

The new bill is a product of the sectarian framework mindset at
Holyrood. Many believe that the new law will be unworkable. This
law, which purports to put manners on planet *fitba*, is an object lesson
in what happens when politicians get panicked into doing something
about a problem they had previously been deliberately ignoring. After
Jack McConnell's well-meaning anti-sectarianism effort, the incoming
SNP Government decided it wasn't a priority. The SNP position, intimated in many private briefings, was that droning on about sectarianism was "running Scotland down". Journalists were called out on their
lack of patriotism.

One of the many ironies of this situation is that in "doing something about the problem" the SNP Government is ignoring the real
issue in Scotland. Of course, there is a problem in Scotland of anti-
Catholic hatred, but it cannot be understood without also factoring in
anti-Irish racism. They are intertwined because of the history of large-
scale Irish immigration in Scotland at the height of the British Empire
when Ireland was very much a colonial possession of the London imperium. Occupational parity was achieved by Catholics of Irish descent
in Glasgow in 2001; in New York the same social progress was reached
in 1901. With large-scale job discrimination finally over, what is left in
Scotland is the attitudinal discrimination arising out of those generations of the Irish being at the back of the bus.

One aspect of this is that there remains little acknowledgement of
the contribution of the Irish to the building of modern Scotland. In
the Scotland of many cultures, somehow Paddy doesn't fit in with the
national narrative propagated by Salmond's Blairite new SNP. Some
legal types believe that this new law may well be tested at the European
Court of Human Rights and within that arena it will founder.

Scotland continues to have an issue around being comfortable with
the Irish and Irishness among it, just as the De Valera generation in
Ireland were not comfortable about sharing a space with people of
British heritage. My native city is full of young men who could be the
next Jason Campbell, driven to violence by acting on an ethnic hatred

that has gestated there since the days of the empire. This is not so much Scotland's secret shame, rather it is Caledonia's inconvenient truth. Throats are cut and statistics shredded. The official denial means that the central issue has yet to be tackled. Scotland has a new law, but it will not defuse the tribal time bomb on the Clyde. This bad law will make more hard cases.

How to be a racist in Scotland and get away with it

10 January 2012

A good friend of mine who is a long-time buddy of Pat Fenlon said he had high hopes for him when he took up the Hibernian job. I said to my big pal from Tallaght that I hoped he would do well but he would have to cope with the racist abuse that would inevitably be hurled at him. "From that Rangers lot?" he asked. "Not just them. I saw young James McCarthy pilloried at New Douglas Park by the visiting St Mirren fans in 2008 and McGeady got it at many grounds in Scotland."

Today in the *Scotsman* we have a report that Fenlon was subject to abuse based on his nationality. "The Irishman was repeatedly subjected to aggressive abuse – much of it centring on his nationality – from individuals within the home support during the Easter Road side's 3–2 victory over the Second Division leaders. However, despite the offenders being clearly identifiable in the stand, no action was taken by police or stewards," the paper reported.

Personal attacks on the basis of a person's nationality are considered by UEFA to be racist abuse. The man himself passed it off as "banter". The reality is that Pat Fenlon was subject to racist abuse from Cowdenbeath supporters and there was no police intervention. The extent to which anti-Irish racism isn't on the political radar in Scotland frames the response of the public agencies and, indeed, the victims to it. Until anti-Irish racism is publicly challenged in the way black players in England have a zero tolerance of racism, it will continue.

The sporting bodies and public agencies have not even begun to create the atmosphere within which an Irish person, subjected to racist abuse, would feel empowered to complain. If Hibernian's new manager was black, English or Spanish would the response from the police on the day have been different? If I took this story of anti-Irish racism to anyone in the Scottish Government for a response they would whirr into action like a Stepford Wife, parroting out guff about "sectarianism". If official Scotland can't even recognise their country's largest and oldest ethnic minority, it should come as no surprise that they wouldn't respond appropriately to an Irishman suffering racist abuse at his place of employment in the presence of scores of police officers.

Jeff Winter

12 January 2012

The trial by Twitter of Jeff Winter in the early hours of 12 January 2012 flags up some interesting issues. At time of writing, his website has been suspended by the hosting company. My first suspicion was that Mr Winter's site had been hacked or what was being circulated through social media was a doctored image.

However, it would appear that Mr Winter has some previous in these matters and that the alleged comments were not atypical of his views. Before his site was suspended I was able to glean the following; in one post, he described young Celtic supporters as "small and skinny, looked dirty, had pointed noses and their eyes were staring and not evenly placed on their rat like faces ... incestuous produce of an illegal act."

I spoke with several sports journalists in England today who have met Mr Winter and they told me that these views have increasingly become his stock in trade in recent years. Back in 2010 during the referees' strike, he commented on his site that "I did a piece on *Talksport* regarding the Scottish reffing situation. I tried to be diplomatic, but as Goughy named names I had to concur, as I suggested earlier, that this whole situation is down to Neil Lennon and Celtic FC. Their complex that everyone is against them is touching on paranoia. Weather permitting, the SPL will go ahead with officials from across Europe."

On the same post he said of the "Dallasgate" affair: "More ructions north of the border as Hugh Dallas, the head of referee development is forced to resign, that coming just hours after the ref involved in Dundee United v. Celtic announced his early retirement. Crazy – Lennon and his Celtic whingers are causing the careers of decent guys to be finished long before their time."

While Mr Winter was still a top-level referee, the then owner of

Rangers, Sir David Murray, said that the club did not want the "FTP brigade". It would appear that Mr Winter is a member of that anti-Papal fraternity associated with Rangers Football Club. What irks me about such "humour", apart from the offence that it causes, is that it makes it increasingly difficult for journalists to tackle this difficult subject.

It is with this in mind that I remember the tragic passing of my sister in the NUJ, Mary Raftery, this week. Brave journalism on the vital subject of physical and sexual abuse endured by children in Irish industrial institutions and residential schools is her legacy. Just before Christmas I interviewed a man who had been at a Catholic-run boarding school in the west of Ireland in the 1970s and disclosed to me that he had suffered abuse from a member of staff there.

This man, now in his forties, finally wanted to "go public" and his psychotherapist (an ex-social work colleague of mine for over twenty years) had suggested that he contact me as I had an understanding of and sympathy for victims of childhood abuse. We agreed that I would put a series of detailed questions to the appropriate church authorities who had run the establishment (now closed). As a journalist, you know when someone is being obstructive, and it is my view that the church functionary I was dealing with was playing for time and didn't want yet another story in the nationals here in Ireland about the church failing to listen to a disclosure that could have prevented further abuse. Contacting Mary was on my "to do list" for this story. May she find her rest eternal.

The recollection process for this man was proving so traumatic that he decided to stop the interviews and return to his private anguish for now. I, of course, respected his wishes and did not proceed further with the story. In time, I hope, he will somehow find the strength to go public, but in truth it is a fortitude that I know I would not have in the same circumstances. There are some topics that should be off limits to "off colour humour" and I believe that child sex abuse is one of them. Clearly, some people in the making-people-laugh business will disagree with me. What is beyond dispute is that this subject should be approached carefully, if at all.

I was told today that Mr Winter has some media work with *Talksport* and Sky, but that he saw his main income coming from after-dinner speaking in the west of Scotland and, occasionally, Northern Ireland at functions in Orange halls and at Rangers supporters' clubs. It was on this "sash bash" circuit that Mr Winter appears to have honed his repertoire mainly around anti-Catholic hatred and "jokes" about clerical child abuse scandals. The *Daily Mail* picked up on the story and ran with it.

The tipping point on Twitter appears to have been reached when journalist Gabriele Marcotti became involved and phoned Mr Winter. This was no "outing" by social media as Mr Winter is very public in his views, but what it does show is that Twitter can push the old media into picking up a story that was waiting to be written for some time. A tip of the hat must go to James Cameron on *The Celtic Network* (TCN) who was the first to blog on this yesterday and set Twitter off on one. My own meagre contribution to the Twitter debate on this was that, perhaps, Mr Winter "had reached his own Ron Atkinson moment". Time will tell. If this is a career-defining moment for the ex-referee then it will be another footnote in the story of the growing power of Twitter to define our world and how we interact with each other.

The view from Strasbourg

20 January 2012

> O wad some Power the giftie gie us
> To see oursels as ithers see us!
> It wad frae mony a blunder free us

Robert Burns' plea for self-awareness seems very appropriate when I read this report from the "advisory committee on the framework convention for the protection of national minorities" for the European Commission:

> Combating racism and intolerance
>
> 18. The authorities have made continued efforts to implement measures to fight all forms of racism and intolerance in society. Significant progress has taken place with regard to data collection on hate crime. This data indicates that hate crime is on the increase since the adoption of the second Opinion of the Advisory Committee, which is a cause for concern. There is a worrying level of hostility against Gypsies, travellers, migrants and Roma, a situation that is sometimes aggravated by certain sections of the media stirring up hostility and prejudices against them and other ethnic minority communities.

There has also been a steady rise in Islamophobia and in hate crime against Muslims, *a rise in incidents of anti-Irish racism reported* in Scotland, as well as attacks against Roma families in Belfast in 2009. This situation is a source of concern.

It is significant and encouraging that anti-Irish racism in Scotland is now on the European Commission's radar. I hope that that the Scottish Government will find it increasingly difficult to cling to the sectarian framework when it realises that the reality of anti-Irish racism in Scotland is now known in arenas like the European Commission. The Irish community in Scotland needs this awareness to grow in places like Strasbourg so pressure can build on Holyrood to engage with them and listen to their legitimate concerns. Until they do that, the government in Edinburgh, who claim they are patriots, remains a parcel of rogues.

A mythical place

9 February 2012

I recently wrote of the response of Ulster unionism to the campaign for Scotland's Claim of Right. Among the more bizarre suggestions by Lord Kilclooney was for Scotland to be partitioned. Well, drawing an arbitrary line through a country based on sectarian attitudes certainly worked remarkably well here on this island …

However, perhaps I was a little hasty with the Lordship's idea. There just might be one wee bit of Scotland that doesn't fancy being independent of Westminster and, indeed, it might be best for all if it doesn't experience freeeddummm. Over the years, since I first heard of local protests at council house doors being painted green, Larkhall has become a mythical as well as a physical place, a bit like Dublin 4 in Ireland. Such places enter the collective consciousness not just as a physical location, but a shorthand term for a worldview.

For me, "Larkhall" conjures up that 1950s smug parochialism where everything in Scotland was in the correct place, especially the Fenians. It is the human condition to resist change, even when that reordering is for the best. This will be immediately understood by anyone who has worked professionally with addicts or has someone in their family with an addiction issue. The addict denies that change is needed.

The dwindling crowds at Ibrox this season might give an indication as to how many in Scotland are addicted to anti-Irish racism and the fading brand called "Britishness". Could Larkhall be the home of the NewCo Rangers? However, outwith Larkhall, Scotland is changing. The days when people of Irish ethnicity would meekly sit at the back of the bus are over. Those times will not return. Young people in Scotland are consistently stating that they view themselves as becoming more Scottish and less British.

The auld sang may once more be heard after 2014 and, in that scenario, the "quintessentially British football club" is something of an anachronism. These are historic times for the country of my birth and for Rangers. Suddenly many things seem possible. Perhaps the NewCo will field a player in their first team who plays for the Republic of Ireland. I doubt Lord Kilclooney or the denizens of Larkhall would approve.

Close to the bone, but from the heart

22 February 2012

This article first appeared in the Irish Examiner

Usually, journalists are quite happy to get a name check from one of their own. We're like that, so I should have been happy to be mentioned in the *Irish Examiner* on Monday by Ken Early. In the interest of full disclosure, I know Ken and I like him. He's always good craic when we bump into each other at the Aviva and I rarely miss his radio show. However, Ken mentioned me as an example of a freelancer who writes about Scottish football and Rangers in particular without anything nasty befalling me.

I beg to differ. I first stumbled into the world of the Rangers internet as a journalist back in 2008. I wrote about a song that had emerged from the Rangers support. It became infamously known as the Famine Song. They chanted the lines at Celtic's supporters (many of them Irish or of Irish descent) "the Famine is over, why don't you go home?".

The Irish Government's consulate in Edinburgh asked the Scottish Government to clarify what steps they were taking to eradicate this racism against the country's Irish community. I wrote a piece for the *Sunday Tribune* and then went onto a Scottish radio football phone-in to explain how this was playing over here. As a Glasgow Irishman (with a Mayo father) now living back home, I was probably well placed to write on the Famine Song. The response was instant. A tsunami of bile hit my inbox and my extinction was discussed on message boards. The extent of the defamatory material published about me was such that if it had appeared in a newspaper I would now be writing this from my private island in the Caribbean and not a cottage in west Donegal.

The Famine Song saga ended with it being ruled racist by the highest court in Scotland. Rangers supporters blamed me. I then broke a story a year later which led to the Scottish FA's head of refereeing, Hugh Dallas, being sacked (Dallas had sent a "tasteless message" relating to the Pope's visit to Scotland). I got an award for that story but it solidified me as a *bête noire* in the Rangers subculture. These smears, utterly without foundation, are now believed by tens of thousands of Rangers supporters.

Then there were the threats. It was now about death, not defamation. When I travel to Glasgow now, I have to be mindful of not telling anyone who doesn't need to know when I'm arriving. This is police advice. Writing about Rangers has changed my life, but not my journalism. Everything in life has a cost. Ken suggested that I had no price to pay for my work. Wrong, buddy. Dead wrong …

Hearing clearly

5 July 2012

Listening is an undervalued skill for journalists in the digital age. When Stewart Regan made his "social unrest" observation most of the hacks in the presser didn't pick up on the significance of it. They ignored what he had said and then barged on with questions about the Scottish Football League, Scottish Football Association application by Sevco and other such insignificant matters next to public order.

Those two words should have stopped everyone in their tracks; instead, Regan was bombarded with breathless questions from airhead hacks. Thankfully, they were not all of such a low calibre. I have spoken to one experienced journalist who was there and he remains quite clear on what the SFA chief executive was speculating about; Regan was concerned about the Ibrox mob's capacity for trouble. That is my guy's settled view of what the Englishman was on about.

The SFA chief executive has tried to row back from the original "social unrest" comments. Mr Regan obviously thinks it is unlikely, in the event of there being no football at Ibrox in the coming season, that the Famine Song choir will take up a genteel hobby and be good citizens. I agree with him on that. Mention the words "social unrest" in connection with supporters of the deceased club and it conjures up images of Barcelona, Pamplona and, of course, Manchester.

Perhaps he is correct that Edmiston Drive is a sort of underclass crèche that provides a genuine social service to the rest of society. However, I take the opposite view; that Rangers (1872–2012) was a gathering point and a source of affirmation for the worst elements in Scottish society. Augmented by the finest specimens of Rathcoole and the Shankill Road, Ibrox has been a culture dish for some very toxic societal pathogens for over a century. Of course, Regan's comment does unwittingly heap greater pressure of the SFL clubs in their upcoming deliberations. Turnbull Hutton and the other chaps may just have had another issue to consider when they decide on the Sevco application to their league: public order. No pressure then ...

Best buddies

26 September 2012

It would appear that the spirit of Lord Rothermere of the inter-war years has not been fully exorcised from the *Daily Mail*. The quintessentially British newspaper famously supported Mosley's British Union of Fascists in the 1930s. This was at the same time as a chap called Billy Fullerton and his street thugs, the Billy Boys, were splashing around in Fenian blood in Glasgow. The Bridgeton sociopath is, of course, still fondly remembered by the Ibrox klan every time they extol him in song. In the late 1930s, Billy Fullerton joined Oswald Mosley's British Union of Fascists and he even started a Glasgow branch of the Ku Klux Klan.

As well as their well-known hatred of people of colour in America, the Klan are also an anti-Catholic and anti-semitic organisation. Many of the Klan's founder members were of "Scots Irish" heritage, descendants of Lowland Scots who had been "planted" in Ulster in the seventeenth century. Like the Ibrox chaps, the *Daily Mail* has got some previous when it comes to xenophobia and far right politics. However, I was still taken aback by this piece which remarked on the physical appearance of the people queuing for the new Apple mobile phone.

[The online article carries a link to a column by the *Daily Mail* columnist Richard Littlejohn published on 24 September 2012, in which he says of the queue of people at an Apple store in London: "No doubt the usual suspects will howl 'racism', but it is remarkable that the only white face belongs to a blonde bird in a hi-viz jacket. And she's probably Polish."]

I had thought that even the *Daily Mail* would balk at publishing such an observation. Inhabitants of planet *fitba* may be interested to know that *Daily Mail* columnist Richard Littlejohn is best buddies with Ramsay Smith; Media House's executive director and the company's main man at Ibrox have shared many a jolly night out and family holidays with Mr Littlejohn.

As Mr Green's statements, many penned by Ramsay, become more spirited, one wonders if he has asked his good friend Richard for advice on vitriol and venom. Leading author David Aaronovitch once described a book by Mr Littlejohn as a "four hundred-page recruiting pamphlet for the British National Party". However, Mr Aaronovitch had actually read the book before giving his judgement, unlike many of the clairvoyant literary chaps who did their own critique of my book before it was even printed!

When Littlejohn was "transferred" from the *Sun* to the *Daily Mail* in 2005, Paul Dacre, the *Daily Mail* editor in chief, said Littlejohn was returning to "his spiritual home". I am reliably informed that Mr Littlejohn has been a guest at Ibrox on match days, so he will be aware of the unique ambience. Perhaps he will write about his impressions of Ibrox in his column. Of course, now that there are no pesky match delegates to report them, the old song sheet may make a comeback down Govan way. If the bears do break into a rendition of the Billy Boys at Ibrox, I am sure that the ghost of old Lord Rothermere from the 1930s would warmly approve …

NUJ motion about the targeting of journalists

9 October 2012

The following is the motion passed at the National Union of Journalists' Delegate Meeting (DM) in Newcastle at the weekend. The motion was submitted by the New Media Industrial Council (NMIC) and was then amended by the National Executive Council (NEC). All of the NEC amendments were accepted by NMIC. I spoke to this amended motion and it was passed unanimously by DM.

LNM 14 (Far right attacks on journalists)

This Delegate Meeting notes with concern the growing targeting of journalists including threats of violence against them and their families by far right groups in the UK using blogs, Facebook, message boards and Twitter. These attacks have grown in the context of the publication on 8 September 2012 of NUJ member Phil Mac Giolla Bháin's book, *Downfall*.

DM notes that the abusive tone of much of the abuse was underpinned by the racism and sectarianism that too often can be heard on Scottish football terraces. This conference instructs the NEC to work with the SEC to examine organising a training programme for NUJ members in Scotland to heighten their awareness of anti-Irish and other forms of racism amongst Scottish football supporters.

DM further notes the statement in September 2012 from the Scottish Executive Council on this matter. This DM believes that any attack on a journalist is an attack on journalism and an assault on democracy. DM notes that this campaign of abuse follows threats against and actual physical attacks on journalists by the EDL and associated groups and, chillingly, death threats against a journalist covering Loyalist paramilitaries in Northern Ireland.

DM notes that many of these campaigns have engaged the tactic employed by many contemporary far right groups of attempting to portray those who seek to expose racism and hatred as being racist themselves, for example, the video on YouTube posted by a UKIP supporter purporting to expose "anti-white racism at the National Union of Journalists".

DM recalls the long-running NUJ campaign seeking to close the far right Redwatch hate site. DM instructs the NEC to examine whether lessons can be learnt from that campaign and to redouble efforts to seek to force the

police to take seriously the issue of online targeting of
journalists in all jurisdictions in which the NUJ works.

Alien intervention

13 October 2012

Outsiders often see the truth about a culture that the denizen cannot. Sociologists refer to a process called a "common sense inventory".
Basically, the newcomer has to ask questions because they don't know
the rules of the culture; those historical set of assumptions that have
been transmitted from childhood.

Alex Thomson is an alien who landed on planet *fitba* earlier this
year. His lack of comprehension of how things are in Glasgow has been
highly instructive. One of the things that Alex has been introduced to is
the extent to which the "RFC underclass", as he styled them on Twitter,
are allowed to bully and intimidate anyone who irks them. The only
remarkable thing about his blog yesterday on the *Channel 4 News* site
was that it has taken this long for someone in the UK media to stumble
upon planet *fitba*'s dirty little secret.

Alex felt no need to genuflect to the Old Firm fiction that there was
some Rorschachian symmetry in the crime count between the two soccer tribes in Glasgow. He simply outlined the facts, and it is impossible
to tell this story within the "one side is as bad as the other" framework,
so the Glasgow media ignore it. As anyone in the public agencies in
Glasgow will tell you privately, it is the blue half of the city that is
overwhelmingly the source of the city's anti-social football problems.
Their *Herrenvolk* swagger imbues them with a sense of entitlement that
they can behave with impunity. They are hardly deluded in this matter
as heretofore they have largely escaped any sanction from the state.

A klan apologist could argue that this is small-scale stuff and people should man up. However, broken windows can eventually lead to
broken lives. When I reported the threats against me in 2010 to An
Garda Síochána (Ireland's National Police Service) they were highly
professional and that is because they know what the outcome can be
when scum start threatening a journalist. Subsequently, they have a zero
tolerance approach to such "banter". My NUJ colleagues in Northern
Ireland have met with a similar professional response from the Police
Service of Northern Ireland (PSNI). These two police jurisdictions have

reasons to take such things seriously; Veronica and Marty, lest we forget.

When little crimes are ignored they are, in effect, tolerated. The perpetrator can then become the serious criminal of tomorrow. What is needed is for everyone who is threatened by the Ibrox klan to report it to the police immediately and demand the protection of the law. This fascist underclass needs to have manners put on them; that is why there are police and courts funded by the taxpayer. I suspect that is what any outsider would expect a mature democracy to do with such people.

Telling the truth about the Ibrox klan

26 October 2012

When I started writing about the Rangers scandal I realised that the Glasgow media were part of the problem. They were too close to those at the top of the marble staircase and too easily cowed by the Ibrox mob. The *Sun* serialisation debacle showed that the klan can wield power in Glasgow.

I knew that the mainstream media outside the city, indeed, furth of Scotland, would be required to break the media silence. That is why I welcomed the involvement of Alex and his Channel 4 colleagues back in March. All of the people in Scotland who want to live in a decent society – which is almost all of the country's population – owe a great debt of gratitude to Alex Thomson and his colleagues on *Channel 4 News*. The man himself has covered twenty-two wars and isn't frightened by what Glasgow has to offer in terms of threats and intimidation.

Moreover, he saw how the local hack pack had wilfully ignored the Rangers story for, in part, precisely the same reasons that he explores in his piece tonight. That is why he saw the value of those outside the Scottish mainstream, including myself, who had been willing to tell the story of the Rangers scandal. As has already been trailed, Gary Allan QC will say tonight that a "criminal underclass" exists around the Ibrox club. Graham Spiers first used the term "white underclass" to describe this element of the Rangers support in the aftermath of the rioting in Manchester in May 2008. This was before I had written a word on the club as a journalist. However, it is an apt term for a group of people, self-selecting, who do not wish to abide by the norms of civilised society.

It is for another day why they find Ibrox to be such a warm house where their hatreds are incubated, but it seems to be the case. What will be screened tonight by *Channel 4 News* will not feature an outside broadcast from Baghdad or Mogadishu. All of those interviewed are resident in Scotland. Therefore, this piece would have been within the production budgets of the Scottish broadcast organisations. However, elements of the local media remain under the toxic influence of the klan so it had to be compiled by people travelling up from London.

The criminality of the klan is now a UK story. How quintessentially British! The Scottish print sector, especially the tabloids, chases the Ibrox demographic. Working to tight margins, editors fear a boycott of their title, or simply a general fall-off in sales. The klan know that intimidating journalists does often bring real tangible results for them. Apparently their belief system is so fragile that they cannot abide anything in the papers that is at variance with that worldview. Subsequently, I have long since given up on the local media tackling this issue in any concerted or meaningful way. That this is allowed to happen in the major city of a mature democracy is a permanent embarrassment and an occasional disgrace.

The decent people in Scotland owe a debt of gratitude to the people at *Channel 4 News* and the brave people who went on camera to denounce the klan. Good journalism draws a line in the sand and that is what Alex Thomson has done on this issue. In the coming days, what side of that line you find yourself on will tell you a lot about what kind of Scotland you want.

The shameful truth on Channel 4

27 October 2012

Last night on *Channel 4 News* there was a piece of television reporting that should be a wake-up call for everyone in Scotland. For it was either seven minutes and fifty-one seconds of an intricately choreographed libel against the reputation of a fine bunch of Corinthian chaps in Govan or it was the shameful truth.

If it was the former, then the conspiracy involved an award-winning TV news channel based in London, their highly decorated war correspondent, a QC, the NUJ's full-time organiser in Scotland, Raith Rovers' big cheese Turnbull Hutton, respected social commentator Gerry Hassan and my book editor, Angela Haggerty. As conspiracies go, you have to admit that's fairly impressive!

For the conspiracy theory to hold water, all of these people would be motivated to besmirch the reputation of such a dignified bunch of supporters. Presumably, there was even some skulduggery in the supporter's audio that was broadcast. Of course, there is one other explanation for the Channel 4 piece last night: that it was entirely factual. The reality is that there is simply no need for any black propaganda to be used against the crazy end of the Ibrox support. They do all of that themselves. Actually, they are very good at it. They lash out in anger at a new social order where they are not "The People" and instead they see an appalling vista where they are consigned to the hellish ignominy of equality.

As the Zeitgeist in Scotland changes, they see their world slipping away. The structures and societal arrangements that affirmed and reinforced their sense of cultural superiority are decomposing in front of their eyes. A new Scotland based on decency and fairness where the worldview of good folk like Turnbull Hutton is the moral compass rather than those who would seek to have a book suppressed is emerging.

Of course, those who, in recent weeks, abused bookshop staff in Glasgow for working in a place that stocked *Downfall* will now be proudly wearing the Royal British Legion poppy. These fine fellows will proudly state that they do so to remember those who died for our freedom. I would wager that they have a rather different concept of liberty than most of us. Their idea of freedom is when they get to decide which books can be sold and which stories newspapers can publish. That is why we cannot allow them to win. Lest we forget.

Graham Spiers and the "rogue angry underclass"

30 October 2012

The initial response from the Fitba Fourth Estate to *Channel 4 News'* groundbreaking piece on the Ibrox klan was depressingly predictable. Some hacks were saying on Twitter that if thirty-two journalists had been threatened then they would know about it.

This was in response to Paul Holleran's assertion on the Channel 4 report that he had been contacted by that number of union members since December, complaining that they had been threatened. I know Paul Holleran and I am also aware of that growing list of journalists in Scotland threatened by the Ibrox klan. That this figure was being questioned by members of the Scottish hack pack was very dispiriting.

Subsequently, huge thanks must go to Graham Spiers for writing a brave piece today on what he has endured for over a decade. Whatever criticisms people may have of Graham's views on the game we all love, no one should doubt his basic decency. As a committed Christian, he called out the Rangers support for their bigoted anti-Catholic chanting when it wasn't fashionable to do so. He was the first mainstream journalist in Scotland to use the *verboten* term "anti-Irish racism" on radio when discussing the Rangers mob. Moreover, he also pointed out that the guy on the throne of the Murray empire had no clothes when such an observation was definitely bad for your professional health as a sports writer. Yet, he persisted. Today he came to the defence of Alex Thomson and *Channel 4 News*.

The ITN folks stand accused of telling the truth about the Edmiston Drive chaps. Graham shared his own experiences for the first time on the subject of being intimidated by Rangers fans. They echo the experiences of Gary Allan QC. Equipped with a "faux Protestant culture", the Ibrox klan is a serious social problem that modern Scotland needs to deal with.

They have a deluded sense of entitlement that leads them to believe they can bully and intimidate anyone who irks them or their tragically fragile belief system. Until these fine fellows feel the full force of the state upon them, they will continue to toddle along believing that they truly are "The People". What they believe informs how they behave. Their sense of entitlement propels their actions.

The recent victory over the *Sun* serialisation of *Downfall* has only exacerbated the situation. In the following week after the *Sun* caved in to them, the klan came very close to forcing the main book retailers to cancel orders for the book. It would have been a huge victory for a racist mob and a serious wound would have been inflicted on Scottish society. Initially, my publisher shielded me from just how close it came to being sold only on Amazon. For those of you who bought the book in Scotland in the old-fashioned way – out of a shop – well, that almost never happened ...

This is an authoritarian mob which considers freedom of thought as thinking only as they do. They tell Orwellian lies about people through the anonymity of social media and target the families of those they consider to be their enemies. Yet, they continue to do so in Scotland with relative impunity. When I spoke at the Changin Scotland conference in Ullapool last year on the subject of being second-generation Irish in modern Scotland I asked my audience – a mixed bunch of Scottish nationalists, Labour people and the politically non-aligned – "What kind of Scotland do you want?"

How the criminality of the Ibrox klan is dealt with in the coming months will go a long way to answering that question. I hope it is a Scotland where people like Turnbull Hutton and Graham Spiers are among the authoritative voices in the national game rather than the online underclass klan who would wish to silence them. On Rangers message boards, Graham is smeared as "the discredited journalist". Perhaps in the eyes of that "rogue angry underclass" he is. However, the good folk in Scotland will view that he has undoubtedly done the state some service. They know't. No more of that.

Respect in the workplace

27 December 2012

As regular readers here will know, I am no stranger to Spain and her people. Moreover, I do not frequent the Costa del Essex, but only auténtico España. In the last two years I have walked El Camino Santiago and visited El Pilar in Zaragoza.

The most relaxing time I had in my adult life was doing not very much in provincial Castile-La Mancha after walking across the north of Spain. Dandering into Azuqueca de Henares and being the only foreigner within earshot was a joy. Only two weeks ago I lunched in el Barrio in La Coruña, so I do not come to this from a position of zero knowledge on España and her people. In terms of full disclosure, I have never been to Benidorm or Ibiza.

I reckon there are very few people in Spain under forty-five years of age who are in any way remotely religious. However, you do see quite a lot of young people making the sign of the cross in public. Perhaps another two generations or so of non-believers in Iberia will excise this religious reflex, but, for now, people in Spain bless themselves. Spain was, of course, a dictatorship for a large part of the twentieth century and the Catholic Church had a favoured position. Modern Spain is democratic and increasingly secular. However, cultures do not change as quickly as forms of government.

Francisco José Sandaza Asensio was born in Toledo almost a decade after the death of Franco. I do not know if the footballer is Catholic or is religiously observant in any faith and that, of course, is a private matter for him. However, the news today that he has been apparently asked to desist from blessing himself on the field of play is particularly depressing.

In his words: "El primer día me aconsejaron no santiguarme antes de comenzar los partidos." ("The first day I was advised not to cross myself before matches.")

It is not clear who made this request of the Spaniard. My own theory is that it was a Chelsea fan on a tour of the splendid stadium that John Brown played for. I expect that the intrepid chaps on the Scottish sports desks will soon be running this story down and preparing a "big splash". They could start by contacting Lorenzo Amoruso and asking him about what he stated in his autobiography about being advised not to bless himself before matches, especially where he could be seen by the paying customers at Ibrox. In the meantime, I am sure that Sevco's impressive media operation will put out a statement stating that señor Sandaza is mistaken and that it is perfectly okay for him to indulge in the religious observation of his choice while at his workplace.

Facing up to anti-Irish "stealth racism"

31 January 2013
This article first appeared in An Phoblacht

The Scottish Government has appointed a "bigotry czar". Dr Duncan Morrow, of the School of Criminology, Politics and Social Policy at the University of Ulster, will chair a panel chosen to examine the scale and nature of religious bigotry in Scotland, assess efforts to tackle it and advise ministers on policies and initiatives to combat sectarianism. Dr Morrow is also a former chair of the Community Relations Council in the north of Ireland. He gave interviews to the press and spoke of persistent claims of "an embedded anti-Catholicism that isn't going away in Scotland". The words "anti-Irish racism", however, never passed his lips.

I made several attempts to contact Dr Morrow about this apparent oversight on his part, but emails were not answered and phone calls were not returned in the two weeks in between going to print. I would have put to him the proposition that to discuss anti-Catholic hatred in Scotland without mention of the Irish community is nonsensical. The derogatory terms for Catholics in common usage in Scotland mainly have an Irish flavour to them. This is "stealth racism" and no one operating in the mainstream Scottish media seems able or willing to call it as such.

For example, there is an official fiction in Scotland that the Famine Song – a song with its origin in Scotland and urging Irish descendants in Scotland to "go home" because the Famine is over – is a manifestation of sectarianism, not anti-Irish racism. When the Famine Song was at its zenith, a sticker appeared in Glasgow. It was a rip-off of an advertising campaign by the P&O ferry company. The slogan "P&O takes you home" was replaced with "The Famine is over. P&O takes you home." If this had been aimed at any other ethnic group in Scotland there would have been a debate in the Scottish Parliament about it – and rightly so. Taking the ethnic out of the equation is crucial because to do anything else would be to recognise the existence of the Irish community in Scotland.

Academic Tom Gallagher stated in his book *Glasgow: The Uneasy Peace* (Manchester University Press, 1987) that a key objective of the leaders of Scottish society in the early twentieth century was to deny to outsiders that a large proportion of Scotland's biggest city was either Irish by birth or by extraction. The Famine Song makes reference to an event in Irish history and is used as a taunt to people in Glasgow of Irish heritage to go home. Where should they to go home to? Yes, that's right, Ireland. Yet any attempt by anyone in Scotland to celebrate their Irishness today is often met with derision by the same chaps who lustily belt out the Famine Song. The racists who call on the Irish of Glasgow to go home to Ireland simultaneously deny them the right to self-define as being of Irish heritage.

The comparative experience of the Italian community in modern Scotland is instructive. Catholic country? Check. The state is a republic? Check. Flag is a tricolour? Check. Not on the Allied side in World War II? Check. In fact, it is where the Pope has his gaff ... Yet when Italy won the World Cup in 1982, Glasgow's George Square was covered in Italian flags and no one had a problem with it. If that night had witnessed a great triumph for the Ireland soccer team (okay, I can dream) thousands of Irish tricolours in Glasgow city centre would no doubt have been considered provocative, or even sectarian.

In the last ten years, two high-profile players born in Scotland who have chosen to play for Ireland have been subjected to a torrent of racist abuse. Aiden McGeady and James McCarthy dared to be Irish on the sports field and that is *verboten*, even in "modern Scotland". Under the UEFA criteria, what McGeady and McCarthy suffered in Scotland was racism. Cairde na hÉireann have been battling long and hard for official Scotland to formally call this ancient hatred for what it is and to stop hiding the truth within the sectarian framework. Until this stealth racism is addressed openly by the Holyrood elite it will continue to incubate wherever the historically illiterate obsess about "Fenians and flegs". Recent moves from the Scottish Government suggest that their work is not yet done.

Links

http://www.philmacgiollabhain.ie/scotlands-british-problem/
http://www.philmacgiollabhain.ie/ibrox-racist-banner-criticised/
http://www.philmacgiollabhain.ie/
   exclusive-interview-with-james-macmillan/
http://www.philmacgiollabhain.ie/kevin-mcdaid-rip/
http://www.philmacgiollabhain.ie/showing-respect-in-coleraine/
http://www.philmacgiollabhain.ie/rangers-no-irish-need-apply/
http://www.philmacgiollabhain.ie/an-irish-player-for-rangers/
http://www.philmacgiollabhain.ie/there-is-no-team-like-the-glasgow-
   rangers/
http://www.philmacgiollabhain.ie/maurice-edu/
http://www.philmacgiollabhain.ie/an-act-of-rememberance/
http://www.philmacgiollabhain.ie/james-mccarthy/
http://www.philmacgiollabhain.ie/the-unwanted/
http://www.philmacgiollabhain.ie/wanted-as-long-as-youre-not-irish/
http://www.philmacgiollabhain.ie/the-least-desirable/
http://www.philmacgiollabhain.ie/plastic-paraguayans/
http://www.philmacgiollabhain.ie/the-sash-cloud/
http://www.philmacgiollabhain.ie/a-first-step/
http://www.philmacgiollabhain.com/wp-content/themes/original/
   ip280810.pdf

http://www.philmacgiollabhain.ie/returning-to-the-scene-of-the-shame/

http://www.philmacgiollabhain.ie/goerring%E2%80%99s-eleven/

http://politics.caledonianmercury.com/2010/12/13/opinion-scotland-the-irish-sectarianism-and-racism/

http://www.philmacgiollabhain.ie/the-hate-that-dare-not-speak-its-name/

http://www.scottishreview.net/PhilMacGiollaBhain105.shtml

http://www.guardian.co.uk/commentisfree/2011/apr/13/irish-heritage-scotland-cultural-oppression?commentpage=all#start-of-comments

http://www.philmacgiollabhain.ie/helping-rangers/

http://www.philmacgiollabhain.ie/the-best-small-country-in-the-world/

http://www.philmacgiollabhain.ie/laethanta-scoile/

http://www.philmacgiollabhain.ie/the-obdurate-order/

http://www.philmacgiollabhain.ie/attacks-on-the-short-strand/

http://www.philmacgiollabhain.ie/the-irish-governments-failure-to-acknowledge-anti-irish-racism-in-scotland/

http://www.philmacgiollabhain.ie/james-macmillan-calls-on-lamont-to-apologise-or-resign-after-rant-on-catholic-schools/

http://www.philmacgiollabhain.ie/the-colour-orange/

http://www.philmacgiollabhain.ie/sing-a-rebel-song/

http://www.philmacgiollabhain.ie/a-clear-and-present-danger/#more-1759

http://www.philmacgiollabhain.ie/anthony-stokes/

http://www.philmacgiollabhain.ie/an-illicit-ethnicity/

http://www.philmacgiollabhain.ie/a-bad-law/

http://www.philmacgiollabhain.ie/how-to-be-a-racist-in-scotland-and-get-away-with-it/

http://www.philmacgiollabhain.ie/jeff-winter/

http://www.philmacgiollabhain.ie/the-view-from-strasbourg/

http://www.philmacgiollabhain.ie/a-mythical-place/

http://www.irishexaminer.com/sport/soccer/close-to-the-bone-but-from-the-heart-184731.html

http://www.philmacgiollabhain.ie/hearing-clearly/

http://www.philmacgiollabhain.ie/best-buddies/

http://www.philmacgiollabhain.ie/nuj-motion-about-the-targeting-of-journalists/

http://www.philmacgiollabhain.ie/alien-intervention/

http://www.philmacgiollabhain.ie/telling-the-truth-about-the-ibrox-klan/

http://www.philmacgiollabhain.ie/the-shameful-truth-on-channel-4/

http://www.philmacgiollabhain.ie/graham-spiers-and-the-rogue-angry-underclass/

Facing up to anti-Irish 'stealth racism', *An Phoblacht*, 31.01.2012

APPENDICES

In this section, the 1923 Church and Nation Committee report is replicated in its entirety as well as a list of the members of the influential Kirk body at that time.

The final two documents hold both the lyrics of the Billy Boys, the battle hymn of Rangers supporters for generations and outlawed by UEFA in 2006, and the Famine Song, ruled illegal by the High Court of Justiciary in 2009.

REPORT

OF

COMMITTEE TO CONSIDER OVERTURES

FROM

THE PRESBYTERY OF GLASGOW AND FROM THE SYNOD OF GLASGOW AND AYR ON "IRISH IMMIGRATION" AND THE "EDUCATION (SCOTLAND) ACT, 1918"

TO THE

GENERAL ASSEMBLY OF THE CHURCH OF SCOTLAND

29th MAY 1923

COMMITTEE 1923-1924.

The MODERATOR.
The PROCURATOR.
Rev. Professor FULTON.
  „   „ W. P. PATERSON.
  „   „ MAIN.
  „   „ REID.
  „ Dr THOMAS BURNS.
  „ „ R. H. DUNLOP.
  „ „ M'CLYMONT.
  „ „ DONALD MACMILLAN.
  „ „ MITCHELL.
  „ „ GORDON MURRAY.
  „ „ OGILVIE.
  „ „ GEORGE WALKER.
  „ ROBERT BURNETT.
  „ DUNCAN CAMERON (Kilsyth).
  „ A. J. CAMPBELL.
  „ W. M. CAMPBELL.
  „ GEORGE CHRISTIE.
  „ J. D. COCHRANE.

Rev. M. SCOTT DICKSON.
  „ G. H. DONALD.
  „ JAS. FERGUSON.
  „ J. M. FORBES.
  „ SCUDAMORE FORBES.
  „ W. M. GOLDIE.
  „ J. MACLAGAN.
  „ J. S. MACNAUGHTON.
  „ G. B. THOMSON MICHIE.
  „ R. W. RUTHERFORD.
  „ WILLIAM SWAN.
The Right Hon. LORD SALVESEN.
JAMES BROWN, Esq., M.P.
JAMES TENNANT GORDON, Esq.
JAMES MACFARLANE, Esq., LL.D.
JOHN H. MACLEOD, Esq., M.P.
DAVID MEIKLEREID, Esq.
W. H. MILL, Esq., S.S.C.
GEORGE STEWART, Esq.
ALEX. WALLACE, Esq., W.S.

THE HON. LORD SANDS } *Joint-Conveners.*
REV. WILLIAM MAIN }

3 o

750   COMMITTEE ON OVERTURES *re* IRISH IMMIGRATION

REPORT.

THE Overtures on which the General Assembly took action
show that the alarm and anxiety which prompted them have
been occasioned by the incursion into Scotland of a large
Irish Roman Catholic population within recent years. The
question of the Scottish Roman Catholic population has not
arisen, nor is there any reason why it should arise. They
have a right to call Scotland their country, in common with
their fellow-countrymen of the Protestant Faith. Nor is
there any complaint of the presence of an Orange population in Scotland. They are of the same race as ourselves and
of the same Faith, and are readily assimilated to the Scottish
population. The Committee, therefore, interpret the Remit
from the General Assembly as being an instruction to consider and to report on the problem of the Irish Roman Catholic
population in Scotland. They cannot be assimilated and
absorbed into the Scottish race. They remain a people by
themselves, segregated by reason of their race, their customs,
their traditions, and, above all, by their loyalty to their
Church, and gradually and inevitably dividing Scotland,
racially, socially, and ecclesiastically.

It is necessary to dispose of the possible objection that
a considerable proportion of the Roman Catholic population
in the industrial area of Western Scotland is of purely Scottish
lineage. Statistics show that the only two counties in which
a purely Scottish Roman Catholic population of any size
exists are Inverness-shire and Dumfriesshire. The number
of Roman Catholic school children on the Rolls of the Inverness-
shire Education Authority is 1800, out of a total enrolment of
12,800. The number of Roman Catholic children on the Rolls
of the Dumfriesshire Education Authority is 534, out of a

total enrolment of 12,711. The native Roman Catholic population in the uplands of Banffshire and in Aberdeenshire is so small as to be almost negligible. It is clear, therefore, that the surplus of the purely Scottish Roman Catholic population cannot be large, and cannot supply many recruits for the industrial areas of the country. Besides, it is well known that the Highland Roman Catholic clings to his home and his native soil, and therefore the relatively small number who do come south when spread over the centres of population form an insignificant section of the community. The problem, therefore, that has been remitted to the Committee for consideration is almost exclusively an Irish problem ; and though recognition should be made of a certain number of Poles in the coal-mining districts, the fact remains that this is a question arising out of the abnormal growth of the Irish race in Scotland.

In no other European country did the Reformation have a more complete triumph than in Scotland. Sooner or later practically the whole body of the Scottish people adopted the principles of the Reformed Faith. Owing to the difficulty of providing preachers, certain isolated communities in remote parts of Inverness-shire adhered to the old Faith, and the influence of powerful Roman Catholic families in Dumfriesshire succeeded in keeping sections of the peasantry within the fold of the Church of Rome. It is true that the Reformed Faith did not adopt the Presbyterian form of Church government to the exclusion of every other form. Among many of the nobility and the landed gentry the Episcopal Church had devoted adherents, and in certain counties— notably Aberdeenshire and Forfarshire—a certain number of the humbler classes adhered to the Church of their territorial Superiors. But, generally speaking, the result of the Reformation was that the Roman Catholic Church was practically extinguished in Scotland, which thereby became homogeneous in Faith and ideals.

It was not until large numbers of Irish Roman Catholics came over from Ireland that the Roman Catholic Church began to grow, to feel her power, and to assert her influence, and this was the beginning of the destruction of the unity and homogeneity of the Scottish people. With the industrial

752   COMMITTEE ON OVERTURES *re* IRISH IMMIGRATION

development of Scotland in the nineteenth century a demand
for cheap labour arose. Industrial firms and great contractors
advertised for labour in the Irish Press, and crowds of Irishmen and their families emigrated to Scotland to engage in
building railways, to work in coal mines, in the great shipyards on the Clyde, and in the jute mills of Dundee, and to
labour in the construction of public works, such as the Loch
Katrine water scheme. When they had settled down they
invited relations and friends to come across to Scotland,
promising to find work and a home for them. All were welcomed by the employers of labour. The Irishmen worked
well, accepted almost any kind of habitation, and were content with small wages. It was in the great plain of Scotland,
stretching from the Clyde on the west to the Tay on the east,
where is the mineral wealth of Scotland and where are her
great cities, that the Irish race found their livelihood and
made their home.

Meanwhile there was going on a great exodus of the Scottish race. They wished for better conditions of life, higher
wages, and wider prospects. Compelled by the economic
pressure of the Irish race, young Scottish men and women—
the flower of the nation—left their native land, and sought
to build up their fortunes in America and the Dominions.
It was certainly to the advantage of the countries to which
they went that the best of our Scottish people should have
gone there, but it was a grievous loss to the land of their
fathers. Their places were taken by a people of a different
race and a different Faith, and Scotland has been divided
into two camps—a Scottish and an Irish.

There is no parallel to these movements in modern or in
ancient times. It is a thing unprecedented that one race
should gradually by peaceful penetration supplant another
in their native land. For this is what is happening. According to the ' Roman Catholic Directory ' there is a total population of 2,070,000 in the Roman Catholic diocese of Glasgow,
embracing Lanarkshire, Dumbartonshire, Renfrewshire, North
Ayrshire, and a small part of West Stirlingshire. Of this
great population at least 450,000 are Irish—that is to say,
that in the crowded industrial area of the west almost every
fourth person is Irish. In Lanarkshire alone, the most populous

county in Scotland, soon every third person will be Irish. It might be possible for the Scottish people to contemplate this situation with a certain equanimity were there the least likelihood that the Irish population in Scotland would not grow out of all proportion to the growth of the Scottish population. But, unfortunately, the evidence is overwhelming that the Irish race in our midst will increase, while the Scottish race decreases. The following statistics are eloquent ; they tell their own tale :—

IRISH POPULATION IN SCOTLAND.

1881.	1901.	1911.	1921.
327,239	432,900	518,969	601,304

The Irish population has almost doubled in the last forty years. What of the Scottish population? In the twenty years, 1881 to 1901, the Irish population increased by $32\frac{1}{3}$ per cent, while the Scottish population for the same period increased by only $18\frac{1}{2}$ per cent. In the twenty years, 1901 to 1921, the Irish population increased by 39 per cent, while the Scottish population increased by only 6 per cent. That is to say, that from 1881 to 1901 the increase of the Irish population was nearly twice as great as that of the Scottish population, and from 1901 to 1921 the increase of the Irish population was $6\frac{1}{2}$ times as great as that of the Scottish population.

Statistics as to marriages show that the power of the Irish race in Scotland to increase more rapidly than the Scottish race will become greater in the future than it has been in the past.

The Report of the Registrar-General shows :—

	Total Marriages.	Roman Catholic.	
1861-65	109,063	10,378	1 in 10
1881-85	130,879	13,009	1 in 10
1901-05	159,192	16,712	2 in 19
1919-21*	130,176	16,204	1 in 8

* Only three years are given, so as to avoid the abnormal years of the war.

The statistics of the Education Authorities of Glasgow, Lanark, Dumbarton, and Renfrew also provide evidence of

754   COMMITTEE ON OVERTURES *re* IRISH IMMIGRATION

the certainty, under existing circumstances, of a still more rapid increase of the Irish population in Scotland in the future.

GLASGOW AUTHORITY.

	1919.	1920.	1921.	1922.
Scottish children on Roll	148,364	147,299	146,552	142,293
Irish Children on Roll .	42,297	42,870	43,334	42,909

Decrease of Scottish children	6071
Increase of Irish children	612

Had the proportion remained unaltered there would have been an Irish decrease of 1211 and a Scottish decrease of 4246.

LANARKSHIRE AUTHORITY.

	1919.	1920.	1921.	1922.
Scottish children on Roll .	76,962	78,934	79,898	76,787
Irish children on Roll .	23,042	24,291	25,370	26,000

Decrease of Scottish children in three years .	173
Increase of Irish children in three years . .	2958

Had the proportion remained unaltered there would have been an Irish increase of only 641 and a Scottish increase of 2344.

RENFREW AUTHORITY.

	1919	1920.	1921.	1922.
Scottish children on Roll .	41,164	42,351	42,367	41,465
Irish children on Roll .	11,118	11,399	11,528	11,535

Increase of Scottish children in three years .	301
Increase of Irish children in three years . .	417

Had the proportion remained unaltered there would have been an Irish increase of only 153 and a Scottish increase of 565.

DUMBARTON AUTHORITY.

	1919.	1920.	1921.	1922.
Scottish children on Roll .	18,614	19,308	19,162	21,042
Irish children on Roll .	5,520	5,695	5,777	6,729

Increase in Scottish children	2428
Increase in Irish children	1209

Had the proportion remained unaltered there would have been an Irish increase of only 831 and a Scottish increase of 2806.

There is a widespread impression that the rapid increase of the Irish population relative to the Scottish increase is due to the alleged fact that the Irish family is, as a rule, larger than the Scottish family. This is not true. The fertility of the Scottish working-class family is just as great as that of the Irish working-class family. The tendency to restrict the size of the family does not—as yet, at any rate—affect the Scottish working-class any more deeply than it does the Irish working-class. In one populous mining parish—where the Irish population is one-fifth of the whole—the Scottish birth-rate for 1922 was somewhat higher than the Irish birth-rate. But there are statistics to show that the increase in the Irish population and the relatively small increase in the Scottish population are due mainly to two causes—immigration of Irish into Scotland, and emigration of Scots from Scotland.

There were in 1901 no less than 205,064 Irish people living in Scotland, who had come over from Ireland ; in 1911 there were 174,715. The figures for 1921 are not yet published, but, assuming that they are 170,000, it is clear that the natural increase of the Irish population in Scotland has been greatly enhanced by emigration from Ireland to Scotland. On the other hand, the emigration of Scotsmen from Scotland has been constant and large in recent years. It was very great between 1901 and 1914, while for this year it is reckoned that it will have reached the huge figure of 30,000. Comparatively few Irishmen emigrate from Scotland.

It is a notable fact that whenever the Irish population reach a certain proportion in any community, whether village, small town, or area of a great city, the tendency of the Scottish population is to leave as quickly as they possibly can. Many areas of the large cities, not a few villages, and even some small towns, are becoming exclusively Irish. In Port-Glasgow the number of Irish marriages in 1921 was 43, while the Scottish marriages were 89 ; in 1922 the number of Irish marriages was 40, while the Scottish marriages were 66—the percentage of Irish marriages increasing from 32·5 per cent

756   COMMITTEE ON OVERTURES *re* IRISH IMMIGRATION

in 1921 to 37·7 per cent in 1922. In the Parish of Old Monkland on the 31st January 1923 the total number of Scottish children attending school was 8018, while the number of Irish children was 5000. The Croy district of the parish of Cumbernauld is practically Irish ; the Scottish mining population, refusing to stay, have gone elsewhere. This social phenomenon has a very sinister meaning for the future of our race. The time is rapidly approaching when, through this racial imcompatibility, whole communities in parish, village, and town will be predominantly Irish. It is, in fact, a sober and restrained prophecy to say that through the operation of the various factors now at work—immigration of Irish and emigration of Scots, disinclination of Scots to work alongside and live among Irish, partiality of Irish foremen for employing Irishmen—the great plain of Scotland stretching from Glasgow in the west to Dundee and Edinburgh in the east will be soon dominated by the Irish race. If, therefore, the Scottish people wish to safeguard their heritage, they cannot afford to lose time in taking whatever steps may be necessary to secure this just and patriotic end.

At present the problem is admittedly most formidable in the western industrial shires. But already there is conclusive evidence that the thorough permeation of the industrial east is merely a matter of time. Educational statistics for Edinburgh and Dundee tell their tale of a growing Irish population, overtaking—more gradually than in the west, it is true, but as surely—the Scottish population.

DUNDEE AUTHORITY.

	1919.	1920.	1921.	1922.
Irish children on Roll	5,439	5,532	5,612	5,609
Scottish children on Roll	23,098	22,561	22,165	21,663

Irish increase in three years	170
Scottish decrease in three years	1435

Had the proportion remained unaltered there should be an Irish decrease of 241 and a Scottish decrease of 1024.

EDINBURGH AUTHORITY.

	1920.	1921.	1922.
Scottish children on Roll	57,668	56,766	56,320
Irish children on Roll	5,854	5,999	6,029

Decrease of Scottish children in two years .   1348
Increase of Irish children in two years .   .   175

Had the proportion remained unaltered there should be an Irish decrease of 108 and a Scottish decrease of 1065.

The approximate increase of the population of Fifeshire for the past ten years is 25,000. Of this number 5382 are Irish. The Irish, therefore, account for approximately 22 per cent of the total increase, a percentage that is much higher than the Irish percentage of the population of Fifeshire, which is about 6 per cent. Wherever industrialism prevails the Irish race increases. West Lothian has one Irishman for every eight Scotsmen; East Lothian one for every twenty-five Scotsmen. Given the continuance of the present conditions, there is every certainty that the industrial east will soon become as Irish as the industrial west. Meanwhile the population of rural Scotland—in the Highlands and southern uplands, where the Scottish race is unadulterated—goes steadily down.

There are still some factors to be taken into account in estimating the relative positions of the two races in Scotland in the future. It is not likely that the establishment of the Free State will cause any return of the Irish race in Scotland to their native land, or that the Irish people will hereafter remain in Ireland. There are few important industries in Southern Ireland, and the Free State is always likely to remain a pastoral and agricultural country. Such a land cannot provide for the maintenance of the natural increase of a prolific race. The lure of reconditioning Scotland—to use the phrase of a prominent Roman Catholic layman—appeals strongly to the Church of Rome. If Scotland be won for the Roman Catholic Church, a mighty lever for the control of England—the greatest prize of all—will have been put into the hands of the Church. Already the Roman Communion is the largest in Glasgow, the second city of the Empire. This achievement could only have been regarded as the

758   COMMITTEE ON OVERTURES *re* IRISH IMMIGRATION

dream of a visionary fifty years ago. But when such dreams come true, who can say that dreams of yet vaster triumphs will never be realised ? The spiritual guides of the Irish people encourage them to come over to Scotland, and they are astute and far-seeing men. Within forty years the number of the Irish race in this historic home of the Reformed Faith has been almost doubled. It is not unreasonable to say that within the next forty years the Irish population in the industrial area of Scotland will approach 1,500,000, and the Scottish race will then have lost control of the populous and wealth-producing parts of their country. What will follow must be plain to any thinking mind—the rapid permeation of the whole of Scotland by an alien people.

Even now the Irish population exercise a profound influence on the direction and development of our Scottish civilisation. Their gift of speech, their aptitude for public life, their restless ambition to rule, have given them a prominent place in political, county, municipal, and parochial elections. They have also asserted themselves in co-operative and benefit societies. They have had an unfortunate influence in modifying the Scottish habit of thrift and independence. An Irishman never hesitates to seek relief from charity organisations and local authorities, and Scotsmen do not see why they should not get help when Irishmen receive it. Indeed, it must be said that the social problem has been complicated and increased by the presence of the Irish population. Generally speaking, they are poor partly through intemperance and improvidence, and they show little inclination to raise themselves in the social scale. The Irish race too modify admirable Scottish customs. The Scottish reverence for the Sabbath day is passing away : it has now become a day for political meetings and for concerts. It may be that there is in the Scottish mind a tendency towards the secularisation of the Sabbath, but indubitably this tendency has been increased and stimulated by the influence of the Irish race. It is not alone the unconscious influence of a large alien population in our midst that is changing the spirit and form of our Scottish civilisation : the Roman Catholic Church has definitely committed herself to the task of converting the Scottish nation. She has her missioners in Glasgow, able men, who exhibit the doctrines of Rome in guises calculated to persuade and convince Protestant minds. As yet the fruits of their labours are not plentiful, and it may be urged that the Protestant Church should make an effort to win over the Irish population to the Reformed Faith. It may be assumed, however, that neither Church will achieve much by the way of propaganda—the Irish will remain true to the ancient Faith, and the stubborn Scot will not forsake the Church of his fathers. This is recognised by the authorities of the Church of Rome, and their hope and method are the capture of Scotland for Rome through the incoming of the greatest missionary race on earth by the way of the great gates of the west—the ports on the Clyde.

The Education Act of 1918—passed through Parliament when Scotland was deeply and painfully preoccupied with the problem of the war—has proved an immense boon to the Roman Catholic Church. It has made her in proportion to her numbers the most richly-endowed Church in Scotland, and has securely entrenched her in the very schools she has either sold or leased to Education Authorities. Her control over these schools that are not now hers is as great as it was when they were her own property, and an over-taxed and financially distressed Scotland has to pay immense sums for the lease or purchase of buildings, which the Scottish people control only to a limited extent. The Glasgow Education Authority pays the Roman Catholic Church £25,000 a year for the lease of the Roman Catholic schools, and has paid £47,000 for their fittings and furnishings. The Education Act of 1872 made no such generous provision for the transference of the schools built by the Church of Scotland or the Free Church of Scotland. They could be transferred, it is true, to the newly-established School Boards. But no sums were paid by the School Boards to either Church for their purchase. Nor could any annual rent be offered for their lease. Every year £283,023 are paid in salaries to the Roman Catholic teachers of Glasgow, and the expenditure per annum on rates and taxes, fuel, light and cleaning, books and stationery, and repairs reaches the enormous sum of £107,225. Such an endowment of denominational schools in one city alone for the children of an alien race is surely unprecedented. The

760   COMMITTEE ON OVERTURES *re* IRISH IMMIGRATION

financial burden on the country is wellnigh intolerable, and economy has to be practised, as some think, to the detriment of education. The salaries of the teachers are reduced, only absolutely necessary repairs are effected, additional building is engaged in only under the spur of the direst necessity, yet the annual rents are paid to the Roman Catholic Church for her schools, which are as useful for her purpose as they ever were. But this is not all. Under the Act of 1918 the Roman Catholic Church can claim that primary and secondary schools shall be erected wherever she thinks they are required. The Education Authority of Fifeshire have built a large secondary school in Cowdenbeath for the Roman Catholic children in the county. The Church will not allow the children of her people to attend Protestant secondary schools. The Authorities must either build or pay for the education of the children in the nearest Roman Catholic secondary school. And this has to be done when the economic life of the country is almost crushed out of existence under the burden of taxation. Meanwhile the Roman Catholic Church, loaded with wealth received from an overburdened nation, is using it for the purpose of securely establishing a Faith in their land that is distasteful to the Scottish race, or of supplanting the people who supplied these riches by a race that is alien in sympathy and in religion.

What, then, is to be the future of our land and of the Scottish people ? The incursion of the Irish race has been a misfortune for themselves and for Scotland. Scotland is a small country. A small country divided by creed and race has never proved to be a happy or harmonious country. Ireland affords a striking illustration of the truth of this. Its racial and sectarian antipathies have embittered the soul of two peoples, and impeded the high enterprises of civilisation. The Dutch and the Belgians, under diplomatic pressure, entered into union in 1815—the one a Roman Catholic, the other a Protestant country. They failed to harmonise, and in fifteen years the union was dissolved. Fusion of the Scottish and the Irish races in Scotland—just as it was in Ireland—will remain an impossibility. The Irish are the most obedient children of the Church of Rome ; the Scots stubbornly adhere to the principles of the Reformed Faith. The Irish have separate schools for their children ; they have their own clubs for recreation and for social intercourse ; they tend to segregate in communities, and even to monopolise certain departments of labour to the exclusion of the Scots. Already there is bitter feeling among the Scottish working-classes against the Irish intruders. As the latter increase, and the Scottish people realise the seriousness of the menace to their own racial supremacy in their native land, this bitterness will develop into a race antagonism, which will have disastrous consequences for Scotland.

The loss of the Scottish race to civilisation would be immeasurable. In science, theoretical and applied, in art, poetry and prose, in government and industry, in philosophy and theology, their contributions to the advancement of knowledge and civilisation have been remarkable. It is idle to say that though they leave their native land they will still be Scotsmen, and will still maintain the traditions, ideals, and Faith of their fathers. When Scotsmen settle in other lands they become good citizens of those countries ; and though they remember with warm affection and great pride the land of their fathers, still generations succeed them that know not Scotland. The formative and inspiring influence of the home land no longer shape the characters of their children. For them Scottish song and legend, the haunting memories of parish, village, or town, the social and spiritual atmosphere of the old land, are remote and ineffective influences.

It may be said, and, indeed, has been said, that on Christian principles the Scottish people should not object to the presence of the Irish in their midst. " Christ died for all." " We are all the children of the One Heavenly Father." There is no surer test of the validity of the application of a commonly accepted truth in all circumstances than its application all round. Would the Irish race, would the Church of Rome, welcome the incursion of half a million Scotsmen into the counties around Dublin ? Would the English people receive with open arms five million Poles into the industrial areas of Yorkshire, Staffordshire, and Lancashire ? God placed the people of this world in families, and history, which is the narrative of His providence, tells us that when kingdoms are divided against themselves they cannot stand. The

762 COMMITTEE ON OVERTURES *re* IRISH IMMIGRATION

nations that are homogeneous in Faith and ideals, that have maintained unity of race, have been ever the most prosperous, and to them the Almighty has committed the highest tasks, and has granted the largest measure of success in achieving them. It is incumbent on the Scottish people to consider, before it is too late, the grave situation in their native land, and to devise means which, while they do no injustice to the Irish people whom they allowed to come into their country, shall preserve Scotland for the Scottish race, and secure to future generations the traditions, ideals, and Faith of a great people, unspoiled and inviolate.

In name of the Committee,

CHRISTOPHER N. JOHNSTON (SANDS), } *Joint-*
WILLIAM MAIN, } *Conveners.*

Extract Deliverance of the General Assembly of the Church of Scotland on the foregoing Report.

At Edinburgh, the Twenty-ninth day of May, One thousand nine hundred and twenty-three years,—

Which day the General Assembly of the Church of Scotland being met and constituted,—*inter alia,*

The General Assembly called for the Report of the Committee to consider Overtures on Irish Immigration and the Education (Scotland) Act, 1918, which was given in by Mr Main, the Convener, who moved—

1. The General Assembly receive the Report, thank the Committee for their diligence, and discharge them, and commend the Report to the earnest consideration of the ministers and members of the Church.

2. The General Assembly, impressed by the facts set forth in the Report, urge the Government to appoint a Com-

315

mission to inquire into the whole situation, with a view to the preservation and protection of Scottish nationality and civilisation.

3. The General Assembly call upon the Government to amend the Education (Scotland) Act of 1918, so that the right to impart religious instruction shall be accorded to all public schools as is accorded in transferred schools; and further, the General Assembly request that Section 18 of the Education (Scotland) Act of 1918 be so altered as to bring it into line with Section 38 of the Act of 1872, with the addition of the provision of Section 18 of the Act of 1918 as regards the appointment of teachers and religious instruction in transferred schools. The General Assembly also consider that sub-Sections 7, 8, 9, and 10 of Section 18 should be revised and altered.

4. The General Assembly remit the whole Report to the Committee on Church and Nation for further consideration, and report to next Assembly.

The Motion was seconded.

It was moved and seconded as an Amendment—

For Paragraph 4 substitute: "The General Assembly instruct the Committee on Church and Nation to take action as indicated in paragraphs 2 and 3, and to invite the co-operation of other Churches and any Associations interested in the question, and report to next Assembly."

The Amendment was with the permission of the Assembly accepted by the Convener, and the Motion, as amended, was agreed to.

Extracted from the Records of the General Assembly of the Church of Scotland by

DAVID PAUL,
Cl. Eccl. Scot.

Tuesday, 29 May, 1923. Item 10.

Report of the Committee to consider Overtures on Irish Immigration and the Education (Scotland) Act, 1918

Committee Members 1923–1924

The Moderator
The Procurator
Rev. Professor Fulton
Rev. Professor W. P. Paterson
Rev. Professor Main
Rev. Professor Reid
Rev. Dr Thomas Burns
Rev. Dr. R. H. Dunlop
Rev. Dr. M'Clymont
Rev. Dr. Donald Macmillan
Rev. Dr. Mitchell
Rev. Dr. Gordon Murray
Rev. Dr. Ogilvie
Rev. Dr. George Walker
Rev. Robert Burnett
Rev. Duncan Cameron (Kilsyth)
Rev. A. J. Campbell
Rev. W. M. Campbell
Rev. George Christie
Rev. J. D. Cochrane

Rev. M. Scott Dickson
Rev. G. H. Donald
Rev. Jas. Ferguson
Rev. J. M. Forbes
Rev. Scudamore Forbes
Rev. W. M. Goldie
Rev. J. Maclagan
Rev. J. S. Macnaughton
Rev. G. B. Thomson Michie
Rev. R. W. Rutherford
Rev. William Swan
The Right Hon. Lord Salvesen
James Brown, Esq., M.P.
James Tennant Gordon, Esq.
James Macfarlane, Esq., LL.D.
John H. Macleod, Esq., M.P.
David Meiklereid, Esq.
W. H. Mill, Esq., S.S.C.
George Stewart, Esq.
Alex Wallace, Esq., W.S.

Joint-Conveners
The Hon. Lord Sands
Rev. William Main

Source: *The Principal Acts of the General Assembly of the Church of Scotland convened at Edinburgh, May 22nd, 1923 with the Abridgment of the Proceedings of that Assembly* (published by William Blackwood and Sons, Edinburgh and London, MCMXXIII)

Extract from Business held on Tuesday, May 29, 1923. Session 7.

Education (Scotland) Act and Irish Immigration.

Accepted.

The General Assembly called for the Report of the Committee to consider Overtures on Irish Immigration and the Education (Scotland) Act, 1918, which was given in by Mr Main, the Convener, who moved.

1. The General Assembly receive the Report, thank the Committee for their diligence, and discharge them, and commend the Report to the earnest consideration of the ministers and members of the Church.
2. The General Assembly, impressed by the facts set forth in the Report, urge the Government to appoint a Commission to inquire into the whole situation, with a view to the preservation and protection of Scottish nationality and civilisation.
3. The General Assembly call upon the Government to amend the Education (Scotland) Act of 1918, so that the right to impart religious instruction shall be accorded to all public schools as is accorded in transferred schools; and further, the General Assembly request that Section 18 of the Education (Scotland) Act of 1918 be so altered as to bring it into line with Section 38 of the Act of 1812, with the addition of the provision of Section 18 of the Act of 1918 as regards the appointment of teachers and religious instruction in transferred schools. The General Assembly also consider that sub-Sections 7, 8, 9, and 10 of Section 18 should be revised and altered.
4. The General Assembly remit the whole Report to the Committee on Church and Nation for further consideration, and report to next Assembly.

The Motion was seconded.

The Billy Boys

Hullo, Hullo
We are the Billy Boys
Hullo, Hullo
You'll know us by our noise
We're up to our knees in Fenian blood
Surrender or you'll die
For we are
The Brigton Derry Boys

[In the final line the word "Brigton" (Bridgeton in the East End of Glasgow) is often replaced by the name of the singer's hometown/estate. Example, "Govan Derry Boys".]

The Famine Song

I often wonder where they would have been
If we hadn't have taken them in
Fed them and washed them
Thousands in Glasgow alone
From Ireland they came
Brought us nothing but trouble and shame
Well the famine is over
Why don't they go home?

Now Athenry Mike was a thief
And Large John he was fully briefed
And that wee traitor from Castlemilk
Turned his back on his own
They've all their Papists in Rome
They have U2 and Bono
Well the famine is over
Why don't they go home?

Now they raped and fondled their kids
That's what those perverts from the darkside did
And they swept it under the carpet
and Large John he hid
Their evils seeds have been sown
Cause they're not of our own
Well the famine is over
Why don't you go home?

Now Timmy don't take it from me
Cause if you know your history
You've persecuted thousands of people
In Ireland alone
You turned on the lights
Fuelled U boats by night
That's how you repay us
It's time to go home.